BOR
DRIBBLE

Football Gaffes, Chants, Injuries and Insults

Liam McCann
Cartoons by
Niki

BORN TO DRIBBLE
Liam McCann
Cartoons by Niki

Published by
Facts, Figures & Fun, an imprint of
AAPPL Artists' and Photographers' Press Ltd.
Church Farm House, Wisley, Surrey, GU23 6QL   UK
info@ffnf.co.uk   www.ffnf.co.uk
info@aappl.com   www.aappl.com

Sales and Distribution
UK and export: Turnaround Publisher Services Ltd.
orders@turnaround-uk.com
Australia & New Zealand: Peribo Pty
peribomec@bigpond.com

Paperback edition first published 2009

ISBN 9781904332930

BORN TO DRIBBLE

Football Gaffes, Chants, Injuries and Insults

Contents

*"He dribbles a lot and the opposition don't like it.
You can see it on their faces"*
RON ATKINSON

1234567891011

The Beautiful Game

Introduction – A Brief History

It seems likely that the modern game of football derived from the ancient Chinese art of Tsu'chu that existed in the first three centuries before Christ. Military papers dating from the Han Dynasty describe a game where soldiers kicked a feather-filled leather ball towards a hoop approximately a foot (30 centimetres) in diameter, backed by a small net supported thirty feet above the ground by a couple of bamboo canes. Sometimes defenders were allowed to obstruct the ball striker, though he was permitted to protect the ball with parts of his body, namely the shoulders and back. The game was certainly played on Emperor Che'eng Ti's birthday in 206 BC because records tell us the head of state was a keen participant. It wasn't a good idea to be on the losing side when he was playing though for flogging was the best you could hope for, and executions were also not uncommon. A text from 50 BC holds that an international contest using these techniques was held between China and Japan.

In fact writings from over five hundred years later (611 AD) tell us that this form of the game had evolved into the popular Japanese sport of Kemari, which is still practiced today. The emphasis was on art and style rather than bodily contact or physical exertion, however. Essentially the players control the ball and pass it to one another without it ever touching the ground. Though the feet are used, the game involves slightly different skills to the common game. It is likely though that both the far eastern versions were passed across central Asia to India and the Middle East. Then they spread to Europe following trade routes and other games such as chess.

These accepted versions of the origins of the game have been challenged by the discovery of a team sport practiced in ancient Mexico by Mesoamericans and then the Mayans some 3,500 years ago. The rubber ball was competed for by four or five players a side and then aimed at a scoring area. The losing captain would typically be sacrificed on an altar next to the pitch. It was a brave man who volunteered to lead his side.

The Romans and Greeks developed their own codes of the Asian variant, both of which placed the emphasis on physical contact and the movement of the ball to scoring areas by way of the hands and feet, primarily with the Roman Harpastum using the hands in a precursor to the game of rugby. The Greek Episkyros didn't survive more than a few generations, though an Olympic event lasting an hour and contested by teams of twenty-seven players is chronicled, while the Roman variant travelled to Britain and beyond with the conquering armies and appears to have lasted almost a millennium, being supported by bastardising the Norman game of Soule that arrived in 1066. In fact, legend has it that the modern game developed after Julius Caesar crossed the Brent near where Griffin Park now stands and kicked the decapitated head of a dead Briton! (It is perhaps not surprising that this story has been handed down the generations when you consider that Brentford's ground is the only one in the country to have a pub at each corner…)

The English adapted the kicking and carrying form of this pastime to transport the ball over great distances, frequently between towns or villages, with the entire population of the competing hamlets sometimes taking part. Though the feet were used, they were more commonly employed to fell or beat an opponent, and it was often quite by chance that they made contact with the ball. As Philip Stubbes, a 17th century writer, tells us (twice):

"Football causeth fighting, brawling, murder, homicide and a great effusion of blood!"

"For as concerning football playing, I protest unto you it may be rather called a friendlie kinde of fyght than a play or recreation, a bloody or murmuring practice than a fellowly sporte or

pastime. By this means, sometimes their necks are broken, their noses gush with blood, sometimes their eyes start out, and sometimes hurt in one place, sometime another"

He was also totally against the notion that the game should be played on God's day of rest:

"Lord, remove these exercises from the Sabbath, for any exercise which withdraweth from godliness either upon the Sabbath or on any other day is wicked and to be forbidden"

Injuries were common as the sport was extremely brutal before laws governing equipment and tactics tempered the violence. A manuscript from Workington suggests that players in the annual Shrovetide match (played on Shrove Tuesday) could use any tactics other than murder or manslaughter to win. This style of football is still played today in some parts of England and Scotland (notably Ashbourne in Derbyshire and Kirkwall north of the border), where it has been chronicled since 217 AD, and even though the towns are boarded up for the safety of the residents, and paramedics are on hand, there are still some serious injuries. Legend has it that the first of these annual games - in Chester - used a severed Danish Prince's head as the ball, while a hogshead was then used for the next few hundred years.

Though there are a few references to these games being played in Anglo-Saxon times, the weight of evidence suggests the Normans brought a kicking game across the Channel in 1066, and this variant, played primarily in Brittany, then merged with the 'mob football' practiced in Britain. Whereas the game already played in Britain was based on physical domination of the opponents, the Norman variation had its roots as a spiritual and religious exercise. The ball, which needed to be carefully controlled, signified the Sun, and it had to be moved across fields for there to be a bountiful harvest. This spawned similar contests, such as that between married men and bachelors to promote fertility and thus increase their chances of finding a spouse. Females, too, were permitted to play; a match between married and unmarried women is chronicled in Inveresk in Scotland in the 1690s. Perhaps this event prompted us to first refer to it as 'The Beautiful Game'. Oscar Wilde was not so sure:

"Football is all very well as a game for rough girls but it is hardly suitable for delicate boys"

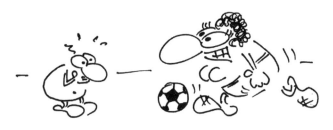

"...a game for rough girls"

Despite the obvious popularity of football amongst the masses, the authorities were less enamoured. In 1314 the Lord Mayor of London, with Edward II's backing, issued an order banning it as a public nuisance:

"For as much as there is a great noise in the city caused by hustling over large balls from which many evils may arise, which, God forbid, we command and forbid on behalf of the king on pain of imprisonment, such a game to be used in the city in future"

King Edward III vowed to imprison anyone breaking this law in 1331. It distracted the common man from practicing his archery, a far more valuable skill. This became evident during the Hundred Years' War, and both Richard II and Henry V were forced to try and stamp the game out so that the French could be beaten on the battlefield.

Scottish King James I decreed that 'Na man shall playe at the fute ball' in 1424 and this sentiment was backed by monarchs across Europe as the game spread to the far reaches of the continent. Elizabeth I then had all footballers jailed for a week, if caught playing, with a follow up punishment of serving the church on the next Sabbath:

*"No foteball player be used or suffered within the city of London,
and the liberties thereof, on pain of imprisonment"*

The Italians had other ideas though and were keen to ensure the game's
survival. They believed that basic rules and different outfits for each side
could bring order to the chaos. A game called Calcio Fiorentino had
developed in Florence and Venice around 1530, and teams of servants
dressed in brightly coloured uniforms contested matches in the Piazza
di Santa Croce on public holidays. Thousands turned up to watch this
bloody, violent contest, a variation of which still exists today, though the
ball is largely ignored in favour of the two teams having a good old scrap.
In fact so dangerous has the annual contest become, that paramedics are
on hand, and they are frequently called upon to remove the unconscious
combatants from the makeshift pitch. Legend has it that in one of the
first games Morticino degli Antinori refused to pass to team-mates - one
of the conditions of the game was that the ball must be kept in motion
- so an opponent, the strongman Dante, picked him up and ran towards
the goal, eventually throwing both man and ball into the makeshift net
for a score.

It is held that the head of St. Paul's School, Richard Mulcaster,
witnessed one of these matches in 1581 and realised that it promoted
health, strength and vitality, through courage, skill and passion. He knew
that all that was needed was a little organisation and the game could
find refuge in the English public schools, and he even advertised for a
'Trayning Master' to bring structure to the boys' exercise periods. This
didn't happen for over a century because both the monarchy and Oliver
Cromwell's government outlawed the game still further in the mid 17th
century, this despite another attempt by Count Albermale to introduce
the game to the Royal Court. The Lord Protector of the Commonwealth,
himself a keen player in his youth, decided that the rules of not exercising
on the Sabbath must be upheld, and this was largely adhered to for the
next two hundred years, though the game didn't disappear completely,
it merely went underground before finding its way into the schools.
As there was a limited playing area inside a school's boundary, rules
were needed to govern the size of the pitch. When teams from different
parishes played the goals could be as much a three miles apart, whereas

this was clearly not possible at school. In 1801 teams from the London schools agreed that a playing surface approximately 100- by 50 yards was acceptable. In 1815 Eton boys drew up a basic list of rules governing numbers of players and match duration. The bonus of this more organised version of the game was that boys could release their pent-up aggression on the field of play rather than terrorise the residents of nearby towns. Religion also played a part, with the emphasis being on turning these young men into muscular Christians.

Two variations then began to emerge. At Charterhouse, Westminster and Harrow the emphasis remained on using your feet to beat opponents, both by dribbling and by hacking their legs if they had the ball. This is alluded to in an old Charterhouse song from around the turn of the 18th century:

"I challenge all the men alive to say they were ever gladder, than when they were boys all striving to kick the most wind out of the bladder"

The Cheltenham and Rugby rules allowed players to handle the ball, to carry it briefly, and, after the supposed intervention of one William Webb Ellis in 1823, to run with it. By the 1840s the head of Rugby School, Dr. Thomas Arnold, openly promoted the playing of their version as he believed it promoted team spirit, a willingness to make sacrifices in working for one another, and overall physical well-being. The two forms of the game then evolved separately, with Eton and Winchester favouring the dribbling game over the Cheltenham and Rugby handling version. This didn't stop the two codes clashing though. Inter-school rivalries meant that teams playing both versions were pitted against one another. Clearly this was unsatisfactory as the sides were playing to different rules and some common ground had to be established. A meeting between former public school boys was held at Cambridge University in 1848 but they couldn't agree on the tripping, hacking and handling areas, and it wasn't until 1863 that the split between the codes finally came. Football, championed by the father of the sport, Ebenezer Cobb Morley, essentially adhered to the Cambridge Rules.

On October 26th eleven clubs and schools sent representatives to the Freemason's Tavern in London to try and resolve the issue. They failed, but a series of subsequent meetings culminating on December 8th - at the founding of Morley's brainchild, the Football Association - saw the Rugby camp leave the fold as they couldn't envision a game without hacking opponents or being allowed to carry the ball in hand. Blackheath were the principle champions of hacking as it was said to be "so much fun", and they, of course, helped found the RFU in 1871. Interestingly they didn't ban hacking for another eight years, prompting the Chancellor of Cambridge University to observe:

"Football is a gentleman's game played by hooligans, while rugby is a hooligan's game played by gentlemen"

The split between the codes was further bolstered when even touching the ball with the hands was forbidden by the FA six years later. It had still been reasonably common in the intervening years for the first half of matches to be played under football rules and the second half under the rugby code. And the schism was complete when, in 1871, the FA Cup was introduced by Charles Alcock (based on an inter-house competition at Harrow), the first organised football competition in the world. The first final (1872) pitted amateur sides Wanderers against the Royal Engineers, which the Wanderers won 1-0, the goal being scored by Morton Peto Betts, a member of the FA committee which had organised the tournament.

By 1888 twelve clubs based in the Midlands and northwest were in a position to form a league, a system for playing each other on a home and away basis during the winter months (this was based on the American baseball model). The regional disparity could be traced to the industrial centres granting a half-day's work on Saturday, which allowed the working classes time for leisure, time they needed to develop the game. Thus football became a sport for the masses instead of remaining as a public school hobby.

Having recruited the top Scottish players of the time, Preston North End became the first League champions, and they managed the first 'Double' when they claimed the FA Cup later that season. It took another four years before a club from London (Woolwich Arsenal) was accepted into the top flight. The same year saw a number of new teams emerge, enough, in fact, to warrant a second tier in English football. Division Two was thus formed for the 1892-93 season.

In 1897 the famous Aston Villa side completed its historic 'Double', claiming the honours over teams that now represented a broad cross-section of the whole country. Then still in the lowly Southern Leagues, Tottenham Hotspur became the only club from outside the structured League to take the FA Cup, which they did in 1901, the first of many triumphs in a year ending with a one.

"I say, that man just kicked the ball with his head"
PRINCE EDWARD AT THE 1889 FA CUP FINAL

The organised game now spread back across the world because British businessmen and missionaries were required to manage the empire, and thousands made the long sea journey to Australia and New Zealand, to India and Pakistan, to Africa and South America. Of course sailors on the ships, even though they were from a completely different class, also needed to let off steam having arrived in the ports. Football thus reached the masses on every continent, no doubt helped by the arrival of the railways which took the game inland. Games in India became so popular that crowds of over 100,000 were common. As there were no stadiums, only the front few rows could actually see the game. But the Indians, with typical ingenuity, devised a way to let the crowd know how it was progressing. Carrier pigeons had small pieces of paper tied to their feet listing the scorers. They were then sent to the back so that everyone could follow the match!

The First World War slowed the game's development and the Football League cancelled all fixtures for its duration. By 1919 however, there were a huge number of clubs waiting to explode onto the scene and two Third Divisions (North & South) were formed as a result. In the top flight some truly remarkable milestones were reached. Huddersfield became the first outfit to win three Championships in a row, a feat emulated by Herbert Chapman's great Arsenal side in the early 1930s. Sadly Chapman died before their 1934-35 title was assured though.

The Second World War took its toll amongst players and teams but with the post-war euphoria and the promise of prosperous times ahead, crowd numbers increased and the game became hugely popular. The arrival of European competition in the 1950s allowed the best home-grown talent to showcase their skills to a much wider audience, and there was a period of great rivalry between the club sides. The World Cup, back after the war break, also provided a much needed boost to the game, with the home unions, now affiliated to FIFA, finally invited to take part.

Globally, the Austrians and Hungarians passed the baton to the South Americans when it came to advancing the game both as a skill and a spectator attraction. Brazil should probably have won the 1950 World Cup but faltered at the final hurdle. They would have to wait another eight years before finally realising their vast potential. Once at the top of the world game, only West Germany and Italy posed a long-term threat to that dominance, at least from a European perspective, while Argentina mounted the only serious challenge throughout the rest of the world.

Closer to home, the newly created European Cup quickly established itself as the World's premier club competition, with Real Madrid dominating the early years. Gradually though the British sides began to make their mark on the continent. Sadly the Munich air crash in 1958 robbed Manchester United of ten fine players (seven died immediately, Duncan Edwards passed away shortly afterwards in hospital and two players were forced to retire), but Matt Busby's new babes were destined to take Europe's biggest prize eventually. Their southern rivals Tottenham Hotspur were the first to achieve success on the continent, however. In 1961 they became only the third club to perform the League and Cup

Double, and two years later they won the European Cup Winners' Cup, a feat also achieved by West Ham in 1965. Celtic managed the unthinkable in 1967 and took the European Cup against the mighty Internazionale, and the following year United finally fulfilled their promise by beating a strong Benfica side 4-1 at Wembley.

Liverpool dominated the domestic club scene throughout the 1970s and early 1980s, taking eleven titles in sixteen years. They backed this up with success abroad, winning four European Cups. Brian Clough's Nottingham Forest took two and Aston Villa another one in this period of dominance for English teams. But the 1980s were troubled times for domestic football. Aside from the scourge of hooliganism, tragedy struck with the Bradford fire, Heysel riots and Hillsborough stadium disasters. Football in England had reached its lowest ebb and something needed to be done to resurrect the sport. Cue the television revolution, all-seater stadiums and cash by the bucket load.

Football now seems to be more about the money. Players' wages are, let's face it, ridiculous, but someone at the top (presumably the chairman) deems the outgoing to be acceptable. Chelsea's wage bill, to take one example, rose from £107 million to £114 million last year alone, but the club registered an £80 million loss, admittedly a drop in the ocean for wealthy backer Roman Abramovich who is reportedly worth around £10 billion. Where does the rest of the money come from then? The fans of course. It's a bit sad but admission prices to matches, as well as season tickets for that matter, have increased with the dawn of the Sky TV era, particularly with the saturation of all terrestrial and satellite channels with football since the advent of the Premier League in 1992. And what's happened as result of all this TV revenue? The big clubs have taken a bigger share and grown in value, while the small clubs have to fight day to day for survival.

The lower leagues found a way to fight back and make some money for themselves with the play-off system. The top two clubs are automatically promoted while the next four contest virtual semi-finals and finals to see who joins them. Of course the matches are played at the biggest venues - the Millennium Stadium standing in for Wembley while it underwent its over-budget facelift - to increase revenue and TV coverage. By 2004 the structure of English football read as follows:

Premiership, Championship, League One and League Two. Below the 92 League clubs, a number established in 1950, are the various other club sides who all do battle for that coveted League spot come the end of every season.

Since the advent of the Premier League, Manchester United and Arsenal have proved to be the dominant sides. Chelsea's extra cash and Liverpool's recent run in European Cup competitions have promoted these two into that elite group, and the 2007 League table simply enforced this view. Even though the top four swap positions occasionally there is a distinct gulf in class between them and the remainder of the division.

Player Speak 1

"Mirandinha will have more shots this afternoon than both sides put together"
MALCOLM MACDONALD

"If I had a blank piece of paper, there would be five names on it"
KEVIN KEEGAN

"If Glenn Hoddle had been any other nationality he would have got seventy or eighty caps for England"
JOHN BARNES

"Batistuta gets most of his goals with the ball"
IAN ST JOHN

"I'll be surprised if all twenty-two players are on the field at the end of the game. One has already been sent off"
GEORGE BEST

"I am not sure exactly why the winter break started but I think it has something to do with the weather"
OWEN HARGREAVES

"Whenever these two teams meet it's always a great game, but this wasn't a great game"
LEE DIXON

"He starts anticipating what's going to happen before it's even happened"
GRAEME LE SAUX

"That kind of ball is meat and two drink for the Palace defence"
DENIS IRWIN

"I don't know why we aren't scoring as we are keeping clean sheets"
EDWIN VAN DER SAR

"He's not unused to playing in midfield but at the same time he's not used to playing there either"
EMLYN HUGHES

"If someone in the crowd spits at you, you've just got to swallow it"
GARY LINEKER

"Steve McManaman once described Zinedine Zidane as 'ridiculous' and you can't get a higher compliment than that"
JASON MCATEER

"He's unpleased about that"
Mark Bright

"Paolo Di Canio is perfectly capable of scoring the goals he scores"
Bryan Robson

Coming to America

By the 1880s football was beginning to spread across the globe, primarily by way of the Commonwealth. Such was the sport's popularity though, that most nations it passed through adopted it. Strangely, when FIFA was formed in Paris in 1904, the seven nations present did not include England.

The Americans favoured the rugby-style version of the two sports, carrying the ball in hand being deemed a more entertaining game to watch. A variant of this had in fact been played at the university of Harvard since the 1820s. In 1876 teams from both there and Yale met to draw up a set of rules that ended up being similar to rugby, but not identical. The Intercollegiate Football Association (IFA) was the end product of the union and the name football stuck even though the game didn't really use the feet. Yale's Walter Camp further revised the rules in 1880 and the way the modern game is now played is effectively down to these changes.

With the formation of the National Collegiate Athletic Association (NCAA) in 1910, the sport in the US gained a structure and a credibility as an organised sport to rival baseball. In 1920 ten teams met at Canton, Ohio, to form the American Professional Football Association (APFA), the forerunner of the National Football League (NFL) which still exists today. During the meeting it was agreed that a few minor rule changes should be made and that players should be paid to compete.

The success of televising the 1966 World Cup immediately prompted financial backers to invest in the game in the US, and the North American Soccer League was born out of the United Soccer Association and the National Professional Soccer League. Several Canadian sides were also included in the venture to broaden its appeal but the first season in 1967 was very poorly received. A change was needed, and it was decided to try and lure the best players in the world to the NASL once their main careers were over. Pelé and George Best arrived in 1975, with Franz Beckenbauer joining a couple of years later. The experiment worked, and crowds of 70,000 turned up to watch these megastars. By 1980 there were 24 clubs and things appeared to be looking up. Sadly, however, the following year scheduling difficulties, problems with TV rights, falling standards and lower than expected gates all contributed to the sport's decline.

It was hoped that the 1994 World Cup would revive the game in North America, and though attendances were good, the game still refused to catch on in a big way. The latest to try his luck there is David Beckham, the out-of-favour Real Madrid star signing for LA Galaxy for five years in 2007 in a deal reported to be worth £128 million!

From the time the first ball was kicked in anger to the present day, the sport has conjured up countless heroes and villains, any number of idiots, a million snippets of trivia and an abundance of magic moments. Here now are some of the very best, and worst, from over a century of the beautiful game.

1 2 3 4 5 6 7 8 9 10 11

Domestic Disasters

"What they say about footballers being ignorant is rubbish. I spoke to a couple yesterday and they were quite intelligent"
RAQUEL WELCH (COMPARED WITH YOU, LOVE....)

What is the definition of a football gaffe? It's an interesting point, and clearly there are a wide variety of clangers that can be dropped. Of course there are the verbal slips that commentators, players and managers like to inflict on us. Some are very funny, particularly when the metaphors are mixed or the line ends up with a non-intended sexual meaning, others are downright bizarre and only the person responsible can have any idea what was meant. There are also the tactical blunders that have cost teams vital matches, the cases of wild overconfidence, the own goals, shocking misses, the horrendous refereeing decisions, and, of course, the goalkeeping nightmares, to name just a few…

The 1877 FA Cup Final was won by the Wanderers, yet again. However, they were a goal down early on in the match when goalkeeper Lord Alfred Kinnaird caught the ball from a long range Oxford shot and then stepped back over his own goal line before punting the ball up-field. A number of Oxford players appealed and the umpires ruled that the ball had crossed the line. You might have thought that with the Wanderers going on to win the incident would have been forgotten, but Lord Kinnaird wasn't prepared to have his name in the history books, so he went to the FA and forced them to agree that the umpires could not have seen the ball over the line! How many 'keepers wish they could do that today, I wonder? Kinnaird, incidentally, remains the only person to have played in FA Cup Finals in and out of goal and appear on the score sheet in both matches. In nine appearances overall, he won five winners' medals, scored three goals (as well as the celebrated own goal), and in 1911, acknowledging his contribution to the game, the FA presented him with the cup itself.

Preston were so confident of beating West Bromwich Albion in the 1888 FA Cup Final that they arranged for the team photo before the match to be taken with the cup. Some reports state that the referee refused them permission to take the snap, but it didn't matter anyway as they lost, 2-1. The word Albion, incidentally, succeeds many English club names, and appears to derive from the Latin *albus,* meaning white - from the cliffs at Dover - which is where many early settlers came ashore.

Andrew Baird suffered the misfortune of getting one of his hands stuck in the back of the net at the beginning of Queen's Park's cup tie with Rangers in 1894. Opposing centre forward David Boyd showed no mercy and scored while the hapless Baird was still trying to disentangle himself.

Aston Villa won the 1895 FA Cup against old rivals West Brom, and so proud were they of the achievement that they displayed the trophy in the window of William Shilcock's sports shop in Birmingham. One night in September thieves broke in and stole it. The cup was never found, and the Villa had to pay £25 for a replacement.

Referee Charlie Sutcliffe was known to be a Burnley man to the core, but some Blackburn fans suspected his allegiance lay with Liverpool. In the 1896 Blackburn - Liverpool tie, the score was listed as 1-0, though Sutcliffe somehow managed to disallow six perfectly good strikes from the home team.

In the days before pampered players were transported to away grounds by luxury coach, chauffeur-driven limousine or private jet, they had to make do with the train or their own car. In 1897, one West Brom player was valued so highly that a train was specially commandeered to collect him after he missed the scheduled departure. The club footed the £50 bill. And nine Bristol City players got lost on their way to Southampton for a match in 1941. The home side generously lent the west-countrymen their coach and five reserves, while a soldier, local schoolmaster and spectator also got a start! Not surprisingly Southampton won (5-2), though their trainer did score against them.

Lancashire side Darwen were renowned as one of the finest League teams in the country in the latter quarter of the 19th century. They held Old Etonians in the FA Cup and were one of the first sides to pay their players covertly. By 1899 though the club was on the slide, and in that season they set a rather poor record. In all they lost 18 consecutive Second Division matches, the worst run by any League team before or since (non-Leaguers Princes Risborough lost all 30 games of their 1953-54 season and Doncaster Rovers lost 34 of 46 games in 1997-98). Sadly Darwen occupy the 'top' spot in another category. A 12-0 defeat against West Brom in 1892 remains the heaviest top flight loss in English football, though it was equalled by Leicester Fosse when they were trounced by the same score in 1909.

The club was also famous for a visit to Blackburn's Ewood Park in the early 1890s. The home side, confident of an easy win, fielded only three 1st XI players, and the Darwen crowd felt cheated and humiliated. They proceeded to defecate on the pitch before removing the goalposts, smashing windows and stealing carpets.

The 1901 FA Cup Final pitted non-League side Tottenham Hotspur against Sheffield United in Bolton. Expectations were high for a giant kill and a huge gate was predicted. However, the railways refused to offer cheap tickets for the event, and previous crowd disturbances at the ground had led to some unpleasant congestion. In short, the fans stayed away, the eventual gate being only 20,470 instead of the forecast 80,000. As a result the local bakers had a nightmare. They'd prepared thousands of meat pies but there was no one to eat them and many had to be given away after the match. That Saturday became known as Pie Saturday in the town as a direct consequence! You would have thought that with the legendary twenty-stone 'keeper William 'Fatty' Foulke in attendance a surplus of pies would have been a most welcome problem.

Spurs won the match 3-1.

Oldham Athletic were pushing hard for the First Division title in 1915 when their left back, W. Cook, was sent off against Middlesbrough. Unfortunately for the Latics, Cook refused to leave the field and was banned for a year, his loss contributing to Oldham's defensive frailties in their run in to the end of the season and costing them the championship by two points.

The notion of having pre-match entertainment is nothing new. As far back as the 1920s Watford fan Joey Goodchild would perform dance routines on the roof of Cassio Road's main stand. Sadly for him the show was discontinued when he overbalanced and toppled into the crowd, causing minor injuries to himself and two spectators. The club coughed up £20 by way of compensation, while Goodchild coughed up a lung.

Charlton decided to build a massive new stadium in 1919, but the main stand was only completed in 1922. Good reviews and a chance to host a number of Cup Finals followed but then, citing a lack of local support, the club decided to move! This left the reserves playing in an empty stadium that could accommodate well over 50,000. Over the years the ground fell into disrepair, but the fans somehow managed to save it and it reopened as the Valley in 1992.

Stockport County needed to win or draw against Stoke towards end of the 1927 season to ensure their promotion to Division Two North. Chairman Ernie Barlow knew that local rivals Bolton might be willing to let ageing England striker Joe Smith change clubs and negotiated his transfer. Stockport duly pulled in a big crowd, as Smith was still a draw player, and the match ended 2-2 thanks largely to his heroics. However, shortly after the game it emerged that the Football League had contacted Barlow to remind him that Smith would need to be registered in time to play. Barlow placed the important telegram in his pocket and forgot all about the rules. When the League found out they docked Stockport two points and fined them heavily, the double punishment scuppering their plans for promotion.

The first game to be broadcast locally was the 1926 FA Cup Final between Bolton and Manchester City, though only a few public halls in both towns were included in the loop. The Arsenal - Sheffield United match mentioned a little later was the first to be broadcast nationally in early 1927.

It was in that year that the FA Cup left England for Wales, the only time in its history that the trophy has not been won by an English side. Cardiff City scored the only goal in the final against Arsenal, the ball somehow squirming under Dan Lewis (a Welshman)'s body after a shot from Hughie Ferguson midway through the second half. The ball might not have made it over the line but Lewis accidentally helped it on its way with a nudge from his knee. Charlie Buchan and Jimmy Brain both had chances to equalise but, with the goal at their mercy, they left the ball to each other and the Cardiff 'keeper re-gathered it. Celebrations in Cardiff were on a scale never before seen. This was the first final to be broadcast nationwide on the radio and hundreds of thousands had gathered in the parks to listen. Arsenal, however, couldn't even drown their sorrows afterwards; their case of champagne was stolen during the last minutes of the match!

There have been other cases of daylight robbery while matches have been taking place. During the Scarborough - Gainsborough Trinity match on Easter Day in 1949, the home players went to their changing room at halftime to discover everything but their clothes had been stolen. All wallets, keys, train tickets and jewellery had disappeared, though the Gainsborough dressing room had not been touched. The match announcer used the public address system to ask if there were any detectives in the ground, but not even Officer Bond could apprehend the crooks and every penny of the money disappeared. A similar situation arose during a Devon derby match a few years before, but this time the robbers were caught in the act at halftime. Though they fled the ground, players and supporters quickly rounded them up and gave them a good kicking!

The referee for the 1930 Huddersfield - Sheffield Wednesday FA Cup Semi-final looked down at his watch and blew for fulltime just as the ball was entering the Huddersfield net. As he couldn't be sure if the ball had crossed the line while his gaze was averted, the ref adjudged that the 'goal' should not stand and Wednesday were denied a visit to Wembley as a result.

The 1932 FA Cup Final will be remembered for a goal that should never have been allowed to stand. Arsenal were hot favourites against Newcastle and were a goal to the good inside fifteen minutes. Twenty or so minutes later Newcastle's Richardson beat a defender and took the ball to the dead-ball line before crossing for front man Allen to nod home. Arsenal's players were convinced, however, that Richardson had allowed the ball to cross the line and they'd marched up-field to await the goal kick. They should have played to the whistle because none of the officials spotted the error and the goal stood. Photographs taken of the incident show the ball to be well out of play, but neither the linesmen or referee were close enough to spot it. Allen scored again with a quarter of an hour to go and underdogs Newcastle claimed the trophy.

Cardiff City's Ninian Park, named after financial backer Lord Ninian Crichton Stuart, was built on the site of an old rubbish tip in 1910. Players falling over after tackles frequently cut themselves on glass shards sticking out of the ground and many teams were wary of playing there. The Main Stand was destroyed by fire in 1937 after thieves tried to blow up the safe they thought held the day's takings. The explosion destroyed the empty safe while the resulting fire took care of the stand. And it was here that the great Jock Stein had a heart attack and died having just watched Scotland qualify for the 1986 World Cup. The ground, it would seem, had some sort of curse on it. And it certainly saw its fair share of garbage.

An enormous number of UK grounds have been rebuilt after being damaged by fire. The blaze that destroyed the main stand at Birmingham's St Andrew's ground during the Second World War, however, was started accidentally, by a fireman! He was probably fired...

Goalkeeper Albert Iremonger once barged team-mates aside so he could take a penalty for Notts County. He smashed the ball so hard onto the crossbar that it rebounded to the halfway line. Desperately chasing back to beat the opposition forwards to the ball, he threw a hopeful boot at it to try and clear it but instead watched helplessly as he thumped it into his own net sixty yards away.

You couldn't fault Port Vale's ambition in the mid-1940s. Buoyed by recent success, the directors decided to build a 70,000 capacity ground dubbed 'The Wembley of the North'. By 1945 the money had run out however and most of the main stands hadn't even been built. Those that had been suffered fire damage and neglect, and capacity was then limited to just 16,500.

Charlton lost the 1946 FA Cup Final 4-1 but they returned the next year with a far better chance of claiming the trophy. This time they were up against Burnley, and manager Jimmy Seed's tactics worked perfectly. In fact, the only thing he got wrong the entire day was dropping the cup and breaking the lid!

Manchester City's 'keeper Frank Swift liked to place his cap on the ground behind him before inspecting the goalmouth prior to matches in the 1940s. Sadly for him, in their match against Preston in 1949 he was still going through this ritual when he had to pick the ball out of the net. The referee had forgotten to check if he was ready for the kick-off and Swift had not noticed that the game had started.

Apologies to all the goalkeepers out there, for this section continues with another few moments best forgotten by the man between the sticks. The first is also a moment completely forgotten by the man who scored, too, as Arsenal's Ronnie Rooke was knocked senseless by a wayward goal kick from Middlesbrough's Rolando Ugolini in 1948. The ball, of course, rebounded from Rooke's face into the unprotected net. Bangor's Timothy Dalton knows exactly how Ugolini feels, for some half a century later he smashed a back pass into the face of an opposing striker and couldn't recover in time to stop the goal. A slightly poorer back pass from Barnet's Mark Newsome did for his own 'keeper, Phillips, the ball bobbling over his attempted hoof up-field and nestling in the bottom corner. Carl Muggleton is another who knows how it feels to whack the ball into the opposing striker. He gifted Oldham a game by default in the 1990s just as the commentators were giving opposite number Paul Gerrard the man-of-the-match award. And so did Ipswich's Kelvin Davis in their match against QPR. He had plenty of time to take a free kick before deciding to smash it into the back of the striker's head. Dundee's Robert Douglas will also be practicing his clearances. He calmly chipped the ball onto the opposing striker's head and then watched it rebound into his net. Kevin Pilkington went one better in 2005, deciding that placing the clearance off his own defender, David Pipe, meant he could claim he hadn't scored the own goal.

Manchester City's Andy Dibble arguably went one better than accidentally cracking the ball against the opposing striker when he tried to nutmeg Newcastle's Keith Gillespie. Of course the 'keeper got it completely wrong and ended up gifting the Magpies an easy goal. And even the great Peter Schmeichel wasn't immune to dropping the occasional clanger from a back-pass. Team-mate Gary Pallister knocked an easy ball back to the Dane, only to watch in horror as the big man sliced his attempted clearance into Barnsely striker Hendrie's path.

It wasn't until 1939 that players were forced to wear numbered shirts, but they didn't always correspond to the player's position on the field. In 1952 Liverpool swapped their left winger with their striker in the hope that the Wolves defenders would become confused. The plan worked, the Wolves players not knowing who to mark, and Liverpool scored two early goals!

The Gravesend referee who officiated for an inter-army match in 1955 will be best remembered for not checking his watch. Despite the occasional glance he failed to realise it was broken and the first half of the contest lasted 70 minutes!

In the same year, Arsenal's Dennis Evans thumped the ball into his own net and started celebrating after hearing the final whistle in their match against Blackpool. Sadly for him, the whistle had been blown by someone in the crowd and the own goal was allowed to stand. Luckily for him Arsenal had already scored four by then.

"Sadly for him the whistle had been blown by someone in the crowd"

Barrow in Lancashire were due to host Gillingham in October 1961, but the Londoners decided, somewhat strangely, to travel the three hundred miles on the day of the game. Their 0915 train from Euston would get them there an hour before kick-off, which seemed safe enough, but they hadn't bargained on sitting on a bus in traffic until nearly ten. The next train wouldn't get them to Barrow in time, and travelling by car or coach was out of the question in the days before motorways. The only other option was to charter an aircraft, at considerable expense, and fly to Blackpool, the scheduled airlines to Newcastle and Manchester being fully booked. With time running out, four cars and a police escort had to be employed to race them to the ground. They arrived at 1730, fifteen minutes after the scheduled kick-off time. The team changed hurriedly and ran out onto the field. They probably wish they hadn't bothered. Barrow were seven goals to the good before the match was abandoned due to bad light. The League, of course, ruled that enough of the match had been played to allow the result to stand and Gillingham went home tails between legs.

Leeds United's goalie Gary Sprake was a great servant to the game but he'll be best remembered for a tremendous howler at Anfield in an FA Cup replay in the early '70s. Jack Charlton passed the ball back to Sprake, waited for him to gather it and then made himself available for the long punt up-field. Sprake had other ideas though. He collected the ball and made as if to hurl it up one of the wings. Sadly for him, the ball clung to his hand and only came out when Sprake was facing his own goal. An amused announcer then played 'Careless Hands' over the public address system.

Though younger readers will only remember George Best for his off-field antics, the drinking binges in particular, those who were lucky enough to watch him play will recall that he was a supremely gifted footballer, a genius. Sadly he never showcased his talent on the World Cup stage, but he did play many internationals against the other home nations when there was still a championship at stake. England were perhaps lucky to be 1-0 up against Northern Ireland in 1971 when the ball rolled through to another great, England's Gordon Banks. The goalkeeper shaped to punt and then, before he knew it, the ball had been craftily stolen by Best before he could kick it. The Irishman knocked it into the English net and started celebrating the equaliser. Banks looked embarrassed; he hadn't been impeded and the ball was in play. Goal, you might think. Wrong. Inexplicably, the referee disallowed the strike and England held on to win. The Irish 'keeper and good friend of Best, Pat Jennings, commiserated with his mate afterwards and discussed how the goal should probably have been allowed to stand.

By a quirky twist of fate Tottenham were playing Manchester United later on that season when a similar situation unfolded, but this time Jennings was in goal for the opposition, Spurs. He gathered the ball, went to punt, and Best nicked it as it was between his hand and foot. Best then rolled it in and shrugged at Jennings. Sadly for the goalie the referee and linesmen had turned up-field to await his punt. When they heard the crowd reaction and saw the ball in the net, they had no choice other than to award the goal.

Time now to visit our first selection of verbal gaffes, from the aptly named gaffers, and you won't be surprised to learn that there are many more on the way. Of course team managers can't really help once the whistle has gone to start the match, but they are supposed to be able to bring the best out of their players during training and at the pre-match and halftime team talks. Footballers are easily confused at the best of times, so imagine them having to listen to this lot.

Manager Speak 1 – Utter Nonsense

"We can't replace a player like Gary Speed. Where do get an experienced player like him with a left foot and a head?"
BOBBY ROBSON

"When you are 4-0 up, you shouldn't lose 7-1"
LAWRIE McMENEMY

"The Spaniards have been reduced to aiming aimless balls into the box"
RON ATKINSON

"The underdogs will start as favourites for this match"
CRAIG BROWN

"I felt a lump in my mouth as the ball went in"
TERRY VENABLES

"When I go to the press conference after the game, the game has not yet finished"
JOSE MOURINHO

"You can't do better than go away from home and get a draw"
KEVIN KEEGAN

"We didn't underestimate them; they were just a lot better than we thought"
BOBBY ROBSON

"Zero-zero is sometimes a big score"
RON ATKINSON

"I wouldn't say he's the best left winger in the Premiership but there are none better"
RON ATKINSON

"Football isn't a matter of life and death. It's much more important than that"
BILL SHANKLY

"For some games you've just got to pick your eleven best players, and sometimes that means leaving out your best player"
LAWRIE SANCHEZ

"We won 5-1, but that was because we were winning 1-1 at halftime"
DAVID ARCHER

The Own Goal Hall of Shame

It's immediately obvious that listing every own goal would take several volumes of an encyclopaedia-size book. I've stuck to the classic howlers where the - usually - poor defender smashes one past his goalkeeper, who's standing rooted to the spot.

The first League own goal wasn't long in coming. On the first day of the new competition in 1888 Aston Villa's George Cox scored for Wolves. Middlesbrough's Robert Stuart was an early pretender to be the king of the own goal, a crown later jealously guarded by a certain Frank Sinclair. His name appeared on the score-sheet at the wrong end five times in their 1934 season.

In 1974, Newcastle goalie Tony Bell's first top flight appearance was against a strong Spurs side. He didn't exactly make a good impression, though. Having caught the ball cleanly from a cross, he overbalanced, landed on his arse and threw the ball into the net behind him. Sheffield United's Jim Brown made an almost identical howler against West Ham the following year, the ball bouncing off his chest and over his shoulder into the net. The poor 'keeper then shipped ten against Gillingham towards the end of his career, about ninety minutes from the end as it happens. In 1977 Torquay's defender Pat Kruse achieved the almost unbelievable feat of putting one in his own net (for Cambridge) after just six seconds!

Stuart Metcalf brought the ball down onto his knee, juggled it twice and then buried it past his own 'keeper to Newcastle's delight in a match in the 1980s, while Huddersfield's Steve Jenkins's strike was better still. He lashed a volley into his own net and then started throwing punches at opposition forwards Paul Devlin and Kevin Francis who were baiting him over the error. Jenkins was promptly shown the red card to cap a pretty dire performance.

Spare a thought for the hapless Jorge Nino of Brazilian side Democrata. In a match against Atlético Mineiro in 1982 he managed a hat-trick of own goals. Not surprisingly his side lost, 5-1.

Crystal Palace stopper George Wood had a shocker against Aston Villa in the mid-'80s. He parried a harmless cross into the striker's path, then, when the resulting header was actually drifting a yard wide, he managed to dive headlong into it and put it in his own net! Leicester's Keith Weller had been given the 'goal of the season' the year before after his spectacular strike against Luton, but he bent a thirty-yard shot around his own 'keeper at Kenilworth Road to cancel it out.

Sheffield United's John Pemberton buried a cross from Manchester City's David White that was meant for Mike Sheron in 1993. Pemberton seemed to stumble at the last minute before connecting ruthlessly with his right boot and sending the ball slamming into the roof of the net. Forest Green's Wayne Hatswell can sympathise for he knows that sinking feeling well having directed the ball beautifully into his own top corner with a thunderous left foot.

Portsmouth's Jamie Ashdown can be considered extremely unlucky when he conceded an own goal against Gillingham. The shot he was trying to save rebounded off the post and into his back, then ricocheted into the air. Ashdown stood, desperately scanned the area for the ball, then felt it fall onto his back and watched it roll into the net. Bugger!

Nottingham Forest's Mark Crossley will be remembered as a fine goalkeeper. However, in a match against Blackburn he caught the ball cleanly from a Colin Hendrie header and then rolled over and threw the ball into his own net.

"He rolled over and threw the ball into his own net"

His team-mates had already turned up-field for the punt and did not look too pleased to see the ball behind the goal line when the roar went up from Rovers' supporters.

Leicester and England stopper Ian Walker knows exactly how he feels. He rolled onto and then over the ball in a match against Bolton, the ball eventually squirming out from underneath his body and over the line. And David James, he of 'Calamity' fame, has a number if howlers to his (dis) credit, the 'catch the ball from a weak Blackburn shot and then pass it rugby-style into your own net' being favourite, though not for West Ham fans.

Liverpool's Sander Westerveld came out to claim a Chelsea corner, then decided to punch the cross clear instead. Sadly for him, he belted it straight into his own net with a goal reminiscent of a John Lukic special while the 'keeper was at Leeds. The boys in blue were a little less pleased after Andy Myers' perfectly controlled header beat his own goalie in a Premiership encounter with Liverpool in the '90s.

It was all smiles again at Stamford Bridge though after Manchester United arrived with new £4.5 million signing Massimo Taibi in goal for a Premiership clash in 1999. Taibi had already caused some consternation at Old Trafford by gifting Southampton three goals, one of which, a Matt le Tissier pea-roller, somehow squirted through his legs, so there was no great surprise as howler followed clanger in a 5-0 defeat by the Blues. A joke about personal computer viruses quickly followed, the Taibi virus, of course, not letting you save anything. And when United couldn't blame their 'keeper for giving away their lead to Southampton, they put it down to their grey shirts, one of the many abominable colours sported by them recently. Still, they changed them at halftime and ended up losing anyway, 3-1. It's a bit sad and predictable nowadays when screwing the fans for all they've got seems to take priority, but is changing the strip regularly the only way to keep the coffers overflowing?

Scotland's Willie Donachie will be remembered fondly as a player, except by his international goalkeeper in their match against Wales in the annual home union tournament in 1978. The goalie rolled it out to him and he attempted an immediate back-pass, even though he wasn't under any pressure. Of course he miss hit the simple pass and scored for Wales from twenty-five yards. He never managed a goal for his country at the right end, and he ensured this match finished all square.

Wimbledon's Dave Beasant was chipped beautifully by Wally Downes in 1983. Sadly for the goalkeeper, it was his own defender who'd scored, and from a direct free-kick at that. Here, though, the referee got things wrong by awarding the goal. The correct decision would have been to award a corner.

Spurs were hot favourites to win the 1987 FA Cup Final against Coventry. Sadly for them they weren't able to maintain their 100% record in finals as a Gary Mabbutt own goal cancelled out his earlier strike at the right end and secured the trophy for the Sky Blues. The ball cruelly deflected from his knee and looped over a stranded Ray Clemence (Bert Turner had been the first to score for both sides in the final when he netted for both Charlton and Derby in 1946).

Four years later Spurs were back in the final, only this time they faced Nottingham Forest. The Londoners conceded an early Stuart Pearce thunderbolt free-kick, awarded for Paul Gascoigne's dreadful tackle on Gary Charles. This challenge saw Gazza stretchered off with a badly damaged knee, an injury that turned out to be serious enough to postpone his big-money transfer to Lazio. For some reason the referee took pity on him and didn't send him off though. Spurs then equalised, before Des Walker stepped up to give Spurs the win, the only problem being that he was Forest's best defender. Spurs swung in a corner which wasn't cleared and he headed past Mark Crossley from close range. Walker knew immediately how Mabbutt must have felt against Coventry.

Celtic's Jonathan Gould is yet another goalkeeper who struggled with a simple strike. The Dundee striker nodded the ball towards the goal and then watched in amusement at Gould gathered it, passed it backwards and scored a classic clanger.

Borussia Dortmund's Leonardo Dede scored against his own 'keeper, Jens Lehmann, with a spectacular twenty-five-yard header. And while we're in Germany, Bayern Munich's Jens Jeremies had a complete communication breakdown with goalkeeper Oliver Kahn in a match against 1860 Berlin recently. Instead of letting Kahn claim the rather weak corner, Jeremies decided it would be better to head it past him into his own net. Kahn, usually big, strong and capable, was not amused and the two brushed past each other with curiously serious expressions.

Internazionale's Italian defender Gianluca Festa lobbed his own goalie from all of twenty-five yards with a spectacular strike. He then moved to England, helped Middlesbrough to the latter stages of the

2002 FA Cup and shinned the ball past Australian Mark Schwarzer to gift Arsenal victory and sink their hopes of winning the trophy. Sadly Schwarzer also knows what it's like to gift the opposition victory, only his clanger came in the League Cup Final for Middlesbrough against Bolton in 2004. He managed to spoon an easy shot from Davies over his shoulder and into the net.

Manchester City's defender Jamie Pollock chipped the opposing striker beautifully then beat another man before heading into his own net. If he'd been at the right end of the pitch it would have surely been a candidate for goal of the month. Sadly, it wasn't.

Fulham's French striker Steve Marlet netted at his own end against Arsenal in 2002. He sliced his attempted clearance so badly that it spooned up and into the goal out of Edwin van Der Sar's reach.

We drop a couple of leagues to Weston-super-mare now as Kevin Brown scored an almost identical goal with his sliced clearance. Blackburn's Colin Hendrie wouldn't dare slice the ball; he netted a fabulous, though not very well-received, volley into his own net. Arsenal's Silvinho's was even more impressive in that he smashed a cross back past his 'keeper into the opposite top corner.

Walsall's Charlie Ntamark actually dribbled round one of his own defenders before calmly placing the ball past his 'keeper in their match against West Ham in 1994. Hammers' striker Tony Cottee then had the cheek to claim the goal as his! Arsenal's Ian Wright also had the temerity to claim a defensive howler for himself when Leicester's Steve Walsh lobbed Kasey Keller. Walsh will forever be remembered for a few red cards, especially by David Geddis, who was left with a broken jaw after one encounter (which led to an eleven-match ban), as well as Wolves front-man Steve Bull, who was another sparring partner, literally. Keller was on the receiving end of another own goal when Tottenham's striker turned defender Gary Doherty (the 'Ginger Pelé') beat him with an inch-perfect pass into the roof of the net at White Hart Lane.

Shane Wesley scored an improbable bullet header for Cardiff when he was trying to clear a corner, something even the Premiership's greats aren't immune from. Jimmy Floyd Hasselbank buried a diving header past countryman Ed de Goey in a match against Newcastle, while England's World Cup winning captain Bobby Moore scored a similar stunner while playing for Fulham towards the end of his career. De Goey had a less than auspicious start to his Chelsea career. On his debut he gifted Southampton a goal after trying to dribble a back-pass round opposing striker Kevin Davies. Coincidentally, commentator Alan Parry was just suggesting how it might be the time for de Goey to show off some of his skills. He probably wishes he hadn't now.

Iain Dowie was always going to get a mention in this section. He scored a brilliant header while playing for West Ham against Stockport in 1996, only one of a series of blunders at the wrong end of the pitch. Liverpool's John Arne Riise and Aston Villa's Gareth Southgate can't escape a grilling here either, for they both contributed fantastic headed own goals during their Premiership careers.

Sadly the teams involved were difficult to track down for this next slice of own goal madness, but South American striker Perez scored in the wrong net from sixty yards after a completely miss hit pass went wildly off course and was caught in the breeze.

Ipswich's Eddie Youds had a complete nightmare against Arsenal when he tried to clear a ball trickling towards the corner flag. Instead of thumping it up-field, he almost trod on it, fell over and then hooked it into his own net. The Portman Road crowd thought they'd had enough entertainment for one afternoon when up popped Lee Dixon to back head a stunning own goal past David Seaman in the second half! Arsenal's woes at the back continued a few seasons later against Blackburn, when Edu popped up to chip the ball over David Seaman and into the top corner. Kolo Toure was another to bury the ball, this time it was a fierce drive into the roof of the net against west Ham in 2002. And while playing against Manchester City in 2003 Lauren actually took the time to control the pass he received before charging at full speed back towards his own net and slotting the ball comfortably past Taylor. Let's give Lee Dixon another headache too. He calmly beat David Seaman from all of thirty yards with a brilliant chip while playing against Coventry in 1991.

Sheffield United's Brian Gayle had a nightmare in their match against Leeds in 1992. A Cantona-inspired Leeds were going for the title but they desperately needed a win to consolidate their position. In the dying minutes the teams were locked together at 2-2, when Gayle contrived to clip the ball beautifully past the Leeds striker with his knee before heading it into his own net. This of course gave their Yorkshire rivals the championship and ensured the Blades' defeat.

While playing for Liverpool against Burnley in the 2005 FA Cup, Djimi Traore scored a fabulous own goal in that he actually rolled the rather poor cross into his own net with a beautiful drag back. It was a delightful piece of skill, just not the right end of the pitch. In fact the goal proved decisive, and Rafa Benitez had to watch his side eliminated. Manchester United fans were quick on the uptake at their League meeting a few weeks later:

"Don't blame it on Hamann, don't blame it on Biscan, don't blame it on Finnan, blame it on Traore!"

Duisburg's Dietmar Hirsch scored with an even more impressive piece of skill when he bicycle-kicked the ball into his own top corner!

Aston Villa's Peter Enckelman had a complete disaster when trying to control a throw-in from team-mate Olaf Mellberg during their match against Birmingham in 2002. Instead of trapping the ball, he let it slide under his boot for a calamitous own goal. If he'd had the presence of mind to claim he hadn't touched it - a fact difficult to corroborate even with the video evidence - the goal would not have stood as a player must touch the ball once it's been reintroduced to the field of play for it to be 'live'. Sadly Enckelman's reactions suggested he must have either got the faintest of touches or didn't know the rules, and David Elleray, after consulting the linesman, awarded the goal. Even worse was to follow, some might argue, for a deranged City fan then came onto the pitch and began gesticulating in front of the disconsolate 'keeper that he was a wanker, one occasion where everybody watching just wished Enckelman would lay the idiot out. (A similar incident occurred back in 1938 when Barnsley's Frank Bokas took a throw-in against Manchester United. The 'keeper misjudged the bounce, got the faintest touch and the ball trickled over the line for the score.)

Just to put the smile back on the faces of those from the Midlands, who can forget David Dunn's wonderful piece of skill in the Blackburn - Aston Villa match in 2002. Trying a delightful centre with his right foot tucked behind his left heel, he only succeeded in missing the ball and kicking his own leg out from under him. Luckily he managed a wry smile as he lay face down in the mud, and though manager Steve Bruce had the same initial reaction, he then dropped him for a few games. Crowd reaction to the blunder: predictable.

Howard Wilkinson's beleaguered Sunderland managed to score not one but three own goals in an error ridden first half against Charlton at the Stadium of Light in 2003. The hapless Michael Proctor contributed two goals and an assist in the 3-1 loss.

Crystal Palace's Tony Popovic scored for Portsmouth with a beautiful flick behind his back in their 2004 meeting. If it had been at the right end it would surely have made the top ten list for goal of the season.

Holmbury St Mary's big defender Stuart Turner will want to forget several moments from their 2005-06 season. Though the club gained promotion, some would argue that Turner had money on them not making it into the Guildford and Woking Premier League. He wrong-footed retiring 'keeper Phil King with a beautiful back-pass at the beginning of the season, then smashed a volley past newcomer Liam McCann a couple of matches later at Addlestone, though in his 'defence' he had been drinking until four that morning. He finished off the series with a delightful flick into his own net against a Dutch representative side in Amsterdam in March 2006, though the author, who was in goal again, might have deflected the ball into his foot. I've been asked not to mention his stunning twenty-five yard strike into the right net at Byfleet, so I won't.

Club-mate Dave Archer is also well-known for netting at the wrong end, his finest moment coming in Holmbury's 1999 fixture against Worpelsdon. Goalkeeper Graham Wadey cleared the ball up-field with a huge punt but Archer misjudged its flight in the wind and instead of volleying it towards the opposition penalty area, he ended up lashing it back past the stranded Wadey and into his own top corner from all of fifty yards, for one of the greatest own goals of all-time. Tough to beat, you might think, but that hasn't stopped the defender trying. While playing at left back, he once collected a pass from goalkeeper Phil King on the edge of his own area. Then, making as if to really give it some with his right foot, he watched helplessly as the ball sliced off the outside of his boot. It then curled back beautifully over King's head and into the far left corner of his own goal, the second of two spectacular strikes. Holmbury's limited fan base has been swelling in recent years, in numbers, not in girth, though some might argue. Perhaps they're hoping to witness another Archer special…

Liverpool's Jamie Carragher scored with a delightful step-over in the 2006 FA Cup Final against West Ham at the Millennium Stadium. It was just a shame that it was at the wrong end. The match was a terrific advert for English football and finished 3-3, a Steven Gerrard 75 mph special at the final whistle forcing the game into extra time. West Ham's Zamora, Konchesky and Ferdinand then missed their penalties and the trophy was on its way to Anfield, sparing Carragher's blushes as it went.

Chelsea's Michael Essien helped Tottenham to an early lead in the quarter-final of the 2007 FA Cup at Stamford Bridge when he slid in to clear an Aaron Lennon cross. Sadly, he hadn't read Peter Cech's intentions and placed the ball past the advancing 'keeper. Spurs should have buried the champions under an avalanche of goals but couldn't take advantage of some terrible defending and Chelsea fought back from two goals down to take the tie to a replay, which they then won.

We'll end this section with two extraordinary heroes of the own goal. First up, let's pay a brief homage to the undoubted king of the art: Leicester's Frank Sinclair has a catalogue of errors to his name including a headed 90th minute goal to ensure defeat by Arsenal, another in the next game to gift Chelsea a draw in the final minute, and another, a forty-yard back-pass in a relegation six-pointer against Middlesbrough that left Ian Walker stranded.

If Sinclair stands for quantity then Chris Brass stands for quality. In a Darlington - Bury match in 2006 he waited underneath a high ball before deciding to clear it over his shoulder and up the pitch towards halfway. That was the intention. The reality was that he half-overhead bicycle-kicked the ball into his own face, breaking his nose, then watched helplessly as the ball cannoned off at high speed into the net. Something he could never do again in a million years of trying…

We paid them a brief, albeit un-credited, visit earlier so let's have another listen to the players now. We're well versed on how the managers can confuse both themselves and their teams with their mindless drivel, so let's hear how the athletes themselves respond.

Player Speak 2

"He has just gone behind my back in front of my face"
CRAIG BELLAMY

"My parents have been there for me ever since I was about seven"
DAVID BECKHAM

"I'd like to play for an Italian club like Barcelona"
MARK DRAPER

"I spent a lot of money on booze, birds and fast cars, while the rest I just squandered"
GEORGE BEST

"It took a lot of bottle for Tony to own up"
IAN WRIGHT PRAISES CLUB MATE TONY ADAMS ACCEPTING THAT HE SUFFERED FROM ALCOHOLISM

"The only thing I have in common with George Best is that we come from the same place, play for the same club, and were discovered by the same man"
NORMAN WHITESIDE

"Gary Neville says that Porto are a bunch of girls who go down too easily"
PETER SCHMEICHEL

"I couldn't settle in Italy. It was like living in a foreign country"
IAN RUSH

"I've never made a prediction and I never will"
PAUL GASCOIGNE

"When you make a mistake, it becomes a mistake"
CRAIG BELLAMY

"We're definitely going to get Brooklyn christened but we don't know into which religion"
DAVID BECKHAM

"Ever since I broke my neck I haven't looked back"
PAUL GASCOIGNE

"Fourth spot is what we're aiming for. We don't want to be second best"
PHIL NEVILLE

"Without being too harsh on David, he cost us the match"
IAN WRIGHT

More Domestic Disasters

Prodigiously gifted Scotsman Denis Law had a long and distinguished career with both main Manchester clubs as well as enjoying a spell with Italians Torino. By 1973 he was past his best and Manchester United decided to release him to City for his farewell season the following year. The penultimate game of that season, somewhat predictably, was a

Manchester derby, with United needing a win to avoid relegation. The game needed a spark but didn't have it; Law could have scored a hat-trick if he'd still been with United, but pitifully few chances fell his or the Blues' way. Then, with a certain air of inevitability about it and with only a few minutes left for Manchester United to salvage their season, the ball came to Law inside United's six-yard box. He had his back to goal so surely couldn't score and relegate his beloved former team. But with the deftest of back heels, he consigned the Reds to Division Two. Both teams had to be taken off as pandemonium erupted at Old Trafford and Law skulked off to contemplate retirement.

Rodney Marsh brought about his own 'retirement' from international football with a quip to England manager Sir Alf Ramsay in 1973. In the pre-match team talk Ramsay was asking for more effort from his players:

AR: *"When you play for England you have to work harder. In the first forty-five minutes I'll be watching you, Rodney, and if the effort's not there I'm going to pull you off at halftime"*
RM: *"Really? All we get at Manchester City is an orange"*

Orient's Bill Roffey stepped up to take a free-kick against Arsenal in 1978 and promptly blasted the ball miles over the crossbar. A policeman on the pitch surround back-pedalled to try and catch the ball but only succeeded in tripping over and falling into the crowd.

The 1980s wasn't the best decade for the players or fans of Bristol City. In a League consisting of 92 clubs, they dropped 86 places, including being relegated three years on the trot.

The Manchester City - Tottenham FA Cup Final of 1981, the 100th such event, will be remembered for the fortune and misfortune of City's Tommy Hutchinson. The Spurs side boasting Crooks, Archibald, Ardiles, Hoddle and Villa were favourites to win but Hutchinson put the northerners ahead after half an hour. Ecstasy. Inside the last ten minutes Hoddle curled a free-kick towards Joe Corrigan's goal but it looked to be heading wide. Hutchinson, sprinting out from the wall to charge the strike down, managed to redirect it with his shoulder, however. It wrong-footed Corrigan and ended up in the far corner. Agony. Spurs of course won the replay, Ricky Villa's wonder goal proving decisive. Hutchinson remains one of only three players to score at both ends in the Cup Final, Bert Turner managing it for Charlton/Derby in 1946, and Spurs' Gary Mabbutt ensuring the north Londoners' perfect record in finals ended, after their previous seven triumphs, in 1987 against un-fancied Coventry City.

Manchester United's Kevin Moran became the first person to be sent off in the FA Cup Final when he was given his marching orders for a late tackle in 1985.

Reading's groundsman Gordon Neate dropped a clanger of epic proportions in 1986. He accidentally sprayed the Elm Park pitch with undiluted weed-killer and then watched all the grass die. Spray weed-killer on a pitch nowadays and half the players would wilt and keel over.

Joe Burrell's miss for Tobermore United against Bangor in 1987 has gone down in history as one of the game's finest. He heads a delightful through ball past the fast-approaching 'keeper, beats the two defenders for pace and is left unmarked in front of an open goal. So what does he do next? He slices the ball yards wide, hangs his head in shame, does a forward roll and almost ends up in the net himself. It's painful to watch, but worth finding on Youtube all the same.

The 1988 FA Cup Final was surely David against Goliath. Wimbledon's hackers and long-ball specialists were up against the might of a Liverpool side at their peak. Though Peter Beardsley thought he'd scored after half an hour, referee Brian Hill ruled that he'd been fouled and awarded a free-kick instead. Liverpool failed to convert this chance and Lawrie Sanchez headed Wimbledon ahead barely a minute later. There was still time for Liverpool to pull it back though, and when they were awarded a penalty for a foul on John Aldridge, the striker got up to take it himself. He'll wish he hadn't. Dave Beasant became the first man to save a penalty in the FA Cup Final, and then became the first goalkeeper to lift the trophy as captain.

Lancaster City's inappropriately named Peter Devine couldn't have known that he'd become the star of all football gaffes DVDs when he stepped up to take a penalty against Whitley Bay. Sadly for him he tripped and stumbled during his run up and barely made contact with the ball. It was made even worse for the poor bloke because everyone who'd gone before had scored comfortably. He then limped off, claiming the trip had hurt his ankle, but it was far more likely he was hobbling off with dented pride.

Former football pundit David Icke scored an own goal of sorts when, in 1990, he claimed to be the son of God. Not surprisingly the work in England soon dried up, if only for the fact that he might therefore be related to Maradona.

Stockport's Neil Cutler will wish he'd been paying more attention to the Torquay striker in a lower league match recently. He didn't know the front-man was standing quietly right behind him waiting to see if Cutler would place the ball on the turf. The striker's prayers were answered and Cutler dropped the ball in preparation for the up-field hoof. Then he simply beat the flailing 'keeper with a drag-back and knocked it in.

Step up Manchester City's Andy Dibble. Here's a professional goalie who must have known that for the ball to be considered in your possession, you must have two hands on it. Of course he'd read the rule book, so perhaps the referee hadn't. Dibble's version stipulated the 'keeper must have full control of the ball, which he did, in one hand. No matter, in a match against Forest in 1990, he gathered it, transferred it to his right hand, didn't see Gary Crosby step out from behind him, then watched as the striker nodded the ball out of his hand and placed it in the net.

Norwich's Robert Green is another 'keeper to make the mistake of not keeping a close enough eye on the opposing strikers. He calmly gathered the ball against Nottingham Forest, collected himself and then threw the ball onto the ground before shaping to hit it long. Sadly he hadn't noticed Johnson lurking behind him and the striker stole the ball and nudged it home. Green was also unfortunate enough to allow a routine back-pass from defender Kenton under his foot in a game against Derby at Pride Park. Tottenham's Robbie Keane also benefited from some slack goalkeeping when he was presented with a goal by Birmingham City's Andy Marriott. Everyone in the ground but the poor 'keeper had seen the Irishman lurking behind him and he popped up to knock the ball in when Marriott placed it on the ground.

Newcastle's Shay Given needed eyes in the back of his head when playing Coventry in 1997. He placed the ball on the ground but immediately wished he hadn't when opposing striker Dion Dublin crept up behind him, stole the ball and rolled it in. The joke circulating immediately afterwards of course related to Given, an Irishman, not knowing where Dublin was….

Goalkeepers always come in for the most abuse, and, sadly, it's often warranted. Stan Collymore, when he wasn't watching other people have sex in car parks, was a pretty good striker, but his effort against Blackburn in 1996 wasn't going to trouble England's experienced stopper Tim Flowers as it rolled towards him. Flowers knelt to collect it, then watched in horror as the ball hit a lump of turf and leaped over his shoulder and into the net. The sad thing about this incident from Flowers' point of view is that he'd marked the centre of the six-yard line at the beginning of the match, for positioning purposes, and it was from this divot that the ball leaped. A serious 'own goal' of sorts.

Tottenham's Ian Walker had a similar shocker against Liverpool, the shot from McManaman cutting the daisies before striking a lump and arcing beautifully over his prone body and into the onion bag. More recently Spurs and England 'keeper Paul Robinson had to watch in agony as a Gary Neville back-pass hit a divot and bounced over his foot. And that was on the second biggest stage, a European Cup qualifier against Croatia. Richard Wright of Ipswich gifted Andy Johnson a goal in similar fashion, while Grimsby's Paul Crichton could fill a volume on his own. Bristol City's Steve Philips must get a mention too for being nutmeged by a backpass.

Preston's Tepi Moilanen managed to gift two goals away in the last couple of seasons. For one, he missed the ball with a karate-style kick ten yards outside his own area, and for the next he allowed the ball to bobble under his foot and into the net. Colchester's Aiden Davidson has also suffered the indignity of watching the ball bounce awkwardly before trickling over the line. Leeds and England's Nigel Martyn Martyn was also beaten by an invisible slice of turf when Middlesbrough's Paul Ince's daisy cutter suddenly leaped into the air and over his shoulder. Ooops.

As gaffes go, this next one is right up there with the best. In a lower division club match in New Zealand, Central's Noel Hickie rounded the goalkeeper and then decided to showboat with the ball on the line. He tried a step-over, tripped and then let the ball squirm off the line. He tried to retrieve it for another shot, then passed it to a team-mate who skied it over the bar.

Time for another verbal gaffe now. In 1991 Crystal Palace chairman Ron Noades suggested that the black players at the club gave the team its skill and flare, but that white players were needed to:

"give the team some brains and common sense"

While work on rebuilding Highbury's North Bank was underway in 1992, a wall shielding the site was painted as a stand full of fans. It was soon pointed out to the club that there were no ethnic minorities or women depicted on the mural and it had to be repainted from scratch to include a wider cross-section of society.

David Mellor MP, a prominent member of John Major's government, resigned soon after his alleged affair in 1992. The press pounced on the story and unearthed the fact that Mellor apparently liked to make love while wearing his Chelsea kit. Presumably it was kit that immediately came off…

Arsenal won the 1993 League Cup against Sheffield Wednesday at

Wembley, with Steve Morrow's late goal proving decisive. During the celebrations, Tony Adams hoisted the jubilant Morrow onto his shoulders and promptly dropped him. Morrow missed all further celebrations as he was in hospital nursing a broken arm! What a way to spend the eve of your greatest triumph. He then missed the FA Cup Final and his career never quite recovered.

When Leeds' manager George Graham signed Sweden's Tomas Brolin from Parma for £4.5 million in 1995, he thought he was getting a bargain. He was. A bargain bucket. Brolin, filled to capacity with fried chicken, was estimated to be even heavier than Jan Molby, costing, some said, £1/lb. He only played 19 times for his new club, whereupon he transferred, presumably by freight lorry, to Crystal Palace. After eating too much between sporadic bouts of training he then disappeared completely, no mean feat considering he was one of the only man-made objects visible from space. Someone even suggested he could pose as a slightly fatter look-a-like for another 'Viking', Andy Fordham…

David Seaman dropped a couple of howlers while between the sticks. In the Arsenal - Real Zaragoza Cup Winners' Cup Final in 1995, former Spurs player Nayim let fly with a speculative lob from forty or so yards. Seaman misjudged the flight of the ball and jumped too early to try and catch it. The ball went over his head and in and proved to be a last minute winner. A similar effort from Brazil's Ronaldinho sailed over the hapless 'keeper in 2002 to put England out of the World Cup, though whether the Brazilian magician actually meant the shot has caused many a pub argument since. The player himself always claimed it as deliberate, indeed team-mate Cafu reputedly told him that Seaman usually came off his goal line to collect square balls (whatever that means!). England were caught out again at the back during their qualifying match against Macedonia at St Mary's in 2002. Somehow Artim Sakiri managed to curl the ball over Ashley Cole, Seaman and Paul Scholes to score direct from a corner. The match, which England were expected to win comfortably, was drawn 2-2. (The corner kick, incidentally, was introduced in 1872, but it was not possible to score direct until 1924. Scotland's Alex Cheyne was the first to net from a corner in an international during their 1929 match against England.) Let's not let Seaman off the hook just yet though. Spurs fans delighted in the Nayim effort and resurrected this chant, originally penned to celebrate his arrival in north London:

"Chim-chimenee, chim-chimenee, chim-chim cheroo, Nayim was an Arab but now he's a Jew!"

One of the greatest gaffes in the history of the game occurred at Maine Road, Manchester, on the last day of the 1995-96 Premiership season. Bolton and QPR had already been relegated but who would join them depended on the results of the last game. One would go from Coventry, Southampton or Manchester City, who were all level on points. City were up against third placed Liverpool who had nothing left to play for. Still, they outclassed the woeful Blues in the first half and were soon two goals to the good. The second half was a different matter. Manager Alan Ball instructed the team to go for it as the Coventry and Southampton games were both goalless. The Blues responded and were soon on level terms. Job almost done. Sadly for the players, the message from the touchline was that they were now safe from relegation and could afford to knock the ball about and play out the draw. The players, knowing from these instructions that one of the other matches must be going in their favour, duly obliged. The substituted Niall Quinn was listening to the other matches on a radio in the changing room when he realised the error. City still needed a goal or they would be down on their inferior goal difference. The call to arms came just too late though and City, having wasted so much time casually passing the ball around, were consigned to the First Division.

West Ham manager Harry Redknapp thought £1 million was a pretty good price for Dutchman Marco Boogers when he signed him from Sparta Rotterdam in 1995. It soon became apparent that Boogers *was* worth that figure, only without the six zeros after the one. His second appearance was brief, very brief. He came on as a substitute against Manchester United and was then ordered straight off after a shocking tackle on Gary Neville. Where he went after the match remained a mystery for a while. He was eventually found hiding in a caravan in Holland, earning himself the nickname 'Mad Marco'. Redknapp incidentally went on to even greater 'heights' with the signings of Florin Raducioiu, Dani, and Javier Margas, the latter running to Chile when things didn't turn out as expected. But surely English managers aren't that gullible? Well the pigs are fuelled and ready to taxi…

Graham Souness received a phone call in 1996 touting the talents of one Ali Dia, a Senegalese maestro with 13 international caps, who was endorsed by AC Milan's George Weah no less. Southampton were always on the lookout for a good value signing so they snapped him up, rather too eagerly as it turned out. He came on for just under an hour as a substitute against Leeds and his true 'class' became blindingly apparent. His contract was cancelled and he vanished immediately thereafter, turning up briefly so that non-League Gateshead could transfer list him. Souness claimed afterwards that he hadn't been duped. Of course not. Never. Not in a million years.

In December 1996 Middlesbrough cancelled a match against Blackburn because they claimed they had too few fit players to muster a side. With twenty-three on the unfit and injured list, it looked like they had a point, but the FA didn't see things the same way and fined them £50,000 before deducting three points. When the teams finally met, they eked out a dull 0-0 draw, the dropped points proving crucial to Boro come the end of the season because they were relegated.

Glenn Hoddle brought in faith healer Eileen Drewery during the build-up to the 1998 World Cup. She said she wanted to see the players one at a time to assess their spiritual well-being. When called in, Ray Parlour famously asked for a:

"Short back and sides"

And he was never picked to play for his country by Hoddle again. The manager was next to land himself in trouble, being relieved of his England head coach's position after claiming, somewhat foolishly, in a press conference in 1999 that:

"You and I have been physically given two hands and two legs and a half-decent brain. Some people have not been born like that for a reason; that's karma working from another lifetime. It is not only people with disabilities"

The headline in the *Independent* soon afterwards read:

"Hoddle 0-1 Disabled (Hoddle o.g.)"

Outspoken MP Tony Banks was also quick to pounce:

"He's doomed to be reincarnated as Glen Hoddle"

A trio of world famous players have all achieved the impossible and they, collectively, occupy the number one spot for all-time greatest misses. Feyenoord's Jon Dahl Tomasson could have a number of entries in this section but I'll restrict him to the joint top spot holder with West Brom's Nwankwo Kanu and Tottenham's Milenko Acimovic. All three somehow contrived to put the ball over the bar when they struck it less than a foot from the goal line. Tomasson's effort came against Ajax in 1999 when he made as if to turn in a low cross but the ball just bounced over the bar. Tomasson hung his head, well, who wouldn't, and then forced a rather wry smile. Kanu's effort was perhaps even more 'impressive'. Bryan Robson's side were battling relegation in their match against Middlesbrough in 2004, when Geoff Horsefield directed a low cross along the goal line towards the Nigerian. The laws of physics must have been taking a momentary break because Kanu's goal-bound nudge ballooned over the bar. Robson summed up everyone's thoughts with:

"How did he miss that?"

Acimovic somehow contrived to bounce the ball off the top of the crossbar even when he struck the ball from eight feet directly below it in Tottenham's 2003 match against Fulham. We'd better give Steve Stone, Ryan Giggs (who won a record ninth League title with Manchester United in 2007), John O'Shea and Ronny Rosenthal honourable mentions here for misses that beggared belief.

The fact that no one had explained a simple rule of etiquette to Nigerian Nwankwo Kanu or Dutchman Marc Overmars ensured utter confusion and, ultimately, a replay of a fixture that does now not exist in the game's history. The Blades were playing Arsenal in the fifth round of the 1999 FA Cup when United's Lee Morris was fouled. Goalkeeper Alan Kelly thumped the ball into the stands so he could get treatment, and Arsenal's Ray Parlour threw the ball back towards him after Morris had been cured. This was the done thing after an injury as the ball should be returned to the side who'd deliberately kicked it off. The sporting gesture had first appeared during the Mexico '86 World Cup and was now common practice. Kanu was unaware of this however, and he pounced onto Parlour's throw thinking it was meant for him. He broke free, squared the ball to Overmars and the Dutchman scored while the Sheffield defence jumped up and down protesting. Then manager Steve Bruce intervened and tried to lead his team from the field. There was a considerable delay before players and manangers had calmed down enough to continue the match. Arsenal played out the match to its ill-tempered conclusion, winning 2-1. Immediately afterwards manager Arsene Wenger offered the Blades a replay to try and calm the storm. The offer was accepted and Arsenal again won 2-1. The Gunners, incidentally, had conceded goals to both Spurs and Blackburn in the seasons before because their rivals had contested similar throw-ins. Perhaps the bad blood between the two London clubs can explain the Spurs situation, though the Blackburn incident is less well understood.

A similar situation arose in a Korean League match in 1999 when the Hyundai Blues scored from forty yards while trying to give the ball back to the opposition after a stoppage. Immediately realising they'd scored unintentionally, the Blues then tried to gift a goal back to Pu Chon Yu Kon, but their 'keeper was having none of it and repeatedly saved their attempts at an own goal!

And yet another way of exacerbating this situation was pioneered by Wrexham's Jeff Whitley a couple of weeks earlier. Preston's 'keeper had booted the ball out to allow the treatment staff on, but the referee had blown to stop the game anyway while the ball was in the air. The Preston players then expected the ball to be returned after the referee decided to drop it. They wouldn't, after all, be contesting the drop, but they can't have expected what happened next. Whitley stepped up and half-volleyed the drop into their top corner! Luckily the referee ruled the strike as unsporting and awarded Preston a free-kick.

Ex-Chelsea player Mickey Thomas was apparently chatting to chairman Ken Bates in 2002 when a rather good looking lady walked past. Thomas cast his critical eye over the lady's shapely rear before commenting:

"I'd like to give her one"

Wondering why Bates didn't look too amused, Thomas was then informed that the woman was his daughter-in-law!

Bradford's Gary Walsh had a nightmare against Manchester United in 2001. Despite them holding their illustrious opponents, he miss-controlled a back-pass and only succeeded in giving it the golfing equivalent of an air shot. Teddy Sheringham was on hand to knock the loose ball in.

Three English League games have seen referees issue five red cards. They are: Chesterfield - Plymouth (1997), Wigan - Bristol (1997) and Exeter - Cambridge (2002).

Ipswich (and later West Ham) 'keeper Craig Forrest spent a largely uneventful eleven years at the club, but a couple of games against Manchester United blotted his copybook somewhat. The first, a 9-0 defeat, still stands as the record Premiership loss. Though most of the goals were unstoppable, and he parried or blocked at least three but couldn't keep out the shots from the rebound, the eighth resulted from his handball twenty yards outside his own area. Manchester United's

Paul Ince took the free-kick quickly while the hapless Forrest was still remonstrating with the referee. The second match, at Old Trafford, was not quite as humiliating. This time he only shipped seven.

Swansea City's Walter Boyd (2000) shares the rather dubious honour of being sent off immediately after coming on as a substitute with Sheffield United's Keith Gillespie (2007). In both cases the time played, according to the referee, was zero seconds, the red cards issued for violent conduct before the match had restarted!

Pierre Issa picked up an unfortunate shoulder injury when he tripped and fell on the ball during the Watford - Birmingham City clash in 2001. As he was carried off on the stretcher he must have imagined being seen in the treatment room pretty soon. Sadly, one of the stretcher bearers slipped on the pitch surround and dumped the hapless Issa onto his already painful shoulder.

Manchester United's French goalkeeper Fabien Barthez tried a new tactic to avoid conceding a goal in their FA Cup tie against West Ham at Old Trafford in 2001. He stopped playing and held his hand up appealing for the linesman to give an offside decision while Hammers' striker Paulo Di Canio bore down on him. Di Canio kept his cool and slid the ball past Barthez, who finally decided to react, albeit too late. The error cost United dearly: they were out of the FA Cup on home turf.

Barthez has been responsible for a number of high-profile clangers, not least when he rolled the ball out mistakenly to the opposing striker while at Monaco, a similar error to that when he presented the ball to Arsenal's Thierry Henry with a weak clearance at Highbury. He also dropped two howlers during United's 2001 Champions' League tie with Deportivo La Coruna.

Charlton's Sasa Ilic knows exactly how that feels. He delivered a lovely ball for Manchester City's Shaun Goater to knock in in 2000.

Norwegian striker Egil Ostenstad was transferred from Blackburn to Rangers in 2003 to provide much needed cover for Steve Thompson and Dutchman Ronald de Boer. In 17 appearances he only scored twice and was politely given his marching orders by manager Alex McLeish at the end of the season. Usually this would be the point where the striker complains about the way he's been treated, signs for another club and bangs in 20 goals the next season. Not so with Ostenstad. He, in an interview with *The Observer,* said:

"I'm rubbish. I'd advise any clubs looking at me to go for someone else. Maybe they could use me as a cone in training"

Halifax goalkeeper Ian Dunbavin can feel slightly aggrieved with the referee for the goal scored by Carlisle in 2004. He collected a simple pass, then appeared to deliberately tread on the opposing striker. The referee called him over, but gestured that he should leave the ball behind. As the whistle hadn't been blown Dunbavin felt he couldn't just drop the ball so he took it towards the referee, and in so doing left his area. The referee had in fact been waving play on, but then blew for deliberate handball, and while the hapless 'keeper was arguing, Carlisle took a quick free-kick and scored!

While coming out of the tunnel to officiate for a Celtic - Hearts Cup tie in 2004, referee Willie Young adjusted his earpiece and appeared to give himself an electric shock. In reality, the sound technician had left the volume up too high and when the fourth official tried to contact him, he almost blew Young's eardrums!

Most people in the game had a great deal of respect for the Chelsea manager during the Russian Revolution, Italian Claudio Ranieri. His reputation for fiddling with his formation and employing a bizarre rotation system for his strikers had not hindered the side's progress to the semi-final of the European Cup. In fact they'd only just dispatched the strongly fancied Arsenal, and were flying high at second spot in the Premiership. Despite these results the rumour mill had been circulating stories that Roman Abramovich was going to replace Ranieri at the first available opportunity, a fact known by the manager:

"I know that his sword is stuck in me already"

So with the gleaming blade hanging over his head, Ranieri took Chelsea to Monaco for the 2004 Champions' League semi-final. In the press conference before the game, he clearly saw what was about to happen, greeting the assembled hoard with:

"Hello, my sharks. Welcome to the funeral"

It was 1-1 at halftime and Chelsea had a crucial Hernan Crespo away goal. Things got better for them after Zicos was sent off thanks to a shameful piece of play-acting by Claude Makalele. He conned the referee into believing he'd been pushed with a theatrical dive. Away goal in the bag and up against ten men, there was nothing that could go wrong now, surely. Unfortunately for the Londoners the wheels were now firmly removed from their juggernaut by Ranieri. He started making random substitutions when all they really needed to do was control the game, lock up the defence and score a winner on the break if they could. The grossly unfit Juan Veron was all but useless and when the defence started creaking they had no pace or skill to get themselves out of trouble. Despite being a man short, Monaco bagged a couple of late goals and the tie was effectively over. Abramovich cut the sword loose and Ranieri was frogmarched out of Stamford Bridge, his disappointment tempered a little by the £6 million pay-off no doubt. (It was during this game, incidentally, that Ron Atkinson delivered his rather scathing line about Marcel Desailly. He hadn't realised his microphone was still on and his comment ensured a swift exit from the commentary box and from all football for a time. This was arguably a bigger gaffe than Ranieri's.)

Charlton fans were quick to pounce on the beleaguered manager, chanting:

"Sacked in the summer, you're getting sacked in the summer"

Apparently Ranieri was heard correcting them, replying:

"I'll be sacked in May, actually. I'm a dead man walking"

In 2004, former West Brom striker Lee Hughes was jailed for six years after reportedly being involved in a hit-and-run which left a man dead. Apparently the player fled the scene to avoid a police breath test. The number of players involved in drink-driving incidents is far too high for all of the idiots to get a mention here however, but Jermaine Pennant, who ended up serving three months for driving with no insurance and under a ban, gets a look-in because on his release he took to the field wearing an electronic tracking tag.

Sky TV pundit Rod Marsh was shown the door after making a joke at the expense of the quarter of a million people killed in the Boxing Day tsunami in 2004. Placing his foot firmly between his teeth he mumbled:

"David Beckham says he won't be going to Newcastle given what the Toon Army has just done to Asia"

Stafford Rangers stopper James Lindley collected the ball in their 2004 meeting with Weymouth. Then he tried to smash it up-field but only succeeded in leathering it into Lee Philips' back. The ball cannoned back over Lindley's head and nestled in the net.

When Arsenal's Jose Antonio Reyes received a phone call from Real Madrid sporting director Emilio Butragueno in early 2005, he was delighted to be offered a contract with the 'Galacticos' and with it the chance of moving back to his home country:

"I wish I was playing for Real, otherwise I'm going to have to go on playing with some bad people"

Unfortunately he didn't realise he was actually talking to a practical joker from a Spanish radio station, and the news of his disenchantment with the north London side spread like wildfire.

His side was awarded a penalty during their home tie against Manchester City in 2005. Now we know that City stopper David James had been known to have the odd calamity when trying to collect a deep cross, but as a one on one 'keeper he was highly rated. So Thierry Henry and Robert Pires decided to take a different kind of penalty to fool him. As it is basically a free-kick, they decided that Pires would roll the ball to Henry and he would bury it. Pires stepped up and missed the ball completely, and Henry overran it as a result. Of course City cleared it and the two star men ended up looking pretty foolish. Danny Mills then laid into them with an all-out verbal assault, and who could say they didn't deserve it?

What they should have done was take a leaf out of the master's book. In 1982 Ajax's Johann Cruijff rolled the ball from the spot to a team mate on the left hand edge of the area. Before the Helmond Sport players could react, Cruijff collected the return pass and slotted it home. Perhaps he had just been listening to the great Pelé, who said:

"A penalty is a cowardly way to score"

West Ham striker Todorov celebrated his goal against Manchester City for a good couple of seconds before realising that he'd put the ball miles over the bar and into row Z. This echoed what had happened in a match between Helmond Sport and PSV in 1983. Jurrie Koolhoff casually knocked the ball past the goalkeeper and wheeled away to celebrate. When he turned back five seconds later he realised that the ball had stopped in a puddle of mud on the goal line!

I'd like to promote Freddie Ljungberg's miss for Arsenal against Bolton in 2005 to the joint top miss position, but I'm bound by certain rules and therefore can't give him that honour. Ljungberg was, after all, more than a yard from goal when he spooned over the easiest of chances.

Commentator Jonathan Pierce bestowed an honour on the effort immediately however:

"Oh, goodness me. Well, that's the miss of the season"

A couple more goalkeeping blunders to celebrate now: In the Newcastle - Liverpool fixture in early 2007, home 'keeper Steve Harper cleared poorly and gifted ex team-mate Craig Bellamy a goal. Not wishing to be outdone, Liverpool's Pepe Reina hoofed the ball into Martin for Newcastle's equaliser. Then, after a blatant dive in the box from Taylor, Nolberto Solano stepped up to put Reina the wrong way and give the Toon Army something to cheer about.

Chelsea's Solomon Kalou was preparing to come on against Liverpool in their Champions' League semi-final in April 2007 when he pulled on Shaun Wright-Phillips's shirt instead. The substitution then had to be delayed while he found his own.

The commentary team are bound to make mistakes during a match. More often than not, they have no idea what they've said, but the astute viewer will invariably remember the errors. Sometimes you can feel a little sympathy if a player's name is unpronounceable, or amusing, such as Germany's Kuntz, and occasionally you know what they're trying to say, but, for the most part, all you can do is wonder what the bloody hell they're talking about.

Commentator Speak 1

"He's looking around at himself"
JIMMY GREAVES

"And tonight we have the added ingredient of Kenny Dalglish not being here"
MARTIN TYLER

"Oh, what a time to score! 27 minutes!"
JOHN MOTSON

"Tony Adams stretching, waiting for Seaman to come out"
BRAIN MOORE

"His reign ended with that 0-0 defeat by Switzerland at Lansdowne Road"
COLM MURRAY

"And now we've news of Scotland's 0-0 victory over Holland"
SCOTTISH TV

"The Waterford player's shot was on target, which is an important aspect of a player's shot"
DAMIEN RICHARDSON

"That was the last and final goal from the Turks"
DAMIEN RICHARDSON

"Oldham are leading 1-0, a well deserved victory at this stage of the game"
TOMMY DOCHERTY

"We are about as far away from the penalty box as the penalty box is from us"
TOM TYRRELL

"Russia have beaten Ireland 4-2, Albania 4-1 and now Switzerland 4-1 at home. It would be a wise man who bet against them beating Georgia"
GEORGE HAMILTON

"It's a football stadium in the truest sense of the word"
JOHN MOTSON

"He's very quick for a man of his age. I suppose you'd call him ageless. He's 33 or 34"
DAVID PLEAT

"I'm not going to drag it out or make a point because points are pointless"
SIMON JORDAN

"He'll have a pair of sharp and canny shoulders to listen to"
DAVID PLATT

1234567891011

International Disasters

Now we have the chance to explore the wider world of calamity. If you thought the domestic game contributed a good proportion of clangers, then think again. This lot really do need their heads examined, though what for, we can't be too sure, as there can't be a great deal to find inside.

Swedish football club AIK's Solna stadium in Stockholm was completely redesigned in the mid-1930s. King Gustav was invited to open the new venue in 1937, which he did, with the words:

"I declare this tennis arena open!"

Brazil only needed a draw in the last match of the 1950 World Cup to become champions, the round robin format pitting them against Uruguay in a game their neighbours would have to win. Brazil went a goal up in the huge Maracanã and all seemed to be going their way. Then the Uruguayans scored twice and the dream was shattered. The predominantly white Brazilian side turned on their two black players, blaming them for the defeat. The trophy was presented by Jules Rimet in complete silence, the crowd stunned. In reality, Zizinho and goalkeeper Barbosa had been two of the stars of the tournament, but it would take another eight years before black players were fully accepted by the country. In the meantime many players and fans killed themselves because of the shame of not winning the 1950 event.

Pelé and Garrincha almost weren't allowed to play in the 1958 tournament because the team management subjected the entire squad to a psychological examination, and neither was considered mentally tough enough to take part. Player power eventually saw them take the field in a match against Wales, however, and the legends were born. How tragic it would have been for the game had the results of that pointless evaluation been taken at face value.

English referee Reg Leafe disallowed four of Real Madrid's five 'goals' in the second leg of their second round European Cup tie against arch rivals Barcelona in 1960. He was bundled into a waiting taxi immediately afterwards so that Real fans couldn't find him and exact their revenge. Spurs fans knew how they felt when Swiss ref David Mellet cost them their rightful place in the European Cup Final by disallowing two goals for offside against Benfica a couple of years later. The fact that the inspired Greaves had beaten the full back on both occasions seemed to elude him.

This section continues with probably the most gaffe-related object, Ron Atkinson excepted, in football's history, the Jules Rimet trophy. Designed and crafted by French sculptor Abel Lafleur in the early 20th century, the World Cup was solid gold, twelve inches tall and featured a winged seraphim. The trophy, originally called 'Victory', was renamed after the president of FIFA who founded leading Parisian team Red Star in 1897, and then organised the first global tournament in Uruguay in 1930. Despite Nazi interest during the war, the trophy survived having remained hidden in a shoe box under the bed of an Italian official.

The trophy was then relatively well cared for until it reached England in 1966, where it was stolen from its glass display case in Central Hall, Westminster. Though the police launched an extensive search and recovery operation, the trophy was not found, and the authorities were pilloried for their efforts. At the end of March, however, the lining from inside the top of the trophy arrived at the FA with a ransom demand. Edward Betchley, a petty thief and dock-worker, was then arrested at the supposed exchange, it being ascertained pretty quickly that the rest of the trophy was not in his possession.

Incredibly a dog called Pickles recovered the cup from under a bush while owner David Corbett walked him across Beulah Hill. He was rewarded with a film role, a medal from the National Canine Centre and a year's supply of dog food treats. And Pickles did pretty well out of it too…

Brazil won the trophy for a third time in 1970, and the decision was made afterwards that they should be allowed to keep it. Sadly they were no better than the English when it came to security and the cup vanished from the headquarters of the Brazilian FA in Rio. It has never been recovered. A replica was then made by a West German goldsmith, the original probably having been melted down and sold.

The winners of all the tournaments since have been presented with the FIFA World Cup, a Silvio Gazzaniga-designed and Bertoni, Milano-sculpted trophy depicting two human figures supporting the earth. Unlike the Jules Rimet trophy it will not be presented to a country for keeps if they win it three times.

I'm sure most readers will disagree with me here, but I'm going to put my head on the block and call Azerbaijani (then a Russian state) linesman Tofik Bakhramov's decision to allow England's third goal in the 1966 World Cup Final against West Germany at Wembley a gaffe. (When asked about the 'goal' afterwards, the man himself reportedly only had one word to say on the matter: "Stalingrad".)

Germany led the match after just a quarter of an hour, but Geoff Hurst, in for the injured Jimmy Greaves, equalised a few minutes later. With thirteen minutes of the ninety left, Martin Peters scored and the trophy looked like going to the hosts. The Germans weren't done however, and a Wolfgang Weber goal took the match to extra time, the first time the half hour had been needed since 1934. Alf Ramsey knew the equaliser had taken the wind out of his players and had to rouse them, which he did with this call to arms:

*"You've beaten them once, now go out and bloody beat them
  again"*

Alan Ball provided the pass for Geoff Hurst to start doing exactly that shortly after the restart, but his shot hit the crossbar, bounced down towards the line and then up and out again. The English appealed for the goal, the Germans appealed against it. After consultation with Swiss referee Gottfried Dienst, Bakhramov indicated that the goal should stand and England were on their way. Hurst completed his hat-trick in the last seconds, still the only man to achieve the feat in the final match, which kind of makes the controversial moment academic. It hasn't stopped the arguments though…

So, what about the 'goal' then? The black and white television footage of the strike appears to show it comfortably over the line, while colour pictures filmed for a documentary along the line of the goal appear to show it on the line. The TV footage has caused the most controversy, but many believe there is a simple explanation for the still frames taken from the action. The exact moment of touchdown is not recorded. The frame in question doesn't exist because of the limitations of the cameras used at the time. A frame shows the ball appearing to be over the line because it hasn't actually landed (there is the faintest of shadows on the ground beneath it). The next frame shows the ball in a similar position, the ball having bounced - unseen by the camera - and now on its way back up. The ball is airborne for both stills, and no TV pictures exist of the impact point. This makes the documentary footage more reliable. A considerable portion of the ball is still visible from behind the post on the pitch side, whereas there is no ball to be seen on the goal side. Recent scientific analysis of the incident, including a real-time virtual reality display, confirms what most German fans believed at the time: the ball probably landed on the pitch side of the line, and not over it on the goal side.

As mentioned earlier, many believe that Hurst's wonderful left foot shot into the roof of the German net on the stroke of fulltime makes the incident irrelevant. But if England's third goal hadn't been allowed, the Germans would have had greater belief going into the second period of extra time and would have known that a single goal would have probably won it for them…

The match was restaged in 1985 to raise funds for the victims of the Bradford fire. Geoff Hurst repeated his hat-trick at the age of 46 and England went on to win 6-4.

Having watched from the sidelines as Don Revie's England failed spectacularly to make the 1978 World Cup Finals in Argentina, British fans - the Tartan Army in particular - hoped Ally MacLeod's Scots would give them something to cheer. The manager himself was confident, loudly proclaiming on numerous occasions:

"Scotland will win the World Cup"

If only it were that easy. Even if you don't know what happens next, you can certainly picture the fall after an announcement like that. It was way the Scottish contributed to the tournament that warrants a closer look, however. MacLeod's strategy quickly unravelled. He failed to watch group opponents Peru in their opener and the Scots were dazzled by the brilliance of their wingers, Munante and Oblitas, and they lost easily. The manager also seemed to have forgotten that his key playmaker, Graham Souness, really should be in the starting XI or at the very least on the bench. Iran were up next, and despite their obvious defensive frailties, they somehow managed to draw with the beleaguered Scots. MacLeod's prediction was fast becoming an albatross around his neck, and his luck off the field was not holding up well either. As he pondered the draw against Iran a dog approached him in the street. MacLeod is said to have looked down at the mutt and said:

"My only friend in the world"

The dog thought otherwise and promptly bit him! Even though all seemed lost, the team was handed a lifeline, albeit a frayed one, when they realised that if they beat the mighty total-footballing Dutch by three goals they would be through to the next round. The task was made all the more difficult when they conceded an early penalty. However, all was not lost. The sublime Kenny Dalglish volleyed home from close range just before halftime, and immediately after the break they too scored a penalty. Then came a moment of pure magic, Archie Gemmill cutting in from the right flank, beating three defenders and slotting the ball into the far corner for 3-1. Sadly the miracle fight-back ended there. Holland's Johnny Rep hit a 25 yard thunderbolt and the Scots 'only' managed to win by a single goal. If you then consider that the Dutch went all the way to the final and performed valiantly against the mighty Argentineans, it just shows what the Scots might have achieved had their manager done his homework and played his best team.

Welsh referee Clive 'The Book' Thomas almost caused an international incident when he allowed Brazil to take a corner against Sweden during the 1978 World Cup even though the ninety minutes were up. Brazil scored, but Thomas then disallowed the goal saying that the match had ended as soon as the corner had been taken.

His outspoken nature meant that he always courted controversy, but many of The Book's ideas, considered way beyond the narrow-minded authorities in the 1980s, are now finding favour. He called for radio communications between the officials, and for video evidence to be used in close goal line calls, both of which are now accepted parts of the game.

A Canadian teenager managed to convince his home town that he had scored in the final of the 1981 World Youth Cup in Australia. Feted as first a local then national hero - as captain of the victorious team - it was discovered a couple of days later that there hadn't actually been a tournament that year!

The Kuwaiti national side had become a fully fledged member of FIFA in 1962 but the team achieved little for the next twenty years. Then, somewhat surprisingly, they qualified for Spain '82. Their first match was against the French and though they put up some resistance they were 3-1 down going into the last few minutes. Then someone in the crowd thought it would be a good idea to blow a whistle. The Kuwaitis thought the referee had blown for fulltime and began to trudge off. France, of course, scored another, uncontested, goal in the meantime!

Drug testing in football only really caught on in the 1970s even though it was widely believed that the sport was clean. In 1974 Haiti's Ernest Jean-Joseph tested positive, and Scotland's Willie Johnston was also caught four years later during the World Cup in Argentina. Compulsory random drug testing was introduced to the top flight of English football in 1992, and a number of players have fallen foul of the law. Paul Merson finally tried to face his problems with drugs in 1994, while Mark Bosnich tested positive for cocaine in 2003, and then admitted to a £3,000 per week habit. Of course one player has arguably become more famous for missing a test. Manchester United defender Rio Ferdinand was given an eight-month ban and £50,000 fine for 'forgetting' to turn up for a test in 2003. It has been said that using his forgetfulness as an excuse was right up there with 'the dog ate my homework'.

Back on the international stage, Diego Maradona was vilified for failing a test (cocaine) while at Napoli in 1991, for which he received a 15-month ban. He then failed another at USA '94 (ephedrine).

Spanish goalkeeper Luis Arconada will forever be haunted by his error that gifted victory to hosts France in the 1984 European Championships. Michel Platini, who scored nine goals in the tournament, curled a free-kick round the wall towards the far corner. Arconada went down low to his left and looked to have the ball firmly trapped, but then it squirted out behind him and over the line. Commentators in some countries have actually adopted his surname as another way of describing a goalkeeping howler, as in:

"Oh dear, he's done an Arconada"

When Brazil met Chile in a qualifier for the 1990 World Cup in Italy, no one could have predicted the events that would unfold over the two-leg tie. The first match in Santiago was an ill-tempered draw, both sides having a number of players booked. The return, in Brazil's enormous Maracanã stadium in front of 160,000, was likely to be even feistier. It was reasonably quiet, however, until Brazil scored in the middle of the second period. Of course the crowd went berserk, lighting flares, beating drums and waving flags. One firework was thrown by a young Brazilian woman towards the Chilean 'keeper, Roberto Rojas, otherwise known as El Condor. Though the flare seemed to land some distance away from him, Rojas went down as if shot. When the smoke cleared his head was caked in blood. The Chileans left the field for their own safety and never returned, citing the game and its atmosphere as too dangerous to continue. In Santiago all Brazilian interests, including their embassy, were targeted and vandalised. FIFA were asked to investigate the on-field incident - to decide if and when the match should be replayed - and concluded that the flare was relatively harmless and could not have caused El Condor's injuries. Sometime later it emerged that Rojas had palmed a scalpel in case he had to cause a diversion and have the game called off. As soon as Chile went a goal down, El Condor had his moment chosen for him. FIFA officials were not amused and gave him a lifetime ban, along with the medical staff who'd issued the bogus report on his condition, and then expelled Chile from the tournament, sending Brazil on their way to Italy.

When Feyenoord manager Wim Jansen sent on a substitute in their 1991 match against Willem II Tilburg, he can't have realised how great the sub's impact would be… on the rule book. The player was not Dutch and nor had he been through the club's youth training scheme (see below), so he was Feyenoord's third overseas player at a time when only two were allowed by UEFA. The referee, somehow wise to the nationalities of all those on the pitch, immediately sent him off!

German club side VfB Stuttgart easily won (3-0) their home first round tie against Leeds in the 1993-94 European Cup. However, when the teams met at Elland Road in the second leg, the Germans didn't find their evening going to according to plan, even though they were comfortable at 1-1 with five minutes until halftime. A Gary McAllister penalty and then goals from Eric Cantona and Lee Chapman made it 4-1 to the Yorkshire outfit. But Stuttgart still had that vital away goal, and no matter how hard Leeds pressed, they couldn't score the extra one they needed. Leeds fans no doubt bemoaned Howard Wilkinson for picking the wrong players for the job, but in fact it was opposite number Uwe Hoeness whose selection was coming under the microscope. Some people had spotted that the VfB manager had brought on two foreign substitutes, Jovo Simanic and Adrian Knup, which meant that with

Slobodan Dubajic and Eyjolfur Sverrisson already in the squad he must have named four foreigners in his original team. UEFA rules only allowed three such players, unless they had been at the club for five years or had progressed through the club's youth policy (like Welshman Gary Speed at Leeds). Stuttgart had broken the rules and, even though they admitted the mistake immediately afterwards, had to be punished. Leeds could either be awarded the tie or a 3-0 home victory instead. UEFA officials eventually decided on awarding them the 3-0 win, which meant the score was 3-3 and extra time would have to be played. As this decision had been taken a day after the match had finished, and both clubs thought the extra half hour would not be sufficient for the fans, UEFA then ordered that the match be replayed in its entirety in the Nou Camp, Barcelona. Only 10,000 fans made the trip to a stadium that cold accommodate more than ten times that, but they finally saw Leeds progress to the next round with a 2-1 win.

Football Legends: Ron Atkinson

Big Ron has enjoyed a colourful career both in England and abroad. His achievements as player and manager are impressive (over 600 appearances for Oxford United, two FA Cups with Manchester United, manager of Atlético Madrid), though he sometimes makes the most basic blunders. Appointed manager of Nottingham Forest to try and save them from relegation, he marched out for his first game and promptly sat in the 'away team' dugout. The fans couldn't help but have a good chuckle before gently reminding the tanned one that he was sitting next to the opposition substitutes! It's as a commentator, however, that many will say he'll be best remembered. His peculiar use of the language has the ability to confuse and amuse at the same time, and he's even managed to spawn his own variant of the mother tongue, that known simply as 'Ronglish'. Here are a few examples, not including the line - delivered when he thought his microphone was off - about Frenchman Marcel Desailly that forced ITV to sack him from his punditry position:

"There's a little triangle of five left-footed players"

"You'd think he'd chance his hat there"

"I wanted to give my players some technical advice so I told them
the game had started"

"On another night they'd have won that 2-2"

"Liverpool are outnumbered numerically in midfield"

"This lad throws it further than I go on holiday"

"He's a little twat, that Totti. I can't see what all the fuss is about"

"I think that the replay showed it to be worse than it actually
was"

"He's not only a good player but he's spiteful in the nicest sense
of the word"

"He is without doubt the greatest sweeper in the world, I'd say, at
a guess"

"The 'keeper was unsighted and he still didn't see it"

"Going to Anfield was like being in Vietnam"

"You half fancied that to go in as it was rising and dipping at the same time"

"That was Pelé's strength - holding people off with his arm" (Err, I think he might have been a bit better than that, Ron....)

"Moreno thought that the full back was going come up behind and give him one really hard"

"There are lots of balls dropping off people"

"Every time Zidane comes inside him, Roberto Carlos just goes bonking down the wing"

"I've had this sneaking feeling throughout the game that it's there to be won"

"Woodcock would have scored but his shot was too perfect"

"They must go for it now as they have nothing to lose but the match"

"A ten-foot 'keeper really should have stopped that"

"He's treading on dangerous water there"

"And Schmeichel extends and grows even bigger than he is"

"Now that Manchester United are 2-1 down on aggregate, they are in a better position than when they started the game at 1-1"

"Someone in the England team will have to grab the ball by the horns"

*"They've picked their heads up off the ground
and now have a lot to carry on their shoulders"*

"Carlton Palmer is the worst finisher since Devon Loch"
(Ron's reference here is to Dick Francis's mount that slipped and fell when the finish line of the 1956 Grand National beckoned.)

Next up, a terrific slice of self-tongue-tying madness:

*"You can see the ball go past them - or the man - but you'll never
see both man and ball go past at the same time. So if the ball
goes past, the man won't, or if the man goes past, they'll take
the ball and vice versa"*

Now let's listen to a few brief conversations with long-time sparring
partner, Clive Tyldesley:

Clive: *"So, Ron, who do you fancy?"*
Ron: *"Not you, Clive, that's for sure"*

Ron: *"I tell you what, Clive, Cole has missed a stick-on there. I
would have put my mortgage on him scoring in that situation"*
Clive: *"Tell me, Ron, how much is your mortgage?"*
Ron: *"I don't have one"*

Here the two men discuss either the location of Gianfranco Zola, or the
rather painful injury to his groin:

Clive: *"I'm not sure where exactly he was injured there"*
Ron: *"Just inside his own half I think, Clive"*

Clive: *"Earlier in the season a substitution was delayed because the player had to remove his rings and chains. That didn't happen much in your day, did it, Ron?"*
Ron: *"Not the chains"*
Clive: *"Is that because it would have taken you half the night to get your chains off, Ron"*
Ron: ...

Here Atkinson shares his views on a man he nicknamed the 'Crab', because he supposedly only passed or moved sideways, Ray Wilkins:

"He can't run, can't tackle and can't head the ball. The only time he goes forward is to toss the coin"

And here's Atkinson on women, not literally, thank God:

"Women should be in the kitchen, the disco and the boutique, but not in football"

(Peter Hetherston, manager of Albion Rovers, was equally derisive about having women officiate the men's game: "I knew it wasn't going to be our day when I found out a woman was going to be running the line. She should be at home making dinner for her man after *he's* been to football.")

As Steve McManaman hoisted the 2002 Champions' League trophy for Real Madrid, Ron chipped in with:

"You won't see that again now that the Scouser's got his hands on it"

Let's give the final word for now about Big Ron to himself though, this from 1983:

"It's bloody tough being a legend"

More International Disasters

The Austrian national side was once the most feared outfit in world football. Their fall from the dizzying heights to the subterranean lows, however, happened relatively quickly. In their qualifying group for the 1992 European Championships they found themselves up against Northern Ireland and the Faeroe Islands, the latter being minnows only recently acknowledged by FIFA and with a population of around 45,000. Surely it would be a cake walk for the Austrians against the part-timers, dentists, fishermen, bankers, bakers and carpenters. Not so. With half an hour to go Torkil Nielsen raced through the cocky Austrian defence and planted a low shot into the net. It stayed 1-0 and the Austrians were sent home tails firmly between their legs. To prove it wasn't a fluke the islanders then held Northern Ireland to a draw in their next match in Belfast.

Frenchman David Ginola graced the Premiership with Newcastle and Spurs, though latterly he seemed to spend more time advertising hair care products. Still, he was a popular addition to the English game and was voted Player of the Year in 1999. He was slightly less popular with his countrymen, however. In 1993, and with France needing only a draw with Bulgaria to qualify for the 1994 World Cup in the USA, he dropped one of the games great clangers. France had not performed well in their previous matches but at 1-1 and seemingly coasting they knew they were through. Awarded a free-kick in the Bulgarian half, Ginola should have taken ages lining it up and then put the ball into row Z, but he didn't. He took a short one and set off up the wing alone. The Bulgarian defence dispossessed him, broke through the French lines and scored. Then the referee blew for full time. Merde!

W Venio's Dutch star Mickey Oestreich knows exactly what it's like to beat the 'keeper and then get goal fright. In their 1994 clash with PSV

Eindhoven he raced clear and instead of calmly placing the ball in the net, he half-volleyed it into the stands for three points. Johnny Wilkinson eat your heart out.

Team England scored a huge own goal before the European Championships in 1996. Several of the players were caught in a nightclub downing drinks from the infamous dentist's chair. Though the full story was carefully kept under wraps, it emerged that most of the players were so drunk they didn't know they were being photographed.

England - Argentina clashes are eagerly awaited. The Falkland's War and 'Iland of God' episodes never seem to fade from the national consciousness, and there is much hype whenever the teams are scheduled to do battle on the biggest stage. France '98 pitted two strong sides against one another in St Etienne and, as usual, there were fireworks. Michael Owen had scored a wonderful individual goal, and Argentina had equalised from a clever free-kick, when Diego Simeone fouled England's pin-up boy, David Beckham. He then remonstrated with referee Kim Milton Nielsen for giving the English a free-kick. Beckham, in a moment of petulant madness, thought he'd settle the score himself and flicked his boot casually at the Argentinean. Simeone went down from the lightest of touches as though felled with a chainsaw. The referee, who was no more than a couple of yards away, had no option but to send Beckham off. England then lost and hero had become villain. His family were repeatedly threatened and effigies of him were hanged and burned at grounds around the country. In fact it would take until the match against Greece at Old Trafford in 2001, when he put in an outstanding display to ensure the home side's qualification for the 2002 World Cup in the Far East, that Beckham was fully restored to hero.

Spanish club side Compostella thought they'd scored a perfectly good headed goal and were celebrating with their striker. Little did they realise that the referee had disallowed the goal and was blowing his whistle for a free-kick before waving play on. Their opponents broke up-field and, with only the Compostella 'keeper to beat, Guerro comfortably knocked it past him.

A French team boasting a number of superstars had romped through the World Cup in their home country in 1998, even dispatching the mighty Brazil 3-0 in the final. (It has since emerged that there was a huge bust-up in the Brazilian changing room before the match, supposedly over the inclusion of striker Ronaldo who had been ill earlier in the day and who looked totally out of sorts in the warm up.)

No matter, four years later much the same French team was predicted to demolish all-comers and retain the tophy in the next tournament in Japan & Korea. Players like Zinedine Zidane, Thierry Henry and David Trezeguet would be in their prime and difficult to stop. Inspirational midfielder Patrick Vieira was extremely confident, summing up the thoughts in the camp by saying:

"We have a remarkable team, with fantastic players in every position"

Arsène Wenger was equally patriotic:

"France are above everyone else"

Senegal were the first to face this 'remarkable' team and knowledgeable pundits were predicting a rout. For some reason the French failed to set the game alight, however, and Papa Diop stepped up for the African nation and scored the winner from close range. Things went from bad to worse during the next two matches. France at least salvaged a point against Uruguay in a goalless tie, but then, with Denmark to beat, they came hopelessly unstuck, conceded two goals and were out. The reigning champions were on their way home without even scoring a goal. France *were,* however, briefly above everyone else shortly afterwards, about thirty thousand feet above them as it happens.

Argentina's Martin Palermo - South American footballer of the year - had a game to forget in a Copa America tie against Colombia in 1999. His side were a goal down when they were rather fortuitously awarded a penalty. He stepped up to take it and blasted the ball against the crossbar. The reverberations had hardly died away when Argentina were awarded a second spot kick. With nerves of steel Palermo stepped up again, and did, what has become known in the trade, a Chris Waddle. The ball has yet to be found. You would have thought that if his side were given yet another penalty, there was no way his team-mates or manager would let him anywhere near the ball. They were, he was, and the 'keeper guessed right and saved it. You'd have thought the gods would have had enough of Martin by now and thrown him back, but there were a couple more twists to the story. He was still rated highly enough to warrant a big money move to Europe and had been in talks with a number of top clubs, so you can imagine their reaction when he somersaulted into an advertising hoarding during a goal celebration, ruptured his knee ligaments and then saw his career spiral downwards to the inevitable conclusion. Oh dear! Still, he is Argentinean, which is some consolation for opposing fans.

Charleroi's Mahamoudou Kere scored a bizarre own goal in a South African League tie against Verbroedering in 2000. His goalkeeper saved a fierce shot, but he was three yards outside his penalty box and the referee put his whistle to his lips. Kere knew that the goalie was going to be sent off so casually knocked the ball into his own net to wait out the stoppage. Sadly for him, the referee decided not to blow and played a crucial advantage. The own goal stood, and then the referee sent the 'keeper off!

Another who knows only too well about the dreaded own goal is Franck Queudrue. While playing for Lens against Bastia in 2000 he smashed the ball into his own net from at least forty yards.

A brief stop at the station of verbal calamities now with a misinterpreted line from the great John Motson after England's 5-1 demolition of Germany in Munich in 2001:

"That's England's finest victory over the Germans since the war"

In the 2002 World Cup semi-final between Brazil and Turkey, Hakan Hunsul kicked the ball at Rivaldo while the latter was standing by the corner flag. Rivaldo took the ball on the knee, but then decided to try and get the Turk sent off. He went down clutching his face as if shot and, incredibly, the referee fell for his disgraceful performance. Hunsul was dismissed and Brazil went on to win 2-1.

German goalkeeper Oliver Kahn will go down as one of the game's great shot stoppers. For club Bayern Munich and country he has consistently proved himself to be among the best in the world. How tragic then that he should 'save' one of his worst performances for the biggest game of his life. Germany had quietly progressed through their group and then the knockout stages of the 2002 World Cup in Japan & Korea despite most authorities writing them off well before the tournament began. But, as the final approached, the team was beginning to fire and they'd silenced some of the doubters with their unassuming play. Though Brazil were expected to win, Kahn, voted man of the tournament immediately afterwards, was their worry. If they couldn't get the ball past the big man, Germany had every chance of taking the trophy. Kahn ensured they didn't, however. He could only parry a rather weak shot from Rivaldo into top scorer Ronaldo's path in the 67th minute. The striker slotted the gift home and Brazil held on to take their fifth world crown.

Atlético Madrid president Jesus Gil launched into a foul-mouthed tirade at the players in 2003, claiming that the ones who didn't pull their weight deserved to die. When he was advised to calm down during the interview - because of a recent health scare - he replied:

"Stick my heart up your arse"

Gil, a complete nutcase if you believe Ron Atkinson (now that's a tough one, to be fair), had spent time in prison in 1969 for overseeing a building project that collapsed, killing nearly 60 people. In all he went through 40 managers in just 17 years at the club.

The 2006 World Cup provided us with a number of magic moments, and a couple of absolute nightmares. Let's not resurrect Graham Poll just yet though. Japan's Atsushi Yanagisawa seemed certain to score against Croatia from three yards when presented with an open goal, yet he contrived to put the ball ten yards wide! Perhaps he'd lived up to his Christian name before the match and had a stomach full of raw fish. His coach, Brazilian World Cup legend Zico, didn't look too impressed and probably should have thought about bringing himself on instead.

You could always be sure of finding a paragraph in this section about the woes that befell England manager Sven-Göran Eriksson. Whether it was his tactics against the big sides in vital World Cup and European Championship matches, or his team selection and apparent lack of passion or enthusiasm for the side, one gaffe stands head and shoulders above the rest, and I'm not talking about the affair with FA secretary Faria Alam that almost cost him his job in 2004. (With hindsight that would have been the best news for English football in quite a while.)

Arsenal manager Arsène Wenger must have been delighted to hear that Eriksson was taking youngster Theo Walcott to the 2006 World Cup in Germany, presumably because the untested teenager would hamper England's chances if they ever came up against the French. Rooney was injured, played poorly throughout the tournament and was then sent off. Strike partner Michael Owen injured his anterior cruciate ligaments after only a minute's play against Sweden and missed the rest of the competition. So who was Eriksson going to play upfront? Here comes the manager's next gaffe because Walcott, who hadn't even made a Premiership start, was clearly itching to get on, but Eriksson decided not to play him, relying instead on the other relative novice that was Peter Crouch. Cue England's sorry exit, yet again, from a major championship.

Okay let's not let Eriksson off the hook so quickly then. In the vital games alluded to earlier (Brazil in 2002, France and Portugal in 2004, and Portugal again in 2006), England were 1-0 to the good in all of them inside a few minutes. Any manager with a modicum of common sense would have realised that one goal was never going to be enough against opposition of that quality, but Eriksson had other ideas and decided to tell his players to play out the eighty-odd minutes remaining in the hope that his team was still winning at the end. Of course this naivety was brutally exposed and England lost all these games. His halftime team talk in the 2002 Brazil quarter-final was particularly inspiring according to one of the players:

"We needed Winston Churchill but we got Ian Duncan Smith"

Eriksson wasn't too fussed though; he walked off into the sunset in 2006 with a multi-million pound pay-off. Thanks very much, job done disastrously, and goodbye. He is now able to command up to £50,000 for an after dinner speech. This presumably starts promisingly, then peters out for the next ninety minutes while the audience gradually loses the will to live. (It emerged in early 2007 that Sir Alex Ferguson changed his mind over whether to retire when he heard Eriksson was going to take over at Old Trafford. He must have known something no one else did, until now…)

Still, England had at least one representative left in the tournament. Referee Graham Poll was our nominated official, though he probably wished he was on the flight back from Germany along with the players. In the Croatia - Australia match he sent off Dario Šimic and Brett Emerton, before showing a second yellow card to Josip Šimunic. Poll then inexplicably failed to send him off. It was a high-profile blunder in front of the world's media and Poll's career at the major championships was over. He eventually dismissed Šimunic for a third booking just before fulltime. (Let's not forget Australian Zeljko Kalac's terrific goalkeeping blunder in this match. He spilled the easiest of stops into this own net to gift-wrap Croatia a score.) And Poll wasn't finished with the game yet either. As the ball was about to cross the Croatian goal line, he blew for fulltime, denying the Australians a winning goal with fifteen seconds left *on* the television clocks.

Okay, let's not leave the poor man alone just yet. In 2002 he almost poked Jimmy Floyd Hasselbank's eye out before Chelsea's match against West Ham. And in the 2007 FA Cup tie between Blackburn and Arsenal he was 'tackled' to the ground by Rovers midfielder Goodspeed just as team-mate Benni McCarthy notched the winner. Poll awarded the goal despite being flat on his face in the mud at the time!

Spare a thought for those foreign players who have, to the English at least, comedy surnames. Brian Pinas lasted a single reserve game for Newcastle against Birmingham in 1999, John Motson delighted in talking about Germany's Stefan Kuntz, Celta Vigo have a player named Turdo (who is presumably not much good), Brazil's Rafael Scheidt apparently *is* that good, and Sparta Prague probably haven't won much since the arrival of Milan Fukal. Imagine the problems he has when people try to buy him a drink…

And a certain Brazilian defender moved to Portugal in 2003, to the headline:

"Argel Fuks off to Benfica"

And you can just imagine Pinas's first confrontation with the referee:

*"Okay, son, that was a bad challenge. I'm going to have to put
  you in the book. What's your name?"*

"Pinas"

"Any more of that and you're off, mate. Now, for the last time…"

South Korean club player Prik undoubtedly has the same problem. And Paul Dickov certainly tries to live up to his name, while the opposing fans enjoy chanting:

"Take that, Dickov"

Russia's Titov sympathises. Queen's Park Rangers used to have a Doudou on the pitch, while Watford's Shittu has been known to drop a couple of stinkers in his defence. In 1958, Danish side Frem Copenhagen frequently called upon Bent Koch to keep goal. Having researched the funny names theme for a while, however, I was disappointed not to find a Bell-End anywhere…

League Champions Juventus were only one of several Italian clubs to be punished for their role in a match fixing scandal in 2006. The club was heavily fined, docked points and then relegated as a result of an enquiry. They were also stripped of their Serie A title, but it will be the thirty-point deficit at the beginning of the next season that will be the hardest obstacle to overcome. Of course the relegation to Serie B brings with it other problems, such as reduced gate receipts, and top players wanting to leave, possibly because dwindling cash reserves will not be enough to meet their wage demands. Some in the Italian media are even speculating that Juventus could be relegated again, which for the club of that stature would be unthinkable. The other clubs implicated in the scandal, Fiorentina and Lazio, will also struggle, though Milan got away comparatively lightly, having just fifteen points deducted from their start in Serie A. This was not the first time that Milan had been in trouble with the authorities, however. In 1980 they were relegated because of illegal payments made during another bribery scandal, and in 1991 they were banned from European competition because the players left the pitch without the referee's permission during their game against Olympique Marseille, yet another team with a history of financial irregularities...

Commentator Speak 2

"People will look at Bowyer and Woodgate and say, 'There's no mud without flames'"
GORDON TAYLOR

"Chris Waddle is off the pitch at the moment, which is exactly the position he's at his most menacing"
GERALD SINSTADT

"We'll have more football later. Meanwhile, here are some highlights from the Scottish Cup Final"
GARY NEWBON

"Steve Bruce is like a cat on hot tin bricks"
ALVIN MARTIN

"Kilbane's head is better than his feet.
If only he had three heads, one on the end of each leg"
EAMON DUNPHY

"If you were in the Brondby dressing room right now, which of the
Liverpool players would you be looking at?"
RAY STUBBS

"Real's second goal made it 3-0"
DES LYNAM

"Forest have now lost six matches without winning"
DAVID COLEMAN

"Cristiano Ronaldo hit the ball with every inch of his body
weight"
ALAN DARK

"Liverpool have now really got to win two away: one in
Barcelona and the other at home to Roma"
BOB WILSON

"Poland nil, England nil, though England are now looking the
better value for their nil"
BARRY DAVIES

"We got the winner three minutes from time, but then they
equalized"
IAN MCNAIL

"There's such a fine line between defeat and losing"
GARY NEWBON

"Lampard isn't the first player to run to the crowd with his lips over his mouth"
ADRIAN CHILES

"Ireland have won a corner and it's in a very good position"
RTE COMMENTATOR

Giants Killed: The Magic of the Cups

It's always pleasurable for the neutral supporter when the FA Cup throws up a tie where the minnows of the Second or Third Divisions are pitted against one of the Premiership giants. The same can also be said when two international teams of completely different pedigrees meet in one of the major tournaments. Though the side that appears superior on paper usually goes on to win, there are a number of occasions where the lowly non-Leaguers or international no-hopers pull off a surprise victory. Here are a few wonderful examples that have rocked the sport to its foundations.

The Corinthians side famous at the turn of the last century was composed entirely of amateurs. They were, nonetheless, a formidable outfit as several top clubs found out to their cost. Sheffield Wednesday won the 1896 FA Cup and were promptly dispatched 2-0. Blackburn, one of the biggest clubs in the country, won a hat-trick of FA Cups in the mid-1880s, but they were thrashed 8-1 after the 1884 final. Bury had just recorded the biggest winning margin in the 1903 FA Cup Final, a record that still stands today, when they faced the Corinthians. The amateurs battered them 10-3. The side was responsible for another shock some twenty years later when, having been in decline for some time, they faced the still mighty Blackburn Rovers, and won 1-0.

Celtic were humbled by lowly Arthurlie by four goals to two in 1897, while Sheffield Wednesday also lost by two clear goals to Darlington in 1920.

On their way to the semi-final of the 1927 FA Cup, Reading knocked out both Manchester United and Portsmouth, two teams considered vastly superior to the Biscuitmen. This unusual nickname derives from Elm Park's proximity to biscuit makers Huntley and Palmers, though they are more commonly known as The Royals, after the county of Berkshire. The side set a League record in 1985 when they won their first 13 matches of the new season.

Herbert Chapman's 'Lucky Arsenal' side couldn't live up to their nickname in a 1933 FA Cup meeting with Walsall, the non-Leaguers winning 2-0. It is said that the cheers as the goals went in could be heard two miles away, and that the Arsenal reserves burst out laughing when they heard the score because they thought they were the victims of a practical joke. History repeated itself some half a century later, albeit with a different score-line, when the two clubs met in the League Cup. The Saddlers emerged victorious again and eventually made it to the semi-final.

Third Division Millwall's cup run in 1937 raised a few eyebrows in that they became the first side from that League to make it to the semi-finals. On the way they beat Manchester City 2-1 before eventually losing to Sunderland by the same score-line.

Dick Duckworth's York City were responsible for the slaying of three giants in their remarkable run in the 1938 FA Cup. In reaching the sixth round they dispatched Coventry from the Second Division and West Brom and Middlesbrough from the top flight. Sadly they then went down to Huddersfield in front of 58,000.

Surely the result of the Colchester United - Huddersfield Town fixture in 1948 was a foregone conclusion. Not exactly. The minnows had already beaten Wrexham, then they dispatched Huddersfield 1-0 before beating Bradford Park Avenue. They were eventually thrashed 5-0 by Blackpool however.

Yeovil Town attributed their successful Cup run in 1948-49 to their diet of eggs and sherry. They faced Second Division Bury in a game they couldn't possibly expect to win and then hammered their opponents 3-1.

The following game threw up another chance for the non-League side to slay a giant, only this time the gulf in class was surely insurmountable.

Sunderland were virtually unbeatable, the Black Cats side of the late 1940s and early '50s being known as the 'Bank of England', not only because they could be relied upon to be impregnable in defence, but also because investors were spending large sums of money on improving the already formidable team. It is perhaps somewhat predictable that the side is best remembered for this, its greatest failure, however, the fourth round FA Cup defeat by the 5000-1 outsiders on their famously sloping pitch in early 1949. Sadly the underdogs could not pull the rabbit from the hat in the next round and Yeovil were soundly thumped 8-0 in front of 82,000 by Manchester United.

Most of the entries in this section concern clubs from different tiers in the British domestic game, but there are a number of international sides that can claim to have slain a giant or two. In 1950 England arrived at the World Cup in South America with a number of so-called superstars in the squad. Indeed with Wright, Finney and Mortensen, among others, they were widely acclaimed as the best side in the world and were expected to dispatch their opponents, the 500-1 outsiders United States, with consummate ease. But despite hitting the woodwork a dozen times, they simply couldn't score, overconfidence certainly playing its part in their 1-0 humiliation by a country that barely understood the game. Clearly shell-shocked they then lost to Spain (1-0) in their next match and were on their way home. The English suffered similar embarrassment at the hands of the Eagles when they lost 2-0 in 1993, and who can forget their 3-1 demolition by Frank Farina's Australian Socceroos at Upton Park in 2003?

Port Vale fell just short of ultimate glory in 1954 when, as a Third Division Club, they made it to the semi-final of the FA Cup (they'd almost made it that far by default in the late 19th century when all their opponents dropped out before their matches). Sadly West Brom proved too strong, the winner coming from former Vale signing Ronnie Allen. The Potteries side set a domestic record for the League that season when they went 30 consecutive games without conceding a single goal!

York City's greatest moment in the cup surely came in 1955 when, as a Third Division side, they took on a Matthews and Mortensen strengthened

Blackpool and won comfortably. They also saw off a Blanchflower inspired Spurs and only lost to eventual winners Newcastle.

AFC Bournemouth caused a sensation when they reached the sixth round of the cup in 1957. Reg Cutler's goal gave them a 1-0 over the mighty Wolves, and they followed this up with another victory over supposedly superior opposition when they beat Spurs. Sadly they then came up against Matt Busby's Manchester United and the Cherries were pipped at the post. It was in the Wolves match that the scorer memorably collided with the goalpost and caused the entire structure to collapse. Play was suspended for several minutes while repairs were made.

The Czechoslovakian side of the late 1950s were thought of very highly, as possible world champions elect. Northern Ireland hadn't read the script though and gave them a 2-1 defeat to think about. In 1982, at their own World Cup, Spain came up against a revitalised Irish side and they went down 1-0. In the early months of 2007, Irish fortunes have again been on the rise. New manager Lawrie Sanchez was booed after his first match in charge for the Euro 2008 qualifiers - a 3-0 defeat to Iceland - but within a few months he had guided the side to the top of their group with a fabulous 3-2 win over Spain. His good run also included victories over England (1-0) in a World Cup qualifier and, more recently, against Sweden (2-1).

The third round of the 1959 FA Cup threw up the mouth-watering tie of Worcester City of the Southern League vs. Liverpool of the First Division, a side that had only lost two of its last sixteen matches. The first attempt to play the game at St George's Lane was abandoned because the pitch was frozen solid, the tie being played in the depth of a cold winter. The following Thursday the teams turned out again on a pitch that was still pretty solid. Worcester were 1-0 after ten minutes, some shoddy defending letting Tommy Skuse slide the ball in from close range. Then Liverpool defender Dick White gave them a second after slicing the ball over his own 'keeper ten minutes from time. Although the Merseysiders pulled a penalty back a couple of minutes later, Worcester held on for a deserved win. Sadly for them, Sheffield United put them out in the next round.

Norwich City's 1959 cup run was notable for wins against a Tottenham side that was just a couple of years shy of its double winning form (1-0) and a strong Sheffield United side (3-2).

Newcastle United have a good cup pedigree. At the beginning of the 19th century they could almost claim the trophy as their own, and they've chipped in with another three victories since the end of the war. But they were also susceptible to defeat by supposedly inferior opposition, as they proved against Bradford Park Avenue, Bedford Town (which the non-Leaguers won 3-1 in the 1963-64 FA Cup), Hereford and Wrexham (both after replays), and Chester. In fairness to the lower league sides I can't actually list them all due to limitations of space, so my apologies to those not mentioned in this paragraph. The Hereford tie in 1972 was particularly remarkable - this was the match boasting Ronnie Radford's rocket after all - as the minnows had held United at St James' Park before beating them 2-1 at Edgar Street, the first time a non-League side had triumphed over a League team for nearly a quarter of a century.

Luxembourg might have become members of FIFA in 1910 but they have had precious little to cheer about in their hundred odd years of international competition. That said, they did pull off a surprise victory over a Eusébio-led Portugal in a World Cup qualifier in the early 1960s, a result that shook football to the core. Think also of the North Korean effort against the pre-tournament favourites Italy in the 1966 World Cup, their 1-0 victory sending the Italians home in disgrace.

Peterborough gained something of a reputation for slaying giants in the late 1950s and early '60s. In 1965 they saw off a strong Arsenal side in the FA Cup and followed this up the following year in the League Cup with victories over Newcastle and Burnley. There was some foundation for these achievements, however. In 1959, the non-Leaguers strung together a run of 103 consecutive home wins!

Moving north of the border briefly to Berwick Rangers' Shielfield Park ground, scene of their famous 1-0 win over Rangers in the 1967 Scottish Cup. The minnows upset their illustrious opponents after a fantastic rearguard action, though sadly they didn't make it much further in the competition.

Swindon visited north London in 1969 expecting to get hammered by Arsenal. It was they who dished out the beating though and they went on to win 3-1.

Don Revie's Leeds United side of the late 1960s and early '70s enjoyed a period of great domestic success. They won the League and the League Cup, and also experienced good runs in the European Cup and FA Cups, reaching the semi-final once and the final twice respectively. They also finished as runners-up in the League three times in the years immediately before the 1970-71 season. The fifth round of that year's FA Cup saw them face Fourth Division Colchester United, a team whose manager, Dick Graham, had been down to the beach that morning to prepare mentally for the game:

"It was a beautiful summer's day with blue sky and a calm sea. As I looked out I knew beyond all shadow of a doubt that we were going to beat Leeds. It wasn't wishful thinking, it was total conviction"

The underdogs put in the performance of their lives and were 3-0 up at one point. Leeds pulled it back to 3-2 but the Us held on to win, prompting Graham to make good on a pre-match promise by scaling the walls of Colchester Castle! His side then won the Watney Cup after a penalty shootout against the team that had just denied Leeds the Division One title, West Bromwich Albion. They were soundly thumped 5-0 by Everton in the next round of the FA Cup however.

Leeds were on the receiving end again when they were pitted against Second Division Sunderland in the 1973 final. Ian Porterfield smashed home from 12 yards to give the underdogs a lead they wouldn't relinquish, thanks largely to the amazing performance of their goalkeeper, Jim Montgomery, who made a series of breathtaking saves.

Wales travelled to face Hungary in Budapest in 1975 mindful of the fact that the home side had not been beaten there in more than thirty years. In fact the last British side to beat them, England, had only done so in 1909. In the intervening years it was the Hungarians who finally ended the belief that the English were the best side in the world, the Magnificent Magyars hammering them twice in the 1950s. Wales, of course, upset the apple cart and won 2-1.

Lawrie McMenemy took a virtually unknown Second Division Southampton outfit to the final of the 1976 FA Cup, where they faced Manchester United. Instead of being overawed by the occasion the

Saints played out of their skins and recorded a deserved 1-0 victory, Bobby Stokes winning a car for his goal when he couldn't even drive. McMenemy proved this triumph was no fluke when they reached the final of the League Cup in 1979 and actually finished League runners-up in 1984.

Harlow Town, and yes, I've no idea where that is either, pulled off a shock victory when they beat Leicester by a goal to nil in 1979.

Fourth Division Halifax Town called in stage hypnotist Ronald Markham, of whom more later, in their bid to overcome Manchester City in the 1980 FA Cup. The great Romark, as he was then known, worked his magic and Town came away with a memorable 1-0 victory. City recovered quickly, however. They made it to the final the following year and only lost to a Ricky Villa-inspired Spurs in the replay.

Halifax were responsible for another giant kill when they took on West Brom in the 1993-94 Cup competition. This time they went away from the Hawthorns with a 2-1 win. The Baggies had suffered at the hands of non-League opposition before however, and knew how it felt. They'd been humbled 4-2 at home by cup specialists Woking two years earlier, the non-Leaguers earning themselves a standing ovation both there and after their next match, a 1-0 defeat at Goodison Park. Two other supposed giants from the Midlands probably had no sympathy with their local rivals. Coventry were beaten 2-1 by Sutton United in 1988-89, and as winners of the coveted trophy only two years before after a memorable performance against Spurs, they were expected to bury their opponents under an avalanche of goals. Birmingham City had been dumped out (2-1) by Altrincham a couple of seasons earlier.

Shrewsbury Town managed to knock Wimbledon out of the FA Cup in 1991.

Domestic Oddballs

You might be wondering what defines an 'oddball'. Many hundreds of books have been written about football facts, figures and trivia, but the problem with these is that they're constantly becoming outdated as goal-scoring records fall or number of appearances are bettered. I've tried to compile a selection of stories, both from the UK and, later on in chapter seven, around the world, that stand out because they include rare events. Indeed many have unique and bizarre qualities.

In 2004 researchers at Southampton University announced that they'd discovered a manuscript purporting to be an instruction to buy King Henry VIII a new pair of football boots. At a time when most European monarchs were banning the game, as it prevented the masses from practicing archery, Henry was clearly a fan. Some historians dispute this however, claiming Henry couldn't stand the physical demands of the sport. But perhaps William Foulke (see below) modelled himself on a previous big fella between the sticks.

First played around 1717, the Eton Wall Game is an interesting variation of football. It pitches teams from those who board at the school (Collegers) against those who live in the town (Oppidans) on a pitch 120 yards long by just six yards wide. At least one of these matches used a door in the wall at one end and an elm tree at the other as the goals.

The Harrow version of the game used goals approximately twelve feet wide, but this was doubled if the game was a draw and a replay was required. It was perhaps as a result of this practice that the modern width of a goalmouth has been set at eight yards or twenty-four feet. The teams would also change ends every time a goal was scored though this practice soon died out.

Early forms of the game - at least until 1860 in some places - also included two scoring areas. An outer goal, or 'rouge' as it was known, would count if no inner goals were scored. A single inner goal would, however, wipe out all the opponent's rouges.

The first official football club was formed in Sheffield in 1857. One of the rules they employed was that each player had to carry a half-crown coin in each palm so they could not use the rugby-style hand-off to beat an opponent. Six years later, eleven clubs proposed forming the Football Association, which had an immediate duty to draw up rules governing the size and weight of the ball. The abbreviation assoc was often suffixed with an 'er' in accordance with tradition at Oxford University, where rugby had become rugger. Once the 'a' had been dropped the progression to 'soccer' quickly followed. One Charles Brown replied that he'd rather play soccer when it was suggested that he join the rugger team in 1883.

It wasn't until 1866 that the match length of an hour and a half was introduced, this being decided by teams from London and Sheffield. It is one of the longest standing rules of the game.

The 1875 FA Cup Final became the first major match to see extra time being played. The Royal Engineers drew 1-1 with the Old Etonians but then won the replay 2-0. The 1880 final was awarded to Nottingham Forest after Sheffield refused to play the extra half hour. Italy won the first World Cup Final (1934) to go into extra time, when they beat Czechoslovakia, and Real Madrid took the first European Cup (1958) having beaten AC Milan 3-2 after two hours.

The first game to be played under artificial light took place at Bramall Lane between Sheffield and a locally represented side in October 1878. Most of the 10,000-strong crowd watched the match having sneaked in under the cover of darkness without paying however! It was not for another seventy years that a League match would be played under floodlights though, when Newcastle beat Portsmouth 2-0 in 1956.

As football became more organised and crowd numbers increased, the issue of professionalism was first broached. It is said that two players for club side Darwin, Fergus Suter and John Love, were the first to be paid, in 1879. Six years later the practice was so widespread that the League was forced to legalise payments to players and the professional era began.

At the end of the Zulu Wars in South Africa in 1879 it was decided that money should be given to the families of British soldiers killed during the conflict. A match was organised between the Zulu Warriors and Sheffield, then probably the best-known club in the world. The Zulu side actually comprised the best players from around the country but they were made up to look like African fighting men and were covered in war paint. The touring side won 5-4 at Bramall Lane, then continued their success with victories over Scarborough, Barnsley and Chesterfield. The fact that they never lost sadly didn't ensure their longevity. FA representative Pierce Dix believed that the tourists devalued the game because it wasn't being played in the right spirit, and they were also being paid, which was still against the FA's wishes.

The first recorded instance of the crowd influencing the outcome of a game was in 1881 when a pitch invasion during the Queen's Park - Dumbarton fixture forced the referee to abandon the match. Seven years later an FA Cup tie between Preston and Aston Villa was halted for the same reason. Villa fans had long been known as some of the most boisterous in the country. Indeed their intervention during the 1893 League campaign forced the FA to ban them from the cup competition that year.

Preston earned their nicknames 'Proud' and 'Invincible' after winning the first League Championship - consisting of twelve clubs (Accrington, Aston Villa, Blackburn, Bolton, Burnley, Derby, Everton, Notts County, Preston, Stoke, West Bromwich Albion and Wolves) - in 1888-89 without losing a single match. They then promptly won the FA Cup without conceding a goal throughout the entire competition.

The idea for such a league had been around for a while but it wasn't until the clubs met at the Royal Hotel in Manchester in April 1888 that Scotsman William McGregor finally saw his wishes realised. The first day's action offered a number of highlights, perhaps the finest being Derby's fight-back from 3-0 down to beat Bolton 6-3. Preston's Jack Gordon scored the first League goal though.

The Crewe Alexandra - Kensington Swifts FA Cup tie in 1888 will be remembered for a controversial incident after the game had finished (2-2). Crewe officials complained that the goals were of different sizes. The referee examined the uprights and found that one crossbar was two inches lower. Swifts were disqualified as a result and Crewe went through to the fifth round. From then on all complaints about the pitch had to be made and checked before kick-off. It was discovered in 1989 that one of the crossbars at Portsmouth's Fratton Park was an inch too low, and had been for some time...

Hampden Park is home to Scottish football's Queen's Park. The side was so successful in its youth that it won the domestic cup ten times in twenty years before the turn of the 19th century. In fact they went unbeaten for seven years, with the exception of a couple of games played in England (the FA Cup Finals of 1884 and 1885), and during that run they didn't concede a goal for five years! They were also the first club to appear on television.

Nets were first used at the suggestion of J.A. Brodie for an Old Etonian's match in Liverpool in the early 1890s. They were used in the FA Cup Final in 1892 between the much fancied Aston Villa and local rivals West Bromwich Albion at the Kennington Oval. Villa's goalie Jimmy Warner had a shocker though and West Brom won 3-0. There was some concern about the rigidity of the mesh, however, as balls frequently bounced out and the referees couldn't tell if a goal had been scored. At the end of their 1909 season West Bromwich Albion thought they'd scored and started celebrating, but the referee deemed that the ball had come back off the crossbar and waved play on. The error cost West Brom a point and they missed out on promotion as a result! Strangely a similar incident confined Aston Villa to Division Two as recently as 1970. And a beautiful Clive Allen strike for Crystal Palace in 1980 was ruled out because the referee failed to spot that the ball had rebounded off the stanchion two feet inside the goalmouth.

There was no law governing penalties until 1891. The idea of giving the striker a free-kick was first suggested in Ireland, but the practice didn't become common in England until a few years later. In fact the Corinthians, then one of the most famous clubs, felt the rule was so biased that they instructed their goalkeeper to stand by one post until the penalty had been taken. The idea was then gradually adopted, with various changes being made to the rules over the next decade so that 'keepers were no longer allowed to advance six yards or indeed move along the goal line. The ten yard exclusion zone from the spot (indicated by the arc on the edge of the penalty area) was introduced in the early

1920s. Grimsby were one of the first teams to suffer a referee who was a little overzealous in awarding spot kicks. In 1909 they faced four in quick succession against Burnley but the remarkable Scott saved three of them.

Anfield was home to Everton until 1892, when an argument between the club and the ground's owner, John Houlding, led to the side seeking new pastures. Houlding then formed Liverpool AFC and Anfield became their home. The flagpole mounted above the old Kop End was the mast from Brunel's famous Great Eastern, which was broken up on Merseyside in 1888. To Spurs sides the Liverpool fortress was almost impregnable and they failed to win a single game at Anfield between 1912 and 1984!

When Port Vale were hammered 10-0 by Sheffield United in 1892 you could be forgiven for thinking that they'd just been outclassed. Not so. The heavy snow hampered the busier goalkeeper and then, to make matters far worse, he dropped his glasses and was unable to find them!

"He dropped his glasses and was unable to find them"

Fulham's Craven Cottage ground was named after Baron Craven's hunting lodge, a dwelling that was frequented by royalty. The pitch was laid on an area that had been part of Anne Boleyn's estate and was opened in 1894. The ground staged the first home international away from Crystal Palace in 1907, and was where Pelé made his only club appearance in England, when Santos played their hosts in 1973.

The match between Sheffield Wednesday and Aston Villa in 1898 had to be abandoned with ten minutes remaining because the light had failed (the first game played under artificial light was at Bramall Lane in 1878, but the idea was in and out of use depending on FA preference). The League decided that instead of replaying the fixture, the teams should simply play out the last ten minutes at the next available opportunity. Fifteen weeks later Aston Villa completed a 4-1 win and then went on to take the Championship.

Sadly the player, year or fixture aren't documented for this next slice of oddness, but it has been claimed that one man was brought on as a substitute and was immediately - without him even walking onto the pitch - asked to take a corner. He curled the ball beautifully into the top corner, turned round to celebrate, broke his ankle and was taken off without ever making it onto the field. The goal turned out to be the winner!

The match between Burnley and Blackburn in December 1891 was not exactly a thriller. It was so cold that the Blackburn players almost didn't make it out of the dressing room, and they wished they hadn't after conceding three goals in the first half. After the break only six Rovers players came out to play. Referee Clegg deemed that was enough for the match to restart and they got underway. There followed a couple of scraps that saw Clegg send two players off, and then all of Blackburn's players bar 'keeper Herby Arthur marched off in protest. Clegg, of course, waved play on! Arthur shouted 'offside' as often as possible before Burnley realised they'd have to start all their attacks from inside their own half or Clegg would give free-kicks after every pass. When Arthur made a save midway through the half he kept the ball for as long as possible to waste time and no Burnley player could dispossess him. Clegg eventually got tired of the antics and abandoned the match.

The 1894 Stoke - Wolves clash took place in a blizzard. Referee Helme had no option other than to take the teams off after three and a half minutes as the conditions were unplayable. They were not able to return and the three hundred brave souls who came to watch went home very disappointed. The weather also put paid to the Walsall - Newcastle fixture the same month, though the Walsall players, fed up at not being paid, almost caused the game to be abandoned before it had started. When they finally took the field, Newcastle seized the initiative and went 3-0 up. Walsall fought back and scored a couple of second half goals but then the sleet and snow closed in and the game was called off. Sadly for Walsall enough of the fixture had been played to ensure the result stood. Half the team was sacked the following week.

The Spurs - Nottingham Forest clash one hundred years later suffered the same fate, in that the snow forced the referee to call a halt to proceedings. The white ball had been exchanged for orange but the players could not see from one side of the pitch to the other and the commentators had no idea who had the ball, or, indeed, where it was.

Stand-in referee John Conqueror presided over the first half of the 1894 Sunderland - Derby clash which saw the home side go three up. When scheduled ref Mr Tom Kirkham arrived to take over, he bizarrely offered Derby the chance to restart the match, which they accepted immediately. The pressmen at the ground were understandably worried that their halftime reports would be inaccurate, but they needn't have worried as Derby shipped another three in the second first half. Sunderland took full advantage of the wind in the third half and banged in another five goals. The final score in this 'game of three halves' was therefore listed as 8-0 even though Derby's international 'keeper Jack Robinson had let in eleven. He blamed the result on not having his pre-match rice pudding! His defence had clearly deserted him…

As a goalkeeper William 'Fatty' Foulke was head and shoulders above his contemporaries. As a physical specimen he was shoulders and waist bigger than anyone else. Sheffield United signed him at a solid 15 stone in 1894, but by the end of his playing career a decade or so later he weighed more than 23 stone. Chelsea craftily employed two tiny ball boys behind his goal to make him appear even larger. It is said that he once picked up an opposing centre forward, Liverpool's George Allan, and dumped him on his head after being subjected to an illegal shoulder charge. And soon afterwards he fancied testing himself against the opposition striker one on one so he deliberately picked the man up, tucked him under a huge arm and launched him into the net to concede the penalty. Indeed it is said that Foulke only met his match once, when he conceded defeat to the weather. In a match at Aston Villa at the turn of the last century it was so cold that several players had to be resuscitated at halftime. Foulke stayed out longer than most but paid the price and had to be carried off by six men (the stretcher was too small) when finally bowed by the driving sleet.

There are many more stories about the great man but this caught the eye as I trawled through the research material. He took exception to Southampton's late equaliser in the 1902 FA Cup Final at Crystal Palace, but instead of venting his fury while out on the pitch, Foulke decided it would be best to cool off in the bath after the match. There came a point, however, when he could no longer contain his anger, and referee Tom Kirkham and his linesmen were gobsmacked when twenty-three stones of dripping, naked goalkeeper stormed out of the dressing room on the warpath. Kirkham hid in a boot locker, the door of which was immediately ripped off its hinges. Foulke then had to be restrained by groundstaff and the Secretary of the FA himself! Dare I mention the time he made it into the dining room before his Chelsea team-mates and polished off all eleven breakfasts? Probably not.

Another player with the same nickname was Billy Wedlock. The half-back helped Bristol City to promotion in 1906 and played 26 times for England. More recently, Greentown's Thomas Haylock has been targeted for his size, team-mates nicknaming the twenty-stone 'keeper 'Cheesecake'. In 1977 he was dropped by his manager, the gaffer citing 'top of the net work upsets him' as the reason!

Liverpool won their 1895 FA Cup tie against Burnley 2-1 after extra time. It wasn't until sometime later, however, that the referee realised he shouldn't have played the extra half hour because the entire match needed to be replayed. Liverpool then won the rescheduled match 4-0.

Willie Maley managed Celtic for half a century! His tenure started in the late 19th century and he only retired at the outbreak of World War Two. Sheffield Wednesday's Eric Taylor remained with the club as either manager or coach for 32 years up until 1974. Forfar Athletic's Steve Murray wasn't quite as lucky. He 'managed' just three days at the club in 1980.

Founded in 1896, Egham Town are nicknamed the 'Sarnies', for an obvious and quite amusing reason. And here's another instance of wordplay entering the football lexicon. In about 1898 an Irish family, the Hoolihans, moved to Southwark. They were well-known for their riotous parties and all night drinking, and this behaviour, allied with their surname, spawned the word hooligan.

When Stoke met Burnley at the end of the 1898 season they both knew that a draw would guarantee their place in the top flight. So they engineered the most boring football match in history. There were no shots at all during the game and both sets of players seemed quite happy to pass the ball to each other. The crowd, understandably, was less amused and repeatedly stole balls kicked into the stands so that the teams might get the message. The worst match in recent memory was surely the League Cup Final in 1999 between Spurs and Leicester. There was one shot on target in two hours of football, Allan Nielsen's winner securing the trophy for the north Londoners. Yawn. Of course contests involving the Foxes used to be so much more interesting. Four Leicester players were challenged to a penalty shootout in 1899 by the Sanger's Circus elephant. Though the ball was large and favoured the beast, the players were expected to win. The elephant trounced three of the four but William Keech quickly realised it was moving off its line early and placed his four shots into the corners. Still, the animal somehow managed to save two of them. It then scored a couple itself and drew 2-2. Keech's offer of a rematch was accepted with a loud trumpet but this time he read the elephant perfectly and won 3-2.

At the end of January 1900 British forces of the Lancashire regiments engaged the Boers at Spion Kop (an English translation of these Afrikaans words is 'lookout'), a hill in South Africa. It was a particularly bloody battle in which more than 300 Liverpudlians lost their lives, mostly as a result of poor intelligence and leadership. In 1906, journalist Ernest Edwards suggested that the bank of earth at one end of Anfield should be called the Kop in tribute to the city's fallen soldiers, and the name has been associated with the ground ever since.

Bury's 6-0 win over Derby in the 1903 FA Cup still stands as the greatest margin of victory in the final.

Sir Arthur Conan Doyle, he of Sherlock Holmes fame, played in goal for Portsmouth, while Nobel prize-winning physicist Niels Bohr played for the University of Copenhagen.

Stamford Bridge was built in 1905 before there was even a team to play there. Brothers H.A and J.T Mears had acquired the site the year before but had to fend off stiff opposition and a rival bid for the land by the Great Western Railway. No club wanted to move there upon the stadium's completion so a local side was formed instead. During construction some workers chanced upon a stash of old coins. Not realising the value of the Spade Guinea, they buried the hoard under the West Stand.

With a population of just 6,000 Brechin City, formed in Scotland in 1906, prides itself on being the smallest place in the UK to have a representative League side. It is said, somewhat derogatorily, that the club became the first to experiment with professionalism when the locals tried to pay the side to play elsewhere!

During a match at Falkirk's Brockville Park the ball was kicked so hard in the wrong direction that it actually cleared the grandstand. Despite an extensive search it was not immediately found, and only turned up a couple of days later 43 miles away. It had somehow landed in the bed of a railway truck outside before being transported away as cargo.

Falkirk became the first Scottish League side to score more than a hundred (102) goals in a season as far back as 1907. They were also the first club to pay more than £5000 for another player when they signed Syd Puddefoot from West Ham in 1922.

As the new century dawned, Newcastle United were the most feared team in the country, their home, St James' Park, a fortress. In December 1908 they took on sixth placed Sunderland and were expected to win comfortably, but the score was 1-1 at the break. In the first thirty minutes of the second period Sunderland tore up the form book and scored eight times! The 9-1 defeat must have shaken the Tynesiders up though because they went on to win the championship comfortably.

Striking Welsh coalminers took on the soldiers sent to arrest them in a match at Tonypandy in 1910. Major-General McReady's Lancashire Regiment was far too strong however and ran out 4-1 winners.

Captain Robert Falcon Scott took a football with him on his ill-fated expedition to Antarctica in 1910. When progress across the unstable ice floes was impossible, he would organise the party into two teams and they would play a match.

Bradford City beat Newcastle with a highly disputed goal in the 1911 FA Cup Final. So talked about was Jimmy Speirs's strike that fans of both clubs re-enact the game to this day, usually on the morning of the Cup Final itself, though not if one of the teams is involved. The 1991 game helped raise money for the burns unit that had treated many of the survivors of the Bradford fire, which killed 55 and seriously injured 210 at Valley Parade in 1985. All the more tragic is that the stand was due to be renovated, with work starting the following day. (It had been a black weekend for football because another fan was crushed by a collapsed wall during a riot at St Andrew's.)

The 1915 FA Cup Final was the last to be held for four years due to the country's involvement in the First World War. The fact that war had already broken out meant that many of the crowd for the final at Old Trafford between Sheffield United and Chelsea were in their brown uniforms. This led columnists to dub the match, the 'Khaki Cup Final'.

Many believe the Arsenal - Tottenham rivalry merely stems from their proximity in north London. Think again. Arsenal, formerly the Woolwich Arsenal, were formed south of the river but moved north having claimed the crowds in Woolwich just weren't up for it. Spurs, who had only joined the League the year before, in 1908, and north London rivals Clapton Orient didn't like having their space invaded as it meant some of their supporters, and therefore income, would be tempted to join the Arsenal. For the next decade the ill will between the clubs simmered rather than boiled over but it was only a matter of time before another catalyst sparked a furore. In 1919 Arsenal came fifth in the Second Division and could not be promoted. Chairman Sir Henry Norris had invested all his money in their new Highbury stadium but knew Second Division crowds would not be enough to realise anything on this outlay. He had to get them promoted.

Spurs and Chelsea had finished bottom of the First Division and would be relegated in the two down, two up tradition. The danger was that this would leave no London clubs in the top flight and they might form a breakaway league. Norris arranged for Chelsea to stay up by claiming that Manchester United's game with Liverpool was rigged and the Mancunians should be dropped. Then he called a meeting and decided that since the two down rule had obviously been suspended, a vote should decide if Arsenal or Spurs should take the last place in the top flight. The president of the League, John McKenna, was an Arsenal man and the vote, somewhat predictably, went with them. Arsenal thus became the only club to be promoted to the First Division without earning it, and they have never been relegated from it since.

Spurs, understandably, were outraged, but instead of fuming over the decision they replied quickly and decisively on the pitch. They immediately won the Second Division title, and then claimed the FA Cup the following year, 1921, finishing above their now hated rivals for the next two seasons. Sir Henry Norris was then banned from all football for eight years for financial irregularities...

Though it died out for a time between the First World War and the latter half of the 20th century, women's football enjoyed a period of great expansion throughout the 1890s. Indeed Ada Anscombe was so highly rated that an all male team once offered to swap two players just to sign her. England's champion of the game at the same time, Nettie Honeyball, joined forces with Scotland's Lady Florence Dixie to found the Rational Dress Movement, which would go on to organise matches. Sadly, in 1902, the FA intervened and banned all games against women. That didn't stop a fixture going ahead in 1917 however. Injured Canadian servicemen took on their nurses and a number of local women in Reading, though the men were asked to play with one arm behind their back. The ladies went on to record a comfortable victory, 8-5.

Teams from the Royal Engineers devised a handy way of combining two essential skills: fitting their gas masks in preparation for war, and playing football. Dressed in full combat gear, no player was allowed to touch the ball until he'd fitted his mask. The referee would then periodically blow his whistle during the match and the players would have to pack the mask away before they were permitted to continue. It just goes to show how worried the army was about German gas attacks towards the end of the First World War.

The Raith Rovers team were touring the Canary Islands in 1920 when their ship, the *Highland Loch,* ran aground during a storm. The players were forced to take to the lifeboats in order to save themselves. They've had some other memorable moments in their history too. In 1938 they knocked in 142 goals, then a League record. But by 1963 they had plummeted to the other end of the scale and didn't win a single match.

Brentford manager Harry Curtis seized on a meteorological

phenomenon to help his side beat a strong Oldham outfit. They were 2-1 down when fog descended over the pitch and the players were led off. Curtis instructed his players to jump into a warm bath in case the referee decided to call them back out. Just as play was about to get underway, Curtis complained to the officials that going from warm water to cold air could be harmful for the team and the referee believed him! The match was abandoned and Brentford won the replay 4-2.

Fog actually prevented Rotherham from making it to their match against Hartlepool in 1934, the only time a side had cancelled a match due to poor visibility before it had even turned up!

St Albans and Dulwich had contested a 1-1 draw in the fourth round of the FA Cup qualifiers in 1922 and the replay was eagerly anticipated. This game was destined to have slightly more action, helped in all probability by the fact that both teams' first choice goalkeepers had been injured in the original tie and their understudies were deputising. St Albans' Wilf Minter cancelled out an early Dulwich goal and then netted twice more to complete his hat-trick. Dulwich fought back to lead 5-3 after an hour however. The next ten minutes were sensational for Minter though, as he fired home another hat-trick. Dulwich then levelled in the last minutes to force extra time. By the end of the two hours, Minter had seven, all his side's goals. Sadly for him Dulwich had scored eight and they progressed to the next round. It's extremely unlikely that anyone has scored all seven of his team's goals and still ended up losing at this level.

This wouldn't be the last time that Wilf Minter turned up in football's rich history, however. In October 1926 the sport held its annual equivalent of cricket's Gentlemen vs. Players fixture at Manchester City's Maine Road ground. The Professionals were a strong outfit boasting five full internationals and they were confident of winning the coveted Charity Shield, while the Amateurs were just that, amateurs, except for one Wilf Minter perhaps. He created two and scored two as his supposedly inferior side ran out comfortable winners 6-3.

Random Balls 1

"He'll probably wake up having sleepless nights about that one"
ALAN PARRY

*"Hodge scored for Forest after twenty-two seconds, totally
against the run of play"*
PETER LORENZO

"This is going to be a very long 30 minutes with 26 minutes left"
BRIAN MOORE

"He's chanced his arm with his left foot"
TREVOR BROOKING

"We're now in the middle of the centre of the first half"
DAVID PLEAT

*"Don't ask me what a typical Brazilian is because I don't know
what a typical Brazilian is. Romario is a typical Brazilian"*
BOBBY ROBSON

"The World Cup is a truly international event"
JOHN MOTSON

"It was a big relief off my shoulders"
PAUL GASCOIGNE

"Jurgen Klinsmann refutes to earn £25,000 a week"
ALAN MULLERY

"Tony Banks described the English fans arrested in Marseilles as brain-dead louts. That goes for me too"
HARRIET HARMAN

"The only way we will be going to Europe is if the club splash out and take us all to Eurodisney"
DEAN HOLDSWORTH

"Love is good for footballers as long as it's not at halftime"
RICHARD NIELSEN

"I don't think Les Ferdinand was fouled there, Jonathan. I think he went over on his own ability"
ALAN MULLERY

"Viv Anderson has just pissed a fatness test"
JOHN HELM

"Well he's not going to adhere himself to the fans with that"
ALAN MULLERY

"And you don't score 118 goals in 120 games by missing from there"
JON CHAMPION

Oldham's Sam Wynne can't have imagined the impact he would have on their match against Manchester United in 1923. Though his side won the game 3-2, he scored both of Manchester United's goals. Instead of hanging his head in shame, he decided to get forward at every opportunity to try and repair the damage. Oldham were awarded a penalty, so he scored that, and then he buried a long-range free-kick to tie the scores at 2-2. A team-mate then stepped up to notch the winner and spare his blushes. Wynne gets another, tragic, entry in this book for he died when just about to take a free-kick for Bury against Sheffield United at Bramall Lane in 1927. He didn't realise it but he had a severe case of pneumonia and couldn't be revived in the dressing room.

Wynne's four goal 'achievement' pales into insignificance when compared with that of Falkirk's Hugh Maxwell in their game against Clyde in 1962 however. If the final score of 7-3 wasn't odd enough, the fact that Maxwell scored all ten surely defies belief!

Until 1925 the offside rule stated that three defenders must be between the attacking player and the goal when the pass was played through. Of course this made it very difficult for linesmen, and the defensive units soon learned to exploit the rules. Games became fractious affairs with the officials being forced to stop for free-kicks every few seconds. Something needed to be done. Many of the big clubs had been knocked out of the FA Cup early that year so they decided to stage a few friendlies to give them a chance to experiment with the offside rules. Some matches started with a line drawn across the pitch forty yards from each goal, which would be an effective offside line, while others opted for only having two defenders between the attacker and the goal. Clearly one of these was always likely to be the goalkeeper, with the other usually a single defender. The Norwich - Cambridge University fixture was the most successful and the two defender rule, which has remained largely unchanged since, was implemented across the footballing world. The results were spectacular. The following season 6400 goals were scored, nearly 2000 more than the season before.

Celtic's Patsy Gallagher developed a novel way of scoring in their 1925 Scottish Cup Final against Dundee. His side were a goal down when Gallagher collected the ball inside his own half. He proceeded to beat a number of defenders while homing in on goal, but was eventually brought down just inside the box.

Instead of waiting for the referee to blow for a penalty, however, he gripped the ball between his ankles, flipped over backwards and launched the ball over the line. The ref allowed the goal to stand and Celtic went on to win 2-1.

"He gripped the ball between his ankles, flipped over backwards and launched the ball over the line."

Despite a skull fracture after a motorbike crash almost ending his career, Dixie Dean emerged as the greatest striker in the country in the mid-'20s. He helped Everton to two League titles (1928, 1932) - scoring 60 goals in 39 matches in their first championship year - and the FA Cup (1933). In all, he scored 379 goals in just 437 games, including 18 for England in 16 starts. He died having watched the Merseyside Derby at Goodison Park in 1980.

The hymn 'Abide With Me' was first sung at the funeral of its lyricist, Rev Henry Lyte, in 1847. In 1927, the then secretary of the FA, Sir Frederick Wall, knew it to be George V's favourite hymn and asked that it be sung at the FA Cup Final. It is now played every year before the match.

Following the successful radio broadcast of an England - Wales rugby match from Twickenham in 1927, football followed suit pretty quickly. For the benefit of listeners, the Radio Times printed producer Lance Sieveking's diagram of the pitch that was divided into numbered squares. While one commentator described the action (Henry Wakelam), a second (Lewis) called out the number of the square in which the action was taking place so the public could follow the game. The Arsenal - Sheffield United match in the same year was the first to use this system, with the centre circle filling most of square one. The final score was 1-1, and after both Charlie Buchan's and Billy Gillespie's goals, with the ball being replaced for kick-off, Lewis said:

"Back to square one"

Though this simple sentence had probably filtered through from various board games (Snakes & Ladders), the football commentary application ensured it became a well-known phrase. The system lasted for fifteen years and radio broadcasts regularly attracted audiences of ten million, but it died out during the war. This was partly due to the advent of the television. A match at Highbury in 1937 was the first to be televised and this method of communicating with the fans immediately seemed more popular.

Scottish Second Division strugglers King's Park handed out a right royal thrashing to their illustrious opponents Forfar Athletic in 1930. Though some blamed the quality of the pitch and others the Forfar players' hangovers from the New Year's Eve celebrations a couple of nights earlier, their downfall was most likely orchestrated by opposing striker, trainee John Dyet, who'd only been given his chance to impress after injuries had sidelined their first choice forwards. By halftime he'd scored six of his side's seven without reply, and by the end he had eight of their total in a 12-2 pasting. Not surprisingly Dyet was signed immediately afterwards.

The strange game of motorcycle football took hold in England in the late 1920s and early '30s. Played by teams of six-a-side the game was fast and furious and quickly attracted a major following. Though a couple of European tours were organised the fad died out as war approached.

"...the strange game of motorcycle football"

The 1930 FA Cup Final is sometimes known as the Graf Zeppelin Final because the massive German airship passed over Wembley to salute the players during the match.

"The Graf Zeppelin passed over Wembley"

Blackpool's home match against Chelsea in the winter of 1931 was destined to become one of the sport's most talked about fixtures. There was so much water on the pitch that ground staff desperately tried to clear it with buckets and pitchforks (to prod the dirt). It didn't really work and driving sleet and rain only replaced what they'd drained. In fact it was so cold that Chelsea's Peter O'Dowd collapsed unconscious in the changing room at halftime. Two team-mates then refused o play on and Chelsea began the second period with just eight players. Then two more limped off as conditions deteriorated. Of course Blackpool took full advantage and scored four easy goals, Jimmy Hampson bagging a hat-trick.

Port Vale and Charlton drew their first meeting in the 1932 FA Cup, and by the time they stepped out for the replay Jimmy Oakes had been transferred from Vale to the Addicks, making him one of the select few to play for both sides in what was effectively the same match. This happens extremely rarely nowadays as players are declared 'cup-tied' if they have made an appearance for a club during the competition.

King's Park's Alex Haddon scored five consecutive hat-tricks in 1932. He would no doubt have enjoyed a longer future at the club had the ground not been hit by the only bomb dropped on the town of Stirling during the entire war. After the conflict the club folded due to financial irregularities and Stirling Albion sprung up in its place.

Manchester United were desperate to avoid relegation to Division Three at the end of the 1933-34 season, so they changed their traditional red shirts to bring about a change in fortunes. The new cherry and white hoops were given one game, which United won 2-0, and their future in the Second Division was assured.

Referees were not as fit in the 1930s as they are today. Indeed for a couple of games in 1935 it was deemed necessary to experiment with two referees, one to patrol each half. Refs Barton and Wood were unable to cause controversy in either fixture (North vs. South, and England vs. The Rest) as they were both good tempered affairs. The idea was immediately abandoned, though calls for the experiment to be repeated have been heard again recently.

Manager of the great Lucky Arsenal side of the late 1920s and early '30s, Herbert Chapman sadly died of pneumonia having just watched a Third XI match against Guildford in Surrey. His achievements with the club will stand forever though, with five League titles and two FA Cups going to the north Londoners in his nine-year tenure. He was also partly responsible for introducing a number of experimental changes to the game, changes that have now become essential aspects of the sport. Arsenal tried a new white ball, sewed numbers into the backs of their shirts, made great technological leaps with boot manufacture, tried an all-weather pitch and installed permanent floodlights. It is not known yet if Chapman's ghost, which had haunted Highbury, will be noticed wandering the flats now being built on the site.

Derby County's Baseball Ground hosted the annual Crewe vs. Derby Railway Veterans match in 1937, with the home side hoping to retain the trophy won 2-0 the year before. It was to be a match with a few differences, however. The minimum age for the players was set at sixty-five and they were not allowed to run, which was probably a relief for some of the older members of the squad (the youngest turned out to be seventy-three). Thankfully referee Charlie Kingscott, who had officiated at two FA Cup Finals, was not troubled by the pace of the game. Crewe started strongly and looked as though they might walk in a few goals, but Derby soon learned to give their wingers a walk, and they began walking rings round their opponents. Sadly for the 1500 spectators, the game was to finish goalless and the cup was shared.

Sheffield United's away form in the 1938-39 season was so much better than their home form that the management decided to take the team on a long bus journey before their home games. Somewhat surprisingly the tactic worked and the club was promoted to the top flight!

Eton school had adopted the St Helen's Social Club Centre as part of an exercise to improve relations between the hard-working miners in the north and the privileged public school boys in the south. In 1938 it was the turn of St Helen's to travel south and stay at the school for a few days. The St Helen's lads were treated like kings for their time at the school, in that they were accommodated in hotel-style rooms and ate the top class fare dished up by the Eton staff. It was widely believed that the tough northerners would trounce the schoolboys in a prearranged football match, but the Etonians stroked the ball around beautifully and thoroughly deserved their goals in a 2-2 draw.

Having won the FA Cup in 1939, Portsmouth didn't relinquish it until after the Second World War, the longest time any team has had the trophy in its possession.

Charlton Athletic's 'keeper Sam Bartram knew his team had been attacking Fulham's goal for at least fifteen minutes in a match in the early 1940s. The trouble was he couldn't see the action as there was a dense London pea-souper cloaking the ground. It wasn't until sometime later that he realised there was no one else on the pitch. The game had been abandoned due to the poor visibility and his team-mates were all relaxing in the changing room bath!

Liverpool's fame and popularity had spread far and wide by the time war was declared. Even they must have been surprised, however, to receive an application to play for them from the former heavyweight champion of the world, Joe Louis, in 1944. Louis actually signed his professional papers formally linking him with the club but he never made a first team appearance.

During the Second World War many top international players were posted to the military town of Aldershot to do their national service. The lowly side started to perform rather better with the likes of Matt Busby, Denis Compton and Joe Mercer among the XI.

Most people who follow football will be aware of the circumstances surrounding the Hillsborough disaster, when 96 Liverpool fans died and 400 were hospitalised during a crush in Sheffield Wednesday's Leppings Lane enclosure at the beginning of their 1989 FA Cup semi-final clash with Nottingham Forest. Sadly this tragedy was an eerie repeat of what had happened at Bolton's Burnden Park in 1946. Some 85,000 fans had turned up to watch the Trotters' Cup tie against Stoke and still many more were finding ways through and over perimeter fencing. One man, realising the danger of the overcrowding, forced a door open and left with his son. Unfortunately the opening allowed many more fans in and soon they were being crushed at the Railway End. Thirty-three people lost their lives in the tragedy.

These are not the first and, sadly, probably not the last in a series of disasters at stadiums around the world. As early as 1902, 26 people died at Ibrox when a stand collapsed a few minutes after kick-off in a home international, and 80 were injured when a wall collapsed at Hillsborough in 1914. But these pale in comparison with the Lima football disaster in 1964, when 318 were killed at an international between Peru and Argentina. Peru thought they'd scored a late equaliser but the referee disallowed it and all hell broke loose. Police fired into the air in an effort to restore calm but this just caused outright panic. More than 500 were injured alongside the dead. Incredibly the referee said afterwards:

"Maybe it was a goal after all. Everyone makes mistakes"

And 74 were killed at the River Plate stadium in Buenos Aries in 1968. Tragically 66 more lost their lives at Ibrox during an Auld Firm clash in 1971 when a stairway became congested - not for the first time incidentally - and fans leaving the stadium were crushed or asphyxiated.

Despite these disasters being analysed by the relevant associations, and legislation being introduced to combat the problems associated with them, there were still a number of major disasters in the 1980s and '90s. In a match between Spartak Moscow and Haarlem at the Lenin stadium in 1982, some 350 fans were killed trying to get back into the stadium after a late goal, though official reports at the time claimed 'only' 70 had died. Three weeks after the Bradford fire, the Heysel stadium in Belgium hosted travelling Liverpool and Juventus fans for the European Cup Final. Rioting broke out and 39 people lost their lives in the carnage, most when a wall dividing the rival supporters collapsed under the weight of charging Liverpool fans. The tragedy meant that English clubs were banned from the competition for the next six years.

A stampede during a hailstorm caused around a hundred deaths at a match in Kathmandu in 1988, the fans crushed as they tried to leave the locked stadium.

There was no trouble at a match in Corsica in 1992 but 16 people were killed when a section of the stand gave way after the fans' rhythmic dancing caused the temporary steel and concrete structure to deteriorate. And 80 fans were killed during a stampede in Guatemala in 1996.

In 2007 more than a hundred MPs signed a petition to reopen the Hillsborough file, specifically to assess the possibility of reintroducing some standing areas at League grounds. No doubt there will be fierce opposition to the plan from some, but most fans would like to see safe standing sections so they can decide against sitting if they so wish. The problems associated with standing were highlighted once again, however, during Manchester United's Champions' League tie against Lille in Lens in February 2007. Some of the away fans were getting crushed and the heavy-handed police did little to help by stepping in with batons drawn.

Just after the end of the Second World War, Arsenal hosted a game at White Hart Lane - home of legendary adversaries Tottenham Hotspur - as Highbury was still commissioned for war use by the government. The fog was so bad that neither the Arsenal nor the visiting Dynamo Moscow players could see the ball, or each other, but the noises coming out of the mist suggested that there were some late tackles sliding in. The referee, of course, preceding a future Gunners' manager, was unsighted. Dynamo, who reportedly tried to sneak an extra player onto the pitch, won the match 4-3, though no one could be certain if there weren't a couple more goals scored in the gloom.

When Derby County moved in to the Baseball ground in 1895 they had to move a gypsy settlement out. The travellers were none too happy about this and apparently placed a curse on the ground. In 1946 Derby made it through to the latter stages of the FA Cup and the club was advised to try and get the curse lifted in case they made it to the final. The captain sought out a local traveller and asked if the curse could be lifted. The gypsy agreed and Derby went on to take the trophy with a 4-1 win against Charlton. The match is interesting for another reason: Referee E. Smith estimated that the chance of a ball bursting during the final was about one in a million. One burst in 1946 and another the following year! The poor quality leather available after the war was apparently to blame.

A third match to be affected by fog within just a few years took place at Southampton in 1950. The side had toured South America the summer before and had played several matches under floodlights. When it was suggested that lights could be installed at the Dell, the idea was received enthusiastically, the fans coughing up the £600 needed. Local rivals Bournemouth were the opponents, with a kick-off time scheduled for 6.30 pm. Sadly the weather had other ideas and a dense fog enveloped the ground for the entirety. There were no goals, apparently, though anyone who claimed to have actually seen the pitch or the action was branded a liar. Luckily the system survived its first failure, and the first competitive League match under lights was played at the Dell the following year. Indeed many in the ground had been impressed with the experiment, and by the middle of the decade most of the top clubs had installed lights.

The Stockport County - Doncaster Rovers cup tie of 1946 proved to be a rather drawn out affair. The first attempt to settle it resulted in a 2-2 draw, as did the replay at Stockport a week later. After twenty minutes of extra time the scores were still level and, as this was at a time before the dreaded penalty shootout, the teams decided to play until the next goal, which would be the sudden death winner. Death for neither team proved to be sudden as the match dragged on into its fourth hour. The game was finally abandoned due to fading light after 203 minutes of play, though most of the 13,000 crowd had already disappeared by then. Doncaster won the toss for choice of ground in the next match and won comfortably, 4-0.

The Nottingham Forest Jackdaw became famous for catching the bus from Council House Square to the City Ground to watch the match every Saturday in the immediate post war years.

Hinckley Athletic were so desperate for success towards the end of their 1949 season that they resorted to using a hypnotist. Their next fixture was against top side Bedworth Town, who were heading for the Birmingham Combination Championship, and they knew they had to win two of their last four games to ensure survival. Richard Payne was a renowned hypnotist and gladly accepted the challenge, though some of the players and coaching staff balked at his credentials. Six of the side agreed to the experiment and were all put to sleep on stage the week before the match. Payne convinced them they would win, then set up a follow-up meeting for the match-day itself. By then, however, the club's directors had changed their minds and asked him not to attend. With hindsight, they probably wished he had. Bedworth won 2-1 and clinched the title, while Hinckley lost all their games over the Easter period and were doomed. Even manager Bobby Davidson was sacked.

"Hinckley Athletic resorted to using a hypnotist"

Boxing Day 1949 saw more than one and a quarter million fans turn up to watch the 44 League matches that afternoon, an average attendance, throughout every tier of the English game, of just about 29,000! The individual League record attendance had been set the year before, however, when 83,260 saw Manchester United play Arsenal at Maine Road.

The 1923 FA Cup Final between West Ham and Bolton, the so-called White Horse Final because of the efforts of a single mounted policeman (PC George Scorey on Billy) to restore calm amongst the crowd, saw a legal 126,047 paying fans admitted, though it is claimed another 70,000 got in through an open gate without buying a ticket. If these figures are to be believed then this match probably had the highest attendance of any in history.

Ibrox Park has always had the edge on English club grounds in terms of capacity and 118,567 watched the Auld Firm derby in 1939. Hampden boasted an even bigger crowd of 146,433 for the Scottish Cup Final in 1937. The same ground also holds the record for a European tie, with 136,505 admitted for the semi-final of the 1970 European Cup.

One of England's finest players, Bobby Charlton was coached by his mother (a relative of the famous Milburn family) in a local park. She must have done an exceptional job, for when the first scouts came to watch him they fell over themselves to sign him.

"Bobby Charlton was coached by his mother"

The Manchester United representative told her that there was no doubt he would play for England before his 21st birthday. Charlton survived the Munich air crash, helped his country win the World Cup, went on to score 49 international goals, a record, captained United to their European Cup win in 1968, and finished his career with 247 goals in 754 United starts, only five of many remarkable career achievements.

When York City met Stockport County in 1952, the game was remarkable for the simple fact that it was York manager Dick Duckworth's last game in charge. Coincidentally, it was also his first game as boss for their opponents! York had been struggling in Division Three North and, even though Duckworth bolstered his strike force, they were expected to lose comfortably to their more illustrious opponents. You can, of course, predict what happened next. York overwhelmed County with goals from Billy Fenton (2) and new striker Dave Dunmore, and they ran out easy 3-0 winners. Duckworth's career with Stockport proved to be uneventful, his major chance coming with un-fancied Scunthorpe several years later when he almost took them into the top flight, something that had never been achieved.

Ronnie Corbett's cousin was a regular in the Hearts First XI in the 1950s. The comedian himself was offered a trial as a schoolboy but presumably came up a little short…

In the mid-1950s English football was made up of six divisions, there being two north/south options for the middle leagues. Derby's Ray Straw is believed to be the only man to have played in all six, between 1952 and 1960.

While playing for Aston Villa in 1952, Pete Aldis scored with a header from thirty-five yards, a distance that many people believe has never been bettered for a headed goal.

Though the 1953 FA Cup Final between Blackpool (4) and Bolton (3) in Coronation year is remembered as the Matthews Final - on account of Stanley's brilliance in creating holes in the defence and setting up the goals - it is often forgotten that the man who scored most of them, Stan Mortensen, remains the only player to have scored a hat-trick in a Wembley FA Cup Final. Lawrie McMenemy added to the game's myth when he said:

"The last player to score a hat-trick in the final was Stan Mortensen. He even had the match named for him - the Matthews Final"

It was suggested, with a wry smile of course, that when Mortensen died in 1991 he would probably be remembered at the Matthews funeral!

Though it's often believed that Matthews - The Ageless Wonder - was the oldest player (50 years and 5 days) to play League football, this is not the case, though he does remain the oldest man to have contested a top flight game (Stoke vs. Fulham in 1965). New Brighton's stand in 'keeper Neil MacBain played against Hartlepool in 1947 aged 52 years and 3 months.

"Keeper Neil MacBain played a league match
in 1947 aged 52 years and 3 months"

If you count non-League football in these stats then it's difficult to beat the career of Jack Wattam. He began playing in Grimsby in the early 1920s and didn't hang up his boots until aged 74 in the 1980s. During that time it is estimated that he played 5000 matches, but despite spending nearly a full year on the pitch he was not cautioned once in his 60-year career!

In a series of matches that had statisticians the length and breadth of the country scratching their heads, Leeds United were drawn at home against Cardiff in the third round of the FA Cup for three years in a row (1955-56 to 1957-58). The first two ties yielded two victories to Cardiff by two goals to one. It was calculated at the time by one mathematician that the chance of Cardiff winning the third tie by the same score-line was only about one in a billion. However unlikely it might have seemed at the time though, that is exactly what happened, this despite the teams exchanging places in their respective leagues and enduring wildly different fortunes between times.

Manchester City's 1957-58 season can only be described as action-packed. They became the first team in League history to both score and concede a hundred goals in a single campaign. Third Division (North) side Nelson were not fully fledged members of the League when they scored 104 goals and conceded 136 in their 1926-27 season, but the tally is certainly impressive enough to warrant a mention here.

Lincoln City's Bill Anderson had seen his team plummet to the foot of the 1958 Second Division League table and he knew their chances of survival were slim. In fact, City needed to win their remaining six games to be certain of staying in the League. Anderson confidently told his team that they should do exactly that, and then watched in amazement as they won the first five comfortably, quite a surprise given that they hadn't won a game for over four months. Cardiff on the last day of the season was a tough ask though. The Welsh side had been 3-0 up in the original fixture early in the season when it had been abandoned because of snow, so they were confident of sending Lincoln down. However, other results meant that the Imps only needed a draw to avoid the drop. Things didn't look good after seventy minutes though. Cardiff were a goal up and knocking the ball around comfortably. The 18,000 crowd then witnessed the miracle. Lincoln scored three in ten minutes, two from Roy Chapman and a twenty-five yard rocket from Harbertson. Relegation was thus avoided by a point in the most remarkable end to a season.

Arbroath's Gayfield Park was almost destroyed by heavy seas in 1962. The surrounding wall was breached in a storm but thankfully the ground, the closest to the coast in the country, survived. The weather that winter probably affected more games in Britain than in any other year. There were more than 250 postponements during the FA Cup, with the date for Lincoln City's match against Coventry being altered no less than 15 times. Inverness Thistle and Falkirk were to experience even worse in their 1978-79 season however. Their fixture was postponed a record 29 times due to adverse weather!

While playing for Fulham in 1963 Rodney Marsh scored the winning goal with a header, but then butted the post with his follow through. This left him with serious hearing difficulties. Of course injuries to the head were common for at least the first half century after codification because of the considerable weight of the ball. More recently, and at slightly different ends of the talent scale, Brazil's Tostao and Wrexham's Stu McCallum were advised not to head the ball after consulting with medical staff.

Gillingham took the Fourth Division title back in 1964 with a sequence of 52 unbeaten home League games. Three years later Millwall remained unbeaten for 59 home matches. Their enviable record was not bettered until Liverpool's 1980-81 run which included 85 home games without defeat. Nottingham Forest avoided home defeat in all competitions for three and a half years and 71 matches in the early 1950s. Rangers recorded 38 consecutive wins in 1928-29.

Closed circuit television screens were erected at Coventry City's Highfield Road ground to show their away match against Cardiff City in 1965. A number of speakers then allowed the 10,000 or so fans who turned up to listen to commentary by former Spurs great Danny Blanchflower and local journalist John Camkin. George Curtis put Coventry a goal up but the 12,000 at Ninian Park went ballistic when Gareth Williams equalised for Cardiff with an hour gone. Ronnie Rees then stepped up in the dying moments to give Coventry the win. Though the experiment was repeated a few times it failed to catch on nationwide.

Random Balls 2

"Souness gave Fleck a second chance and he grabbed it with both feet"
JAMES SANDERSON

"A game that had been controlled by Argentina has turned 360 degrees"
GLENN DAVIS

"I'm trying to be careful what I say but the referee was useless"
DAVE JONES

*"They've missed so many chances they must
be wringing their heads in shame"*
RON GREENWOOD

"Certain people are for me and certain people are pro me"
TERRY VENABLES

*"We dropped two points against Ipswich and I mean that
sincerely"*
BOBBY ROBSON

"At six foot seven, Peter Crouch isn't quite as tall as he looks"
GABBY LOGAN

"They've tasted the other side of the coin on so many occasions"
ANDY TOWNSEND

"He's caused the Chelsea defence no amount of problems"
JIMMY ARMFIELD

"Ireland will give 99%, which is everything they've got"
MARK LAWRENSON

"The margin is very marginal"
BOBBY ROBSON

"There's a free-kick now in the box, just in that little space between the 18-yard-line and the six-yard-line, that little incomplete rectangle. I don't know what you'd call that geometrically. A three-sided rectangle?"
TOM TYRRELL

"He's cleared that into his own net"
TREVOR FRANCIS

"We're into the second moment of stoppage time, of which there isn't one"
GEORGE HAMILTON

"George will be happy with a draw. I know how ambitious and positive he is"
TERRY NEILL

"England have just scored their second goal from a corner. This will be added to their first goal"
RON JONES

The Fastest Goals Hall of Fame

In this section I'll try and look at the goals that have broken records, whether that be the strikes that have come immediately after kick-off, or the rapid-fire goals scored by individuals and teams alike.

Arbroath's 36-0 win over Bon Accord in 1885 remains the greatest margin of victory in senior football anywhere in the world. So one-sided was the contest that Arbroath's goalie was able to sit and smoke his pipe while watching the action. One newspaper wag wrote of the event, tongue firmly embedded in cheek:

"After conceding the 20th goal, Bon Accord played like a team with no hope"

Unbelievably Dundee Harps beat Aberdeen Rovers 35-0 on the same day! Preston North End made a good fist of trying to beat both in an FA Cup tie against Hyde United at the turn of the same century, but they 'only' managed 26 by fulltime, six of those coming in a seven-minute spell. It is said that the referee in this match actually lost his whistle and didn't finish the game until at least two hours had been played, thus prolonging Hyde's agony by an extra half-hour. Goalkeeper Charlie Bunyan was not amused, though he did go on to have a successful coaching career in Sweden, one of the first to try his hand at the skill abroad.

The Australian national side was involved in an almost equally lopsided match when they met the lowest ranked side in the world, American Samoa, in a World Cup qualifier in 2001. The goals were flying in so often that even the official scorer lost count of the final tally. It has since been confirmed that Australia won 31-0 (or was it 32?), with striker Archie Thompson netting 13, another world record. His individual total beat the 10 scored by Dane Sofus Nielsen against France in the 1908 Olympics. German Gottfried Fuchs - another with an unfortunate surname - also scored 10 against Russia four years later in Stockholm. I wonder who it was who said:

"There are no easy international games anymore"

Preston's J.D. Ross set a new top flight record, a mark that has only once been equalled in the intervening century and a quarter, when he scored seven goals against Stoke City in 1889.

George Hilsdon's Chelsea debut in 1906 was remarkable. In his first League start he scored five goals. Fred Howard's 1913 Manchester City debut was equally memorable. He scored a hat-trick within thirteen minutes and added a fourth in the second half.

Nottingham Forest needed a win against Leicester Fosse to avoid relegation at the end of their 1909 season. They then set about demolishing their opponents, who were considered vastly superior, 12-0. The FA was so surprised by the result that it ordered an enquiry into the match. It turned out that a number of the Fosse players had been to a wedding the night before and had consumed a quantity of alcohol not recommended for pre-match hydration.

Hull City demolished Norwegian visitors Trondheim 16-1 in a friendly in 1912, striker Steve Fazackerley scoring 11.

Everton scored 33 goals in just four matches in 1931. The consecutive games were against Sheffield Wednesday (9-3), Newcastle (8-1), Chelsea (7-2) and Leicester (9-2). They also beat Southport 9-1 in the same campaign, though the game was not part of their incredible run. In 1980 the team became the first to complete 3000 games in the top flight.

West Bromwich Albion striker W.G. Richardson was having a rather lean time in front of goal right up until their match against West Ham in 1931. Despite wasting two early chances he then scored four times in five minutes to set up the Baggies' 5-1 victory. Blackburn's Jimmy McIntyre also managed four in five minutes but his came late in the second half of a game in the 1920s.

Ted Drake of Arsenal was another who found himself enduring a quiet time up front in the 1930s. He was so disappointed with his form that he wrote to hospitalised manager George Allison asking what he should do against Aston Villa in December 1935. Allison is said to have written back telling him to score a sack-full. Wise words indeed. The Villains started well but failed to find the net, so Drake stepped up to show them how it should be done. His first eight shots of the match yielded an astonishing seven goals, the only one not finding the back of the net hitting the bar! Drake scored the winner at Wembley the following year, helped the Arsenal to two League triumphs and went on to have a successful career as manager of Chelsea.

Halifax Town almost folded through lack of finances in the early 1930s, and if League results were anything to go by they perhaps should have imploded after their performance against Lincoln in 1932. Already 2-0 down after a poor first half showing, they hardly needed Frank

Keetley to pop up and score six in the first twenty minutes of the second period. The match finished 9-1, not a good day for the Town.

Luton Town's reserve striker Joe Payne hadn't expected to play in their match against Bristol at the end of the 1936 season, but injuries to the other forwards meant he got the nod from manager Ned Liddell. He scored his first after about a quarter of the match and completed a memorable hat-trick by halftime. He scored another hat-trick before fifteen minutes of the second half were up. Incredibly, Payne ended up netting 10, a new record, eclipsing that of Tranmere's Bunny Tell (9) made earlier that same season against Oldham. In fact nine of Payne's goals had come in a forty-five-minute spell. This remarkable achievement has never been, and is never likely to be, bettered in an English League match. The final score was 12 0. Two years later, at the comparatively young age of twenty-four, he moved to Chelsea for £2000, though by then he'd already picked up an England cap (and two goals). Sadly he broke his ankle during the war which effectively ended a promising career.

England's Willie Hall has been credited with one of the fastest international hat-tricks of all time. He completed the feat in only 200 seconds while playing against Ireland in 1938.

The match between the Football League and a British all-stars XI in 1941 was not as badly affected by the war as many would believe. There were, in fact, twelve full internationals included in the line ups and nearly half had played in at least one FA Cup Final. The halftime score was not exceptional: 3-2 to the League side. The second half, however, yielded a goal every four minutes and the 15,000 crowd were clearly delighted with the League's eventual 9-7 win.

In 1942 Stephan Stanis scored 16 goals in a first class match for Racing Club de Lens in France.

Jock Dodds scored a hat-trick for Blackpool against Tranmere in 1943, the three goals coming in just two and a half minutes. Gillingham's Jimmy Scarth (1952) and Motherwell's Ian St John (1959) also claim to have scored three in the same time, the latter against Hibs.

The mayor of Baden-Baden near Frankfurt in Germany promised two teams from the village that they would receive a bottle of local schnapps every time they scored in a match in 1949. Whether by accident or design

- one suspects design - the teams put on a terrific game, the final score being Baden 25 - Baden 24! You can imagine how the rest of the day panned out… peachy.

"Each team received a bottle of
schnapps every time they scored."

The Wanderers of Argentina had a sit-down strike in the middle of a game in 1951. Even so, they still only managed to lose by the odd seventy.

The Busby Babes recorded a sensational score-line against Nantwich at Broughton in the FA Youth Cup in 1952. The irrepressible Duncan Edwards netted five times in a total of 23 without reply. Curiously, with such a heavy defeat behind him, Nantwich 'keeper George Westwell was then signed by Matt Busby as he was said to have made a series of remarkable saves, and was only being let down by his defensive line.

Bernard Evans scored after just 25 seconds on his debut for Wrexham in 1954, but even this pales into insignificance when compared with 16-year-old Tommy Spratt's debut in the Manchester United 5th XI in 1957. He scored 14 of his side's 25. Welshman Peter McParland scored with his first touch in international football after just 40 seconds in their match against Ireland in 1954.

Jackie Milburn's record for the fastest goal scored in the FA Cup Final (1955) was finally beaten by Chelsea's Roberto Di Matteo in 1997. He bettered the Newcastle legend's strike by three seconds when he scored after just 42 seconds in their match against Middlesbrough.

Stoke winger Neville Coleman established a new record goal tally for a player in that position when he scored seven times against Lincoln in 1957.

Dunfermline seemed certain to be relegated at the end of the 1958-59 season and only an outstanding performance against Partick Thistle could save them. Winger Harry Melrose stepped up to the plate and fired home six times in a 10-1 mauling of their opponents. The Pars lived to fight another season as a result but they did finally drop to Division Two the following year.

Expectation for the Charlton - Middlesbrough match in 1960 was high. Both teams had been scoring freely and there was expected to be a glut of goals. After a frantic first quarter of an hour, in which the action never abated, there were no goals. The next fifty minutes broke goal-scoring records, though. The ball ended up in the nets eleven times, Boro and England star Brian Clough and Valley legend Dennis Edwards both bagging hat-tricks. At 6-5 to Middlesbrough in the last minute it looked like an away victory, but up popped Johnny Summers to level the scores with virtually the last kick of this incredible game.

Manchester City's Denis Law entered their 1961 FA Cup second round tie against Luton in imperious form. The Hatters' were in no mood to be rolled over by their illustrious opponents though, Alec Ashworth putting them 2-0 up after just a quarter of an hour on a typically muddy pitch. Law then decided to take matters into his own hands. Demonstrating remarkable close range ability and awareness, he scored back to back hat-tricks in just three quarters of an hour to put the game well beyond Luton. Sadly for the Scotsman, however, all his goals were about to count for nothing. Chesterfield referee Ken Tuck ruled that the surface had become unplayable and abandoned the game twenty minutes before the end. The replay began in eerily similar fashion, Luton netting twice and Law pulling one back. There the similarities ended, however. Ashworth secured a 3-1 victory for the underdogs in the second half. Sadly for Law and Manchester City, they were out of the cup, this despite them scoring seven goals to Luton's five. George Best equalled his team-mate's achievement nine years later in United's 1970 visit to Northampton Town. Best had just come back from a suspension having had a bust-up with a referee and he was clearly determined to put the episode behind him. He scored six without reply, some of the touches and dribbling defying belief. It was arguably one of his finest moments as a player.

During Fulham's 1976-77 season Best set an unusual record. He'd transferred to the club for just the one season and ended up playing in all four home unions in the space of only ten days. First up was an international for Northern Ireland in Belfast, then came Fulham's visits to Cardiff, St Mirren and finally Crystal Palace. Of course the great man once quipped that he might go and play in North America as:

"Someone once told me to drink Canada Dry"

Bradford Park Avenue's Jim Fryatt scored after just four seconds in a League game against Tranmere in 1965. This is still a contender for the fastest goal in history as the exact time is not recorded, merely rounded to the nearest whole second. What is all the more incredible is that five players touched the ball before Fryatt rounded off the move. For that reason perhaps, it might be suggested that the time was nearer five seconds. Not so with Manchester United's Albert Quixall in their match against Bayern Munich in 1959, his sixty yard thunderbolt being struck immediately after kick-off.

It has been said that the quickest possible goal would be around 2.5 seconds, and indeed some claim, at a level where the TV cameras are nowhere to be seen, that they have scored in about that time.

After 75 minutes of the 1971 Tranmere Rovers - Walsall match the press reporters were preparing to write up another dull, scoreless draw, one of 22 matches Tranmere would tie that season. Then the Prenton Park fans were suddenly treated to a quarter of an hour of absolute mayhem. A Bobby Shinton shot gave the visitors the lead, but this was cancelled out by a Stan Jones own goal. Geoff Morris restored Walsall's lead a few moments later but again Tranmere pulled one back. The trend continued for both side's third goals, the match eventually finishing 3-3! Come the end of the season Tranmere were extremely grateful for those goals, for they escaped relegation, not on goal difference, but on goal average.

Bournemouth had just been given the prefix AFC, to head alphabetical club lists, when they took on Margate in the 1971 FA Cup. The final score was 11-0, which, against lesser opposition, wasn't too surprising. But the fact that Ted McDougall got nine of them set an FA Cup record.

While playing for Argentinean club Independiente against Gimnasia in 1973, Maglioni scored a hat-trick inside 100 seconds!

Ladies football can be equally as exciting as the men's version. In 1975 the Edinburgh Dynamos humbled Lochend Thistle with a 42-0 demolition.

Malcolm MacDonald's finest hour came at Wembley in a World Cup qualifier against Cyprus in 1975 where he scored all of England's five goals.

The great Austrian striker Hans Krankl became one of the most feared front men in the world in the 1970s. In a match against Malta in 1977 he scored two hat-tricks, and was one of the players of the tournament at the World Cup in Argentina the following year.

Substitute Joe Craig made his international debut for Scotland in 1977 and scored with his first touch! He's not the only sub to make an immediate impact, however. Stoke's Brendan O'Callaghan came on in 1979 and notched within ten seconds, while Huddersfield's Phil Starbuck came on as a sub in 1993 and scored after three seconds! Southend's Freddie Eastwood scored just seven seconds after walking onto the pitch for his League debut in 2004.

In Yugoslavia in 1979, two teams vying for promotion reportedly bribed their respective opponents to lose comfortably so they could improve their goal differences. One side won 134-1, the other 88-0!

The Barrow vs. Kettering Town match in 1979 had a couple of interesting sidelines. Barrow's Colin Cowperthwaite scored all of the Bluebirds' goals in their 4-0 victory, with the first coming direct from the kick-off after just 3.65 seconds!

Birmingham's Woodward Wanderers set a record during their 1981-82 season that is unlikely to be beaten for some time. In their 18 fixtures they conceded 422 goals, an average of more than 23 per game!

England were tipped to do well at the 1982 World Cup in Spain, and they started off by scoring the fastest goal ever in the finals themselves. Bryan Robson netted after just 27 seconds against France, and England went on to win comfortably, 3-1. France ended up having the better tournament though, as England imploded yet again and failed to make it to the quarter-final, Kevin Keegan missing a sitter of a header with his first touch against Spain.

San Marino's Davide Gualtieri eclipsed this time, though it was actually in a qualifier in 1993, when he scored against England in Bologna after 8.3 seconds. In the end, Robson's record goal in the Finals themselves stood for twenty years, until Turkey's Hakan Sukur scored after just 10.8 seconds in their third place pay-off match against co-hosts Korea in the 2002 World Cup.

Milton Keynes' Ladies reserves side entered the record books in 1983 when they were thumped 40-0 by Norwich Ladies, the aptly named Linda Curl bagging 23. Just to show that the youth teams can also perform, the Indian Boys Athletic Association based in Calcutta scored 114 times without reply in a 70-minute match the same year!

In 1984 Stirling Albion were pitted against Selkirk in the first round of the Scottish Cup. Stirling had squandered a good few games recently and they knew Selkirk had been scoring freely so they were in no mood to underestimate the Border Amateur Leaguers. Stirling proved their intent by scoring five in the first half, all from different players. David Thompson added to his first half strike with another six in the second period and although there was the suspicion of offside about Stirling's 19th goal, the overall score of 20-0 was considered fair. At one point the Selkirk bench even indicated that they'd like to substitute the entire team!

Robbie Fowler scored a hat-trick in just 4 minutes 32 seconds against Arsenal in 1994.

Adelaide United's Damian Mori scored after just 3.69 seconds of their match against Sydney in 1996. His world record was only beaten when Frederico Chaves Guedes netted after just 3.17 seconds while playing for América Futebol Clube (MG), against Vila Nova Futebol Clube during a Copa São Paulo de Juniores match.

Tottenham's Ledley King scored the fastest ever Premiership goal (10.2 seconds) in their match against Bradford in the 2001-02 season. Newcastle's Alan Shearer equalled this with a strike after a shade over 10 seconds in their match against Manchester City in 2003.

On the last day of the 2007 Ghanaian Second Division season two sides, Narnia and The Great Mariners, were battling for promotion and it was clear that goal difference might become a factor. At halftime both were leading 1-0 but then events took a turn for the more interesting. The Mariners banged in 27 more against the Mighty Jets after the break, but Narnia bettered this by scoring another 30 against Gouw United. The Ghanaian FA somehow sensed that both these matches should be investigated, but decided there wasn't enough evidence to prove beyond doubt that the games were fixed! Inspector Clouseau must have been recruited to lead the investigation…

Random Balls 3

"He's signalling to the bench with his groin"
MARK BRIGHT

"There will be a game where somebody scores more than Brazil, and that might be the game that they lose"
BOBBY ROBSON

"Both side have scored a couple of goals and both sides have conceded a couple of goals"
PETER WITHE

"This is the half of the field where Bayer do most of their damage"
CLIVE TYLDESLEY

"It doesn't endow me to be honest"
ALAN MULLERY

"Fortunately Paul Scholes's injury wasn't as bad as we'd hoped for"
TREVOR BROOKING

"Lombardo speaks much better English than what people realise"
MARK GOLDBERG

"Aston Villa will play a lot worse than this and lose"
ALAN PARRY

"There are some great defenders here. I just don't know their names"
DAVID GINOLA

"It's sometimes easier to defend a one goal lead than a two goal lead"
MARK LAWRENSON

"I can't understand the notoriety of people"
ALAN MULLERY

"If you can't stand the heat in the dressing room, get out of the kitchen"
TERRY VENABLES

"It slid away from his left boot which was poised with the trigger cocked"
BARRY DAVIES

"A game is not won until it is lost"
DAVID PLEAT

"He's about as tall as they get for a goalkeeper of six-foot-five"
KEVIN KEEGAN

*"This is an unusual Scotland side because they have some good
players"*
JAVIER CLEMENTE

More Domestic Oddballs

Oldham's Boundary Park ground is supposedly haunted by Fred, a man
who died at the Chadderton Road End during a match in the 1960s.
The cause of death is not listed, though local rivals might be tempted to
suggest boredom.

During the West Brom - Manchester City Boxing Day clash in 1967
the goalposts collapsed. The incident seemed to unnerve the Mancunians
and, after a lengthy delay, they lost 3-2.

Barrow and Plymouth were locked at 0-0 in their Division Three
clash in 1968 before an unlikely source stepped up to notch the winner
with a quarter of an hour to go. Plymouth appeared to have cleared the
danger from a Barrow corner, but George McLean collected the loose ball
and hammered it back into the box. The shot was going well wide and
'keeper Pat Dunne knew he'd be taking a goal-kick instead of having to
make the save. He hadn't counted on the referee's intervention though.
Trying to get out of the way of the thunderbolt, Ivan Robinson jumped
and turned away. The ball found the inside of his boot and wrong-footed
Dunne to nestle in the corner. A rather sheepish Robinson apologised
profusely but the goal was allowed to stand because the ball remained
in play. Despite a late rally from Plymouth, Barrow held on to win, the
victory seeing them top the table. Robinson was not 'credited' with the
goal to spare him further embarrassment.

Around the turn of the century a referee made a similar error in a
League match. He was trying to avoid a corner when he inadvertently
headed the ball in. He allowed the goal to stand despite the obvious
protestations from the defending team. And then there was the case of the
referee who sent a dumb player off for foul and abusive language…

135

Passionate fans of the game, Bob Wilson and Michael Jones watched a match at each of the 92 football league venues in the 1968-69 season. They were probably the first people to promote the idea of a '92 Club', members of which, since its founding in 1978, have visited every ground. Alan Durban was made an honorary member because he had actually played at every ground by 1976, and Derby County's Jim Smith had managed a side at every venue by 1986.

The match between Tongham and Hawley in 1969 would set new records for bookings. All twenty-two players were shown the yellow card, and the referee also booked one of his linesmen. And whilst we're on the subject, a Scots ref booked all the members of the Glencraig team before they'd even left their dressing room. The squad had penned a chant abusing the referee and he heard them warming up their vocal chords while he was getting changed. He promptly marched into their changing room and showed the entire side the yellow card. Welsh centre-half David Jones was booked in 1978 before he'd even set foot on the field. The referee had heard him make a number of malicious comments to opposition players and officials alike and decided to punish him anyway.

The 1971 Alvechurch - Oxford City FA Cup qualifying tie was not expected to stand out in that year's competition, but it could certainly have benefited from the new European rules where the original deciding coin toss was swapped for a penalty shootout. The first match ended in a 2-2 draw, with the replay another score draw (1-1), as indeed was the third effort to resolve the tie (1-1), the latter two going to extra time of course. The fourth and fifth games also went to extra time but both finished scoreless. Thankfully, the next meeting, at Villa Park, finally settled the issue, in Alvechurch's favour, Bobby Hope's 588th minute header giving them the hard earned win (1-0). One jester suggested that the final might have to be delayed, and another even went as far as to say that the winners of this match should have a bye in the next round and should then play the FA Cup winners themselves as the final would have had to have been played by then. It had only taken eleven hours of football to separate the two sides, and there wasn't a single goal for a 330 minute period of the tie… In the next round, an exhausted Alvechurch squad faced Aldershot for their ninth game in eighteen days. They lost 4-2.

The Arsenal took the coveted FA Cup in 1971 and knew they had to beat Tottenham at White Hart Lane in their last match of the season to give them a historic 'double'. With just three minutes to go, and with their hopes running out, Ray Kennedy stepped up and scored. History would repeat itself eighteen years later, in 1989, when Arsenal were again vying for the League Championship, this time with Liverpool. The last match of the season pitted the two teams against one another and with Liverpool looking comfortable the title looked like being theirs. But with time running out for the Londoners, Liverpool gave the ball away cheaply. Arsenal broke and a Michael Thomas goal in the dying seconds secured the title in the most dramatic circumstances. The Gunners actually ended up winning the League on goals scored because they had the same number of points as Liverpool.

Doncaster Rovers' Belle Vue ground is noted for both its size and the quality of its grass. So impressed with it were the FA in the early 1970s that they tried to buy it. They offered £10,000 to remove the pitch so they could replace the worn out Wembley turf! Doncaster told them to sod off…

One of the linesmen injured himself while warming up for an Arsenal - Liverpool match in 1972. It seemed that the game would not go ahead until someone mentioned that Jimmy Hill was commentating on the game. As he was a qualified official, Hill stepped down from his perch and ran the line for the match, winning considerable praise for his performance.

Though the 2007 Champions' League Final looked set to be between two English clubs, AC Milan sank Manchester United's battleship in the semi-final. They then faced a Liverpool side that had (once again) seen off Chelsea at the same stage, and avenged their 2005 defeat with a 2-1 victory in Athens. English clubs have only met twice in the final of a European competition. Spurs and Wolves clashed for the UEFA Cup in 1972, a Bill Nicholson-led Tottenham proving too strong, while Manchester United beat Chelsea in the final of the 2008 Champions' League.

The fabulous cricket all-rounder Ian Botham played centre-half, albeit briefly, for Scunthorpe in the early 1970s. Kevin Keegan and Ray Clemence also had early career games for the Irons.

Having hung up his boots early due to injury, Brian Clough stepped straight into management, and within a few years he'd guided a rather un-fancied Derby side to the 1972 League title. He followed this up with a 44-day stay at Leeds United, where his outspoken nature was clearly not popular with the board. Clough, along with long-time assistant Peter Taylor, then moved to the club where he'll be best remembered, Nottingham Forest. He led them to the 1978 League championship, thus becoming only the second man, after Herbert Chapman, to take the title with two different clubs. During his tenure he guided Forest through an unbeaten season comprising 19 wins and 23 draws, a feat only bettered a quarter of a century later when Wenger's Arsenal remained undefeated for 49 matches. Clough followed this up with two European Cup triumphs (1979, 1980) and two League Cups (1989, 1990). He was a unique character who demanded everything from his players and was never afraid to speak his mind, a trait that often landed him in trouble with football's authorities. It is perhaps because of this that he was never offered the England job, surely the national team's loss. It was quite fitting that everyone seemed to think his OBE stood for Old Big 'Ead, a point the man himself sometimes liked to prove. When asked how his players were responding to his unique managerial style, Clough replied:

"They tell me I'm doing things wrong, that I'm not the right man. Well we sit down and talk about it for twenty minutes and then decide that I was right after all"

Though Queen's Park Rangers have been around for a hundred and thirty years, they have only ever won one major trophy, the League Cup in 1967. They did enjoy a brief spell as one of the finest sides though, and when I say brief, I mean for about a month at the beginning of their 1975-76 season. In that time they beat the current domestic champions, Derby County (5-1), the Portuguese champions, Benfica (4-2) and the champions of Germany, Borussia Mönchengladbach (4-1).

Tottenham needed a win against Leeds at the close of the 1975 season to stay in the old First Division, but their form suggested a heavy defeat was on the cards. Manager Terry Neill had heard about hypnotist Ronald Markham and decided to give him a try as a last resort. Markham identified three players who could do with listening to his advice. He talked Cyril Knowles through a number of the player's best goals, tried to instil some confidence in Martin Chivers, who'd been out of the squad for a while with an injury, and identified a number of weaknesses in Alfie Conn's game. The response from the team was immediate: Knowles scored a free-kick, Chivers scored the next and Knowles then bagged a penalty. Leeds pulled one back but then Conn scored. Although the Yorkshiremen scored another late on, Spurs held on to win and ensured their survival in the top flight.

Millwall, Halifax (as mentioned earlier), Oldham and Barnet have all reportedly used hypnotists to try and improve their fortunes. It is said that the Oldham side of the 1950s mulled over a proposal to help, but eventually declined the offer, claiming to be "desperate, but not that desperate".

Fulham offered a young man a trial in the early 1970s but they weren't too impressed with his ability and decided against signing him. Football's loss turned out to be Athletics' gain because the boy would win back-to-back Olympic decathlon gold medals (Moscow 1980, Los Angeles 1984). Daley Thompson is now regarded as one of the top five sportsmen ever to have lived.

Pat Dunne became the first woman to referee a men's match in 1976 when she took charge in a Dorset County Sunday League game. Five years later Liz Forsdick officiated for an FA Cup tie between Burgess Hill and Carshalton in Sussex. Since then a number of women have run the line at Premiership matches but none have yet taken control as referee, though Loughborough's Amy Rayner looks like becoming the first to do so if her performances continue to impress.

Scotland manager Ally MacLeod once saw Rose Reilly playing for a boys' team. She was so good that he couldn't believe she was a girl, remarking, once her sex had been established:

"If she was a boy I wouldn't have any hesitation in signing her; she has remarkable talent"

In 1976 Aston Villa's Chris Nichol emulated the amazing feat of Oldham's Sam Wynne some half a century earlier. Villa were struggling in the League and were away to Leicester City when the fun began. Nichol, a veteran who would play nearly 700 career matches, started the scoring by diverting Brian Alderson's stand-bound shot into his own net. He was soon up the other end though, turning in a Brian Little centre to level the scores. Sadly he then gifted Leicester their second when he headed past John Burridge from a Frank Worthington cross for his second own goal. He equalised for Villa a few minutes later after a goalmouth scramble, his goals, the only of the match, all having been scored from open play!

When Nottingham Forest's goalkeeper Chris Woods took the field at Wembley for the League Cup Final in 1978 he had yet to make his League debut.

Football's red card was only formally introduced into the English game in 1976, and it only lasted until 1981. By 1987, though, it was realised that a second colour was needed and the card was reintroduced.

In their 1983-84 season Cambridge United chalked up the unenviable record of not winning in 31 consecutive matches, at the time the longest sequence of failures in League History.

Derby's Robert Wilson was tackled by a Fulham fan in a match between the two in 1983. The crowd had overflowed onto the pitch surrounds towards the end of the game and Wilson was tussling with the defender for the ball when the fan decided he'd seen enough! There was much more to this game than that however. Derby had endured an awful start to the season but had then fought hard to escape the drop zone with a run of fifteen unbeaten games. They needed a win to be sure of staying in the division. Fulham, on the other hand, had had a memorable campaign and needed a win to secure promotion to the top echelon of English football. Bobby Davison volleyed Derby 1-0 up with a quarter of an hour to go and the celebrating fans spilled onto the pitch. Stewards were unable to clear them back into the stands, so several hundred were allowed to stay on the pitch surrounds. With just over a minute left, and with the game frantically seesawing, referee Ray Chadwick blew for an offside. The crowd thought it was the fulltime whistle and invaded the pitch again, and this time nothing was going to clear them. Fulham manager Malcolm MacDonald was incensed, and demanded a replay, but the FA ruled that the result should stand. Derby erected a perimeter fence...

Broken goalposts can usually be repaired in a few minutes. Not so in the match between Chester and Plymouth in 1981. Chester's Grenville Millington dived to make a save from David Kemp's header, got a hand to the ball before colliding with the post, which snapped, and then, while already dazed, suffered the indignity of being smacked on the head by the falling crossbar! The match had to be replayed the following week.

The entire Bristol Rovers squad went to prison in 1982, not, as you might think, as a result of a major scandal though. They played a match against an inmates side from Erlestoke Prison in Wiltshire as a publicity stunt.

A staunch Derby fan, the Rev. Ben Crockett refused to have weddings booked in his church if the side were playing at home. In 1984 one couple took their objection to this practice to the Archbishop of Canterbury as it would spoil their big day. Despite being contacted by the Archbishop, Crockett refused to budge and the ceremony was relocated. Derby beat Plymouth 3-1.

An unlikely scorer made all the headlines after the Knave of Clubs - Newcastle Town Staffordshire Sunday Cup meeting in 1985. Knave's club secretary Dave Hall recalls one of their players collecting a through ball and coming up against the 'keeper one on one. The striker shot early, but sliced the ball well wide, or that's what he thought. Unseen, a dog had scampered across the pitch towards the ball, then leaping like a Scottish Salmon, the pooch headed the ball home from eight yards. The referee was as impressed as the Monks Neil Park crowd and awarded the goal, though the striker didn't stay around long enough to be included in the celebrations! Despite the goal, Newcastle held on to win 3-2.

A fan somehow managed to make it onto the roof of Wembley stadium for the 1986 Liverpool - Everton FA Cup Final. Luckily he didn't suffer the same fate as a supporter who turned up to watch Dunfermline play Celtic in 1968. The ground was filled to capacity and he climbed onto the roof of one stand before falling to his death.

A police dog called Bryn made an unusual contribution to the 1987 Fourth Division relegation battle. Torquay, Burnley and Lincoln all had mathematical chances of being dropped, though, eventually, it all came down to how Torquay could respond having gone 2-0 down to Crewe. They clawed a goal back and then, with just minutes remaining, Bryn, clearly a Crewe supporter, charged onto the pitch and bit scorer Jim McNichol.

The referee had no option but to allow the player treatment and, in the resulting injury time, Paul Dobson fired home Torquay's equaliser. Lincoln were therefore relegated on goal difference, and Torquay chairman Lew Pope sent Bryn home with a juicy steak for dinner!

Formed in 1897 Aylesbury (The Ducks) have a long but not very distinguished history. In fact their biggest game was played against England in 1988, who were, at the time, preparing for the upcoming European Championships. They lost, not surprisingly, 7-0. The Ducks have one of the weirdest goal celebration routines whereby all the players get down and do the 'Duck Walk'.

Apparently West Bromwich Albion's Jason Roberts spelt his own name incorrectly on a transfer request…

Liverpool's John Barnes acquired the nickname 'Tarmac' as an advance on the original 'Black Heighway' honouring the former player. In 1984 he was asked to juggle the ball for photographers while on Copacabana beach in Rio de Janeiro, but he politely declined as there were "so many children doing it better". It's doubtful if any of the children could have scored the goal Barnes managed in England's match against their hosts though. He cut in from the left flank, dribbled beautifully past five defenders and then slotted the ball home from close range for the highlight of his career.

A few other players have been honoured because of their colour, most notably Pelé, who was known as the 'Black Pearl', Russian goalkeeper Lev Yashin (the Black Octopus) and Portuguese striker Eusébio (the Black Panther). Eusébio's real name, incidentally, is Ferreira da Silva, while Pelé was born Edson (after inventor Thomas Edison) Arantes do Nascimento. It is thought that the Pelé name came from his proficiency at a street game called pelada, though a couple of other theories have gained credence, including one that it came from his hairstyle. Here the man himself tries to explain:

"I wasn't too happy to get this nickname. Pelé isn't my real name; my real name is Edson. A classmate wanted to anger me with the name Pelé, so I punched him and got suspended from school. I didn't want the name. Pelé sounds like baby-talk in Portuguese"

And here's another line concerning the great man, this being an old Brazilian saying:

"In Brazil, if you're black and rich, then your name is Pelé"

In 1950 Pelé had watched national team fail at the final hurdle in their decider with Uruguay. His father cried because there would now not be a celebratory party. Pelé, then a brash ten-year-old, comforted his father with these words, that were of course going to come true:

"Don't worry, I'll win the World Cup just for you"

John Trollope played 770 games for Swindon between 1960 and 1980, Harold Bell made 401 consecutive appearances for Tranmere between 1946 and 1955, and Pat Jennings became the first man to play in 1000 first class matches in 1983. Peter Shilton joined him at the milestone having made his four-figure total of appearances between 1966 and 1997. When Tony Ford retired in 2002 the only ground he hadn't played at was White Hart Lane during a 931-outfield-appearance career, most of which were for Grimsby.

Shilton holds the record for England caps with 125, while Jennings has 119 for Ireland. Though not all of them were at first class level, Billy Meredith, the Welsh Wizard, played in over 1100 games around the turn of the last century. He retired aged 49.

In 1959 Billy Wright became the first man to play more than a hundred times for England (105), and since then Bobby Moore and David Beckham (108), Bobby Charlton (106) and Shilton have joined him. Kenny Dalglish became the first Scot to achieve the milestone (102), while goalkeeper Pat Jennings was the first Irishman. (Saudi Arabia's Mohamed Al-Deayea was capped 181 times.) Wright, incidentally, captained England in 90 of those matches between 1948 and 1959, still a record.

Scotland's Billy McNeill played for Celtic for 17 seasons and notched up over 800 appearances. In all he collected 23 trophies with the club (then a world record), a total that surely puts him at the top of the domestic pile. He then guided the club to a further seven trophies as manager!

Perry Groves watched the 1980 FA Cup Final as a ball boy. In 1987 he helped his team (Arsenal) win the League Cup Final! He was once on the bench for the side when he jumped up to celebrate a goal. He somehow contrived to hit his head on the roof of the dug-out and knocked himself out!

Aberdeen's new 'keeper Marc de Clerc had an interesting debut in 1980. After a quarter of the match he hoofed the ball up-field and watched it bounce over his opposite number's head for a goal. Not a bad start to your career. Aberdeen's ground, Pittodrie, translates from the old Gaelic meaning 'Hill of Dung', incidentally, and many visiting fans would say that all they've ever seen there is crap.

Plans for a centenary dance celebrating the anniversary of the Herefordshire Football League in 1989 had to be shelved when it was discovered that the competition was only 90 years old!

The referee for the Crystal Palace - Brighton match in 1989 was not shy of using his whistle. In all Kelvin Morton awarded five penalties, a new British record. (The international record stands at the same mark, the 1930 Argentina - Mexico World Cup tie being equally blessed.) Three of the Seagulls' spot kicks came in a five-minute spell just before the break, but they only managed to score one. Mark Bright hit Keeley's legs with his second and a young Ian Wright hit the post with his having already buried a thirty-yard volley from open play. Curbishley pulled a penalty back just after the interval before Palace's John Pemberton blasted his over the bar. Palace only scored one of their four penalties but they hung on for a 2-1 victory anyway.

In 1990 it emerged that a Danish (where else? once you've read on a line or two) invention was keeping farmyard animals entertained across Europe. The Domino Stress Ball was designed for use by pigs so that the rather intelligent porkers could let off some steam in the pen instead of becoming aggressive when bored. The happier the pigs, the healthier they were, the more they ate and the better value they became. Think Jan Molby meets Emmerdale. Rumours that Franz Baconbauer was going to manage a club (sandwich?) were quashed when Spam Allardyce signed up to coach instead. Big Spam is known to like his sides strong at the back, just as long as they don't keep hoofing the ball up to Hristo Stoinkchkov, the lone styker. As for the name of the club itself: Snout-Hampton, Trotter-ham Hock-spur, Queen of the Sowth and Roast Ham United all spring to mind. Paulo Wanchope has dismissed speculation that he will be appointed captain as pure hogwash, though Pork Ji-Sung - having recovered from a torn hamstring - is known to have signed, the provision being that he's paid in guineas. What their first game wouldn't do for a streaker...

Farmer Bernard Hoggarth saw the value of the ball and tried it out with his 15 pigs in Yorkshire. He noticed immediately that they were extremely good dribblers, and then he let them have the ball. They tended to move the Domino with their snouts, and while able to keep close control, they rarely passed, except wind!

Bradford's Sean McCarthy had an eventful debut for the club in 1990. He started by missing a penalty but made up for it with a goal a few minutes later. He added to this auspicious start with something less impressive though, in that he was then sent off!

Manchester United's Steve Bruce scored 13 goals from his centre-half position in the 1990-91 season. Eric Hayward of Port Vale and Blackpool was less prolific though. He failed to score a single goal in more than twenty years at the back!

Czechoslovakian-born media mogul Robert Maxwell became an important figure in British football via his stakes in Reading, Oxford United and Derby County, to name just three. His generous girth and suspect reliability with other people's cash earned him the nickname 'The Bouncing Czech'. Indeed many believe that his shady business dealings led to his mysterious death while on his yacht off Tenerife in 1991. He then had a posthumous chant dedicated to his memory:

"He's fat, he's round, he's never at the ground, Captain Bob, Captain Bob!"

★

Doncaster Rovers haven't given their fans much to cheer about in recent times so the crowds have resorted to amusing themselves. In 1991, they started chanting "Would you like a piece of cake?" to the visiting fans for no apparent reason. Though the police intervened and tried to quieten the home side, they eventually saw the funny side. Of course the next team to visit, Burnley, brought a load of cakes to the ground and the fans dished them out to the policemen.

The smallest League in the world operates on the Scilly Isles, the two clubs playing each other every weekend.

Wimbledon manager Joe Kinnear had his team vote for the worst player after each match in their 1991-92 season, as opposed to dishing out the usual man-of-the-match award. The player would then be forced to watch the most boring play in the West End at the time so that he wouldn't repeat his poor performance the following week. This unusual approach seemed to work and the 'Crazy Gang' gained Premier League status the following year.

Rotherham's Jason White lost his boot as he was sprinting through on goal but he still managed to slot the ball home. He then spent half a minute looking for his innersole!

"...lost his boot as he was sprinting through on goal..."

Early in his career at Ipswich Keiron Dyer was approached by interviewers while out walking in the town. They had no idea who he was or that he played for the club until they asked him about the rivalry between themselves and Norwich, whereupon he explained that he was a professional footballer in the 'Tractor Boys' First XI.

Chelsea's attack once boasted three of the shortest players in the League. Mark Stein was only five-foot-six, John Spencer the same, and Gavin Peacock claimed to be five-foot-eight, though some dispute this figure as a wild exaggeration! Of course the tiny Dennis Wise (five-foot-five) was in the mid-'90s side at the same time. Chelsea have continued the tradition of finding the best vertically challenged players. Shaun Wright-Phillips is only five-foot-six.

Nottingham Forest's Jason Lee claimed television comedians David Baddiel and Frank Skinner ruined his career by constantly taking the piss out of his striking ability. The man himself, known for having a pineapple on his head on account of his wayward haircut, was incensed when the duo mocked up a spot the ball competition with none of the Xs anywhere near the goal. Most, in fact, were in the stands. Fans chipped in with this (to the tune 'He's Got The Whole World In His Hands'):

"He's got a pineapple on his head, he's got a pineapple on his head"

Partick Thistle manager John Lambie was a touch concerned when striker George Shaw was brought to the sideline suffering from concussion after a clash of heads in the penalty area. His physio shouted over that Shaw had no idea who he was and that he probably shouldn't continue, but Lambie came up with a brilliant solution to his striker's lack of self-awareness:

"That's great. Tell him he's Pelé and get him back on!"

Floodlight failure can always cause problems, especially when the failure is deliberately planned so that the outcome of the game can be altered for financial gain. Police in 1999 were called in to investigate the role played by four men who were arrested as part of an alleged betting scam involving sabotaging the floodlights at Premiership grounds. One Briton and three foreigners were detained on suspicion of burglary at Charlton's Valley ground.

In 1997 a Far Eastern gambling syndicate was accused of causing floodlight failure at a televised match. And a list of floodlight failures was passed to Scotland Yard detectives, who were already investigating a power failure at the Wimbledon - Arsenal match at Selhurst Park that winter. Derby against Wimbledon, and West Ham against Crystal Palace, were also analysed.

The lights also went out on the Olympiakos - AEK Athens fixture recently, which was supposedly another case of sabotage, and not the first time AEK had been involved. In 1982 their UEFA Cup clash with Cologne was held up by a similar failure, so the fans resorted, with little thought for their own safety, to lighting fires on the terraces. The match, of course, had to be replayed. Then, with AEK losing that tie, some sections of the crowd started chanting:

"Turn the lights off, turn the lights off!"

And Rushden & Diamonds' had their lights fail, somewhat predictably, when they were on the verge of losing 1-0. There were other high-profile failures at English grounds in the distant past such as the abandonment of the third round FA Cup replay between Crystal Palace and QPR at Selhurst Park in 1946. The referee called a halt after 117 minutes, though both sides decided that the goalless draw was enough and the match was not played again in its entirety.

Shrewsbury needed to beat Watford by three goals to bolster their promotion aspirations in 1959. After an hour they were well on their way to achieving their goal, in that they were 4-1 up and cruising. Then the lights failed. Someone, it transpired, had deliberately removed the fuses. It seemed unlikely, though eminently possible considering the nature of this strange game, that an Exeter fan was responsible, as they would have suffered if Shrewsbury had won. Referee Denis Howell tried to get the teams to play on but fading light meant the game had to be abandoned ten minutes from time with the score at 5-2. The match had to be replayed. Shrewsbury duly repeated their dominant performance and won 4-1, thus ensuring their promotion to Division Three.

Another game that was abandoned, not because of floodlight failure, more just a case of bad light, was Norwich's second leg League Cup semi-final against Chelsea in 1972. They had taken a 2-0 lead into the match and were assured of going through to Wembley for the first time when, with just six minutes left, fog descended onto Carrow Road and the game was called off. They managed to lift themselves for the replay but lost to Spurs in the final.

One match was abandoned after the full 120 minutes had been played. Malta's club sides Gharb Rangers and SK Victoria were contesting the GFA Cup when the floodlights failed in the dying seconds! French outfit Paris St Germain had played 103 minutes of their 2001 UEFA Cup first-round second leg tie against Rapid in Bucharest when the lights cut out. Rapid were then forced to forfeit the game by UEFA because there was no emergency generator at the ground

Witney Town were drawn against Clevedon Town in the first round of the 1996 Dr Martens Cup. The first leg, at Witney, was drawn 1-1. The second leg a couple of weeks later finished with the same score-line and both teams scored a further goal each in extra time. Witney, of course, had scored two away goals to Clevedon's one so they were through. Or were they? The club secretary, as he was ringing in the score to his opposite number at Dr Martens HQ, discovered that the away goals rule meant they only counted double in normal time. They would need to settle the tie with a penalty shootout, even though the players had changed and the Witney side were heading for their coach home. The news was not greeted with great cheer by the away side as they thought they'd already won, but once the rules of the competition were explained they had no choice but to change back into dirty kit and retake the field. It was now 10.30 pm. Witney Town eventually won the tie 4-2 after the shootout.

While at Luton Town John Hartson, along with pals Jason Wright and Kevin Davis, thought they'd steal a sheep on the way home from the pub one night. They stashed it in a minibus and got the driver to take them home. In the morning they found the sheep in some distress in Hartson's back garden and decided that, rather than have a nosy neighbour call the RSPCA, they would take it back to its field, which they duly did. It is not recorded who felt worse in the morning, the sheep or the players.

A study into the behaviour and intelligence of footballers revealed that players who repeatedly headed the ball had an IQ on average five points lower than players who rarely used their head (to pass the ball, of course). The results surprised many scientists, but they couldn't decide if the difference (108 to 103) was due to the impact of the ball destroying fragile brain cells, or if the players who headed the ball more often only did so because they were too stupid to play in any other position in the first place! A Premier League spokesman voiced his opinion with:

"I don't think heading the ball has got anything to do with it; footballers are stupid enough anyway"

And George Best had an interesting theory about a certain player's nous when he said:

"I think Paul Gascoigne's shirt number (10) refers to his IQ"

Newcastle United's chairman Stan Seymour was equally derisive about Gazza:

"He's George Best without brains"

And Marcus Berkmann chipped in with:

"He has the brain power of an iron filing"

Okay, let's give the man a chance to defend himself. Rangers were 2-0 up against Hibernian at Ibrox when referee Dougie Smith accidentally dropped his yellow card. Gazza saw the perfect opportunity to gain some revenge for the players and calmly raised it in the ref's direction. Smith's sense of humour immediately failed and he booked an incredulous Gascoigne for dissent!

Gazza enjoyed an all too brief stay at the peak of world football. Widely acknowledged as one of the most skilful players of the 1990s, his off the field antics eventually derailed his chances of making it onto the list of all-time greats. He was booked in the semi-final of the 1990 World Cup against Germany and would therefore not have played in the final had England won the penalty shootout. His tears afterwards were lampooned by the press but many thought the passion he showed simply reflected his devastation at the result. He had a couple of indifferent years in Italy before returning home for Euro '96 where he was back to his brilliant best. Scotland's Gary McAllister had just been awarded a penalty at Wembley, but as he ran up to take it the ball rolled a quarter of a turn and Seaman saved the slightly miss-hit shot. England then broke up-field and Gascoigne finished off a wonderful move with a beautiful chip over Hendrie and a low volley past Goram. He immediately ran to the corner flag and lay down - as if settling into the much talked about dentist's chair - while team-mates squirted energy drinks (instead of the usual alcohol) down his throat. A Gazza-inspired England made it to the semi-final where another shootout against Germany ended in more tears.

Arsenal's non-flying Dutchman, Dennis Bergkamp, is not the only player to be afflicted by a fear of using the so-called safest form of transport. (Flying is only statistically the safest way to travel because the distances travelled are so great and the figures are usually compiled using that measurement rather than the more reasonable 'number of journeys taken'. Walking is commonly considered the safest way to travel regular, short distances. Indeed it seems unlikely that many people would fly to the shops or their local pub, and if they did, they'd do so at considerable risk.) Before Bergkamp, Scotland's outstanding winger Jimmy Johnstone only played 23 times for his country in the 1960s because he refused to fly to a number of away matches. It's argued that both men's clubs and countries suffered without them.

In 2001 referee Mike Dean waited while Charlton centre-half Steve Brown was treated for a nasty ankle injury before callously sending him off, even though the player was already being carted away on a stretcher. Brown had misjudged a through ball and decided to deliberately handle it away from the Leicester striker when he turned his ankle over. As the stretcher bearers carried him off, the ref helped him on his way with a straight red card, which he'd been hiding behind his back for the duration of Brown's treatment. Angry fans were somewhat appeased when Dean sent two Leicester players off later on and Charlton went on to win 2-0.

It's not uncommon for the Bolton side to have to eat a strange meal after winning by three clear goals. Usually the restaurant will serve up sheep's testicles with a side dish of snail risotto. Yum yum. And, no, that's not a Thai speciality…

Only two goalkeepers have played in FA Cup Finals for two different clubs. Ray Clemence played for Liverpool (1971, 1974 & 1977) and Spurs (1982 & 1987), while David James played for Liverpool (1996) and Aston Villa (2000), his mistake in the latter gifting the title to Chelsea. James explained the error by saying he'd lost concentration as a result of playing too many video games, which had clearly affected his eyesight... This prompted Switzerland's Bernt Haas to observe, during Euro 2004:

"England have no weak links, except David James"

West Brom's manager Gary Megson watched the ball fly over the touchline in their match against Birmingham City in 2004. Instead of controlling it, he accidentally kicked it into opposition manager Steve Bruce's groin, forcing a chuckle from one and a grimace from the other.

Some 2000 people end up playing football on Hackney Marshes every weekend. The facility hosts 100 matches on the Sunday, can cope with 150 teams at the same time and boasts over 1000 showers.

The Tottenham - Arsenal League encounter in 2004 - Martin Jol's first in charge at Spurs - was notable for an odd score-sheet. Arsenal won the match 5-4, unusual in itself, but the fact that nine different men netted remains unique in top flight football.

How many times has a team surrendered a three goal lead to ten men? Not very often probably, but that's what happened when Spurs met Manchester City in the fourth round of the 2004 FA Cup at White Hart Lane. Spurs were cruising (3-0) at halftime and even prompted beleaguered City boss Kevin Keegan to ask for directions to the nearest job centre. When he got to the changing room he found out that Joey Barton had been given a second yellow card for arguing with the referee as they left the pitch and had been sent off as a result. Incredibly this seemed to kick-start the Blues, and with Shaun Wright-Phillips terrorising the home defence they fought their way back to 3-3. Then, in the last minute, Michael Tarnat crossed for John Macken to score the winner for City. One minute he was looking for a job, the next he'd engineered a remarkable comeback, and Keegan went on the ensure the Blues' Premiership survival as well. Spurs, meanwhile, must have been thinking they were the stars of a remake of 'Groundhog Day'. This was their third 4-3 score-line in four games.

The north Londoners somehow managed to conjure defeat from victory in a similar game against Manchester United in September 2001. Leading 3-0 at halftime and appearing to be in cruise control, they shipped five second half goals in the Premiership's greatest fight-back. Not a good day for manager Glenn Hoddle and 'keeper Neil Sullivan. Sullivan, incidentally, while still with Wimbledon, will be forever remembered as the man caught off his line by David Beckham when the latter scored with a hopeful strike from just inside his own half in 1996.

Charlton's match against Huddersfield Town at Christmastime 1957 was perhaps even more remarkable than either of those mentioned above, however. Centre-half Derek Ufton dislocated a shoulder and was taken to hospital after ten minutes. His side were already a goal down and as substitutes weren't yet allowed, it looked like being a long day for the Londoners. Things got predictably worse and they were trailing 5-2 after an hour. The last half an hour was anything but predictable though. Johnny Summers had moved from outside left to centre forward to balance the side after the loss of Ufton, and he chipped in with four goals in twenty minutes, all with his weaker foot. Huddersfield must have thought they'd salvaged a point when they equalised in the last minute but, incredibly, Charlton scored with the last kick of the match and won 7-6! A record crowd turned up at the Valley hoping for a goal fest in the FA Cup tie between the two a week later but Charlton eked out a dull 1-0 victory.

Referee Chris Foy sent Chelsea's Arjen Robben off in their 2006 match against Sunderland at the Stadium of Light. Foy issued the second yellow card because Robben, who'd just scored the winner, apparently over-celebrated with the Chelsea fans. The ruling on unsportsmanlike behaviour is quite clear and deems that any player reacting in this way, or removing their shirt, has broken the rules. Quite how footballers are supposed to rein in their emotions having just scored a thirty-yard scorcher to win the match in the dying minutes is beyond me.

Robben is not the only player to feel the weight of the law for this type of offence. Hearts' Phil Stamp was sent off by referee Willie Young (thankfully their surnames were this way round) in 2002 after being mobbed by ecstatic supporters having scored an injury-time winner against Hibernian. And Italian bad boy Marco Materazzi was dismissed by Stefano Farina during the 2006 Milan derby, which Inter won 4-3 in the San Siro. Materazzi collected the second yellow for a wild celebration having put them 4-1 up.

In a Luton Town - Liverpool FA Cup tie in 2006, midfielder Xabi Alonso scored from well inside his own half. Luton had held their more illustrious rivals for a good portion of the match and had even chipped in with a couple of goals. But as the tie slipped away from them, Liverpool having scored four, goalkeeper Marlon Beresford decided to try and score from a Luton corner. Of course Liverpool cleared the danger and broke up-field, Alonso dribbling past the stranded Beresford and shooting from distance. Steven Gerrard was less than impressed as the ball left Alonso's boot though, as he was in a far better position to score and the through ball would have been the sensible option. As he was in the middle of berating the Spaniard however, he turned round, saw the ball in the net and began heartily applauding! As a brief aside to this story, it was discovered that Alonso had placed a sizeable bet on himself to score in that match. No shock there then. But the fact that he'd stipulated he would score from inside his own half certainly surprised some. An unnamed punter also collected £25,000 for the same bet.

When Justin Hoyte scored for Arsenal in a League match in early January 2007, he became the first Englishman to score for the club since Sol Campbell in September 2005, almost sixteen months previously.

As the players become fitter and faster, so the referees have to respond in order to keep up with the modern game. While the midfielders tend to do the most running during the match, and have been known to clock up average distances of seven miles, the referees can rely on both good awareness and eyesight to 'clock up' about six miles. It is thought that David Beckham ran nearly ten miles during his one man show at Old Trafford against Greece in 2001, an average speed of over six miles per hour, or a gentle jog for the entire 90 minutes. Strangely, it has been found that the ball is only in play for about half of any given match.

The 2007 Carling Cup Final will be remembered for a number of strange moments. Both Chelsea and Arsenal had played their reserve teams in the preliminary rounds so the big names could concentrate on scoring vital domestic League points as well as progressing in the Champions' League. When it came to the final, Chelsea abandoned the 'kids' and played a full strength side while Arsène Wenger stuck by his Second XI and decided to give them their shot at glory. The Arsenal youngsters then proceeded to show their more experienced rivals how to pass the ball about and they looked good for their one goal lead courtesy of England's youngest ever international, Theo Walcott. Then came the moment Chelsea captain John Terry will want to forget, that is if he remembers it in the first place. While challenging for the ball he received a boot from Abou Diaby - who sounds like he should be captain of the United Arab Emirates - straight in the face. The blow knocked him out cold and lead to play being held up for six minutes while he was revived and carted off to hospital. Then, with 93 minutes of the allotted 90 up, Chelsea's John Mikel tangled with Kolo Toure and a mass brawl erupted. Three players (Mikel, Toure and Arsenal's Adebayor) were red carded by Howard Webb, a former policeman who had no doubt seen a lot worse. The time taken to sort out the guilty from the not quite so guilty, added to the time banked for Terry's injury, ensured the match ran to over a hundred minutes. Two Didier Drogba goals meant that experience told in the end for Chelsea, and manager Jose Mourinho's remarkable record in England continued. Both sides were later fined £100,000 for their part in the brawl, about as much as they've earned while you've been reading this last sentence...

Apparently 17-year-old Paraguayan striker Luiz Paez backed out on a move to Liverpool at the end of the 2006-07 season because the weather in Britain was simply not warm enough for him. Manager Rafa Benitez was not impressed.

In 2007 there were players from 69 nationalities in the English Premier League, but there were only two non-white managers in the entire Football League (92 clubs).

In April of the same year Jacqui Oatley became the first female commentator on the BBC's flagship football program Match Of The Day. Many had predicted she would fall flat on her face but it was the ex-managers and pundits left looking foolish after an impressive debut alongside Jonathan Pearce. On the same day, Portsmouth's David

James kept his 142nd Premiership clean sheet, taking him beyond David Seaman's record. It's strange but you don't usually hear the words 'James', 'goalkeeper' and 'clean sheets' in the same sentence, certainly not when his defenders see him coming out for a cross...

There are some 42,000 clubs now affiliated to the Football Association in England, boasting some 2.5 million registered players. Only angling (see below) can claim more regular participants.

Arsenal Ladies made their usual strong showing in European competition in 2007 on the back of their impressive home League form. In their first 18 matches they scored 102 goals while conceding just six! They then won the UEFA Cup and followed that up with victory over Charlton in the Women's FA Cup Final at the beginning of May.

The Premier League was approached with a novel way of ending games that had ended in a draw recently. The sides would take the usual point each and would then contest a penalty shootout for a bonus point. So far players and managers appear to be against the idea, but surely we should try anything to improve our penalty taking.

It emerged in 2007 that the Queen is an Arsenal fan. Presumably that's because she thinks Henry IX is playing up front.

While football remains the biggest spectator sport on a day to day basis, the Olympic Games are the equal of the Football World Cup when it comes to pulling in viewers during the events themselves. Angling is supposedly the most widely practiced sport globally, with some three million Britons claiming to fish regularly.

Both the Manchester United - Everton and Blackburn - Charlton fixtures at the end of the 2006-07 season provided oddities galore. There were own goals for Hreidarsson and Phil Neville, goalkeeping howlers for Iain Turner and Scott Carson, and defensive mix-ups aplenty. Chelsea, meanwhile, failed to beat Bolton at Stamford Bridge and United secured the Championship a few days later as a result.

Let's go back to the gaffers now. Here's another selection of gibberish delivered by the men in charge.

Manager Speak 2 – Stating the Obvious

"Glenn Hoddle hasn't been the Hoddle we know and neither has Bryan Robson"
RON GREENWOOD

"In a year's time, he'll be a year older"
BOBBY ROBSON

"I've got a gut feeling in my stomach"
ALAN SUGAR

"I'm going to make a prediction: it could go either way"
RON ATKINSON

"The league is all about the league, and the cups are the cups"
RAY HOUGHTON

"If you never concede a goal you're going to win more games than you lose"
BOBBY MOORE

"The substitute is about to come on. He's the player who was left out of the starting line-up today"
KEVIN KEEGAN

"It's raining very hard now and the players are getting wet"
KEITH QUINN

"A deflection - that's what changed the course of the ball there"
JIM BEGLIN

"There's a real international flavour to this World Cup"
JIMMY ARMFIELD

"Alex Ferguson is United. Cut him and he will bleed red"
ALAN BRAZIL

"The crowd, not surprisingly, are standing on their feet"
TREVOR BROOKING

"The first ninety minutes of a football match are the most important"
BOBBY ROBSON

"To play Holland you've got to play against the Dutch"
RUUD GULLIT

"A win would be better than a draw"
DENIS LAW

"Argentina won't be at Euro 2000 because they're from South America"
KEVIN KEEGAN GIVES THE WORLD A WELL-NEEDED GEOGRAPHY LESSON

"If you get a man sent off you can be pretty certain your team is only going to have ten men"
GRAHAM BEACROFT

"Apart from their goals, Norway haven't scored"
TERRY VENABLES

"What I said to them at halftime would be unprintable on the radio"
GERRY FRANCIS

"The difference could be the goals that we conceded"
RAFA BENITEZ

"He's a very honest player who gets seven out of ten every week.
He can head the ball and kick it too"
JOE ROYLE

Goals for the Goalkeepers

Paraguay's José Luis Chilavert was his country's nominated free-kick and penalty taker during the 1990s, and he held the record for the most career goals by a goalkeeper until Brazilian Rogério Ceni came along and bettered his figure of 62 recently. In 1998 Chilavert curled a twenty-five yard dead ball around the wall against Argentina in Buenos Aires (he was helped by a tremendous goalkeeping howler though), and in 1999 he became the first 'keeper ever to score a hat-trick (for club side Velez Sarsfield). One of his special free-kicks was from inside his own half. He received a standing ovation after his side's brave performance against the French during World Cup '98 on a day when none of his free kicks managed to find the mark. Despite most of his team slumping to the turf dejectedly afterwards, Chilavert proudly acknowledged his contribution and then tried to console his own side. Goalies scoring goals is not as rare as you might think, however. Here are some who have made it onto the score sheet:

Morton Betts played in goal for his one England international appearance in 1879, but he had previously been chosen as a striker when turning out for Wanderers in the first FA Cup Final in 1872. He scored the only goal of the match against the Royal Engineers to win the trophy. His side, incidentally, was captained by FA secretary Charles William Alcock, the man whose idea it was to introduce the cup competition in the first place. Alcock had been studying a knockout system at Harrow School and decided the same principle could be applied to a national football tournament. The trophy is now contested by approximately 500 teams nationwide, and they play some 600 matches before the winner is decided.

The first goalkeeper to score from a goal-kick was Manchester City's Charlie Williams against Sunderland in 1900. Until 1912 goalkeepers were allowed to handle the ball outside the penalty box (up to halfway), indeed the rules had to be changed because they were scoring so many goals. Bristol's Peter Roney scored for his side in 1910 and in the Third Lanark - Motherwell fixture the same year both goalkeepers notched, the only time this would happen in a top flight game until 2000, when Chilavert and River Plate's Roberto Bonano both scored penalties.

James Brownlie was given the chance to take a penalty for Third Lanark in 1911. He missed the spot kick but buried the rebound instead!

Scotsman Hamish McAlpine was the first 'keeper to score for two different clubs (Dundee United and Raith Rovers).

Chesterfield's Arthur Birch scored five penalties in the 1923-24 season. Plymouth Argyle's Fred Craig had a similar record, scoring five penalties between 1926 and 1930.

Frank Moss was injured in the first half of Arsenal's 1935 clash against Everton at Goodison. In the days before substitutes, he was deemed important enough to continue as an outfield player and duly repaid the faith by scoring from a Ted Drake cross fifteen minutes from time.

Arthur Wilkie injured a hand playing for Reading against Halifax in 1962, so he went up front and score twice in their 4-2 win!

Having enjoyed a playing career spanning nigh on thirty years, you'd have thought Peter Shilton might have netted more than the one he's credited with. His only goal came during a League fixture for Leicester against Southampton in 1967.

Hartlepool were forced to field Ken Simpkins up front after a spate of injuries crippled the club in 1967. He then proved himself an able outfield player by scoring the winner over Port Vale.

Tottenham's Pat Jennings scored from a huge wind-assisted punt in the 1967 Charity Shield against Manchester United. (It was clearly a good year for the 'keepers.) Alex Stepney was caught flat-footed and the ball bounced over his head and in. Stepney, incidentally, became United's nominated penalty taker after an injury to Willie Morgan in the 1973 season. By Christmas he was their top scorer!

Zimbabwean legend Bruce Grobbelaar netted from the penalty spot while playing for Crewe against York in 1980. Of course he told the York 'keeper which way to go but he still couldn't prevent the goal! The Afrikaans word grobbelaar, incidentally, translates into English as 'clumsy', something the goalkeeper's opponents occasionally wished he had been.

Coventry's Steve Ogrizovic once dived to make a tackle, but then his shorts fell down almost revealing his! Despite the weakness of his elastic, he scored against Sheffield Wednesday in 1986. He was probably hoping to make up for one he conceded to Watford's Steve Sherwood two years earlier.

Colchester's Scott Barrett scored the decisive goal against Wycombe in the last match of the 1991-92 season. His injury time winner was enough to guarantee them the Conference Title and promotion to the League proper. Wycombe, level on points with Colchester at the end of the season, failed to gain promotion because of that single goal. Gutted!

While he was with Total Network Solutions Lee Williams scored a hat-trick, all from the penalty spot. Woking's Laurence Batty netted a total of five, including one from open play in 1991.

Carlos Bossio, nicknamed Chiquito (Tiny) on account of his height (6'5"), became the first Argentine goalie to score with a header in 1996. He nodded the equaliser for Estudiantes in their match against Racing.

Manchester United's Peter Schmeichel scored 13 goals in his career. In 1996 he headed their equaliser against Russian side Rotor Volgograd in the UEFA Cup. His last goal was for Aston Villa in their 3-2 defeat by Everton in 2002. The ball dropped to him after the Toffees failed to clear a corner and the big Dane lashed home the volley from seven yards.

Steve Mildenhall once scored from a free-kick in his own half for Notts County against Mansfield Town in a Worthington Cup tie.

Argentinean goalie Carlos Roa - who also has a nickname (Lechuga, meaning Lettuce on account of his vegetarianism) - scored a penalty for Mallorca in 1998 during the Spanish Cup Final. He was pretty useful between the sticks too, as England's David Batty found out to his cost during the penalty shootout at France '98. Aussie Mark Bosnich also scored for his national side, the last goal in a 13-0 rout of the Solomon Islands in a World Cup qualifying match. He was back at the other end for a howler, however, when he slipped while trying to make a routine clearance against Newcastle. He compounded the error by dropping the ball at Lee Clarke's feet and then had to watch him score. Bosnich was the subject of many a tabloid headline. He once aimed a one-armed salute at the Spurs fans - appearing not to appreciate the scale of the gaffe (much of Tottenham's fan base is Jewish) - and he was then caught with cocaine in his system after a drugs test. His countryman Adam Federici scored the winner for Reading against Bromley after being played up front in 2006.

Carlisle were spared the indignity of playing non-league football by their loan star Jimmy Glass at the end of the 1999 season. With only seconds left on the clock, Glass charged the full length of the pitch and buried a close range effort against Plymouth Argyle. His heroics sent Scarborough plummeting from the League instead and the fans stormed onto the pitch celebrating with unbridled emotion. By a strange coincidence Glass's replacement, Peter Keen, scored from his own box a year and a half later in the match against Blackpool, only this time Carlisle were three down and heading for defeat.

Dagenham & Redbridge's Tony Roberts scored a last gasp equaliser against Basingstoke Town in an FA Cup qualifier. The Daggers won the replay and went on to reach the third round, eventually falling to Ipswich, then a Premiership side.

Former Everton great, and still considered a legend on Merseyside, big Neville Southall moved down the managerial ladder a couple of rungs to coach part-timers Canvey Island. He also played up front for 'The Bull Fossils' in the Dover & District Sunday League. He notched just the once for Everton, in a League Cup penalty shoot-out against Charlton.

There is a great story concerning the big man before he'd made it to Everton though. In 1981 he was with Bury and was reputed to be so good in training, saving practically everything, that he was banned from a couple of sessions so the strikers could rebuild their confidence. Amazingly, with Southall taking a backseat for a couple of weeks, Bury began to claw their way up the league!

Mart Poom scored for Sunderland against his previous club Derby in 2003. In the dying moments Sean Thornton curled a beautiful corner onto his head and Sunderland salvaged a 1-1 draw.

Future Spurs and England 'keeper Paul Robinson scored a last minute equaliser for Leeds against Swindon Town in the Carling Cup in 2004. His strike forced the game to extra time, after which he proceeded to save a penalty to win the match. Robinson popped up on the score sheet again in their League match against lowly Watford in March 2007. With Spurs winning 1-0, he was appointed to take a free-kick on the edge of the pitch in line with his own area. He thumped the ball all of 95 yards, where, after being left by defender Shittu, it bounced over Ben Foster's head and nestled in the net. The irony here has nothing to do with the Watford defender's name, though it's certainly worth a good laugh, more that Foster had replaced Robinson in the England line-up for the previous international, that against Spain. Of course Robinson was then selected to take over international duties for the European Championship qualifier against Israel later in the month. As far as bizarre incidents go, however, this match wasn't finished. Spurs' Egyptian striker Mido missed surely the easiest chance of his career when Foster could only parry a weak Huddlestone shot into his path. He somehow contrived to hit the keeper with his shot rather than bury it from a couple of yards.

Portuguese 'keeper Ricardo killed off England's chances of victory at Euro 2004 when he scored the last penalty of their quarter-final clash. Arsenal's Jens Lehmann was no stranger to the other end either. He netted twice for former club FC Schalke, the first, a penalty against 1860 Munich, the second a diving header against Borussia Dortmund. Fellow countryman Jörg Butt hit nine goals for SV Hamburg during 2000-01. Not to be outdone, Blackburn's American star Brad Friedel netted from a corner against Charlton. Sadly for him the goal didn't change the outcome of the match as a Claus Jensen strike for the Addicks half a minute later proved to be the winner.

Middlesbrough's Jim Platt scored a hat-trick for their reserves against Lincoln City in the 1970s, and Sheffield Wednesday's Kevin Pressman has also scored several penalties during shootouts. Pressman holds another, rather dubious honour. In their match against Wolves in 2000, the first of the season, he was sent off for handling the ball outside his area after just 13 seconds. He'd charged out of the box to intercept a through ball but, when he realised it was going to make it to the striker, he stretched to make a conventional save, which left the referee no choice.

Bristol City's Ray Ashley (1973), Glentoran's Andy Paterson (1989), East Fife's Ray Charles (1990), Maidstone's and Iain Hesford (1991), Walton & Hersham's Phil Smith (2000), Preston's Andy Lonegan (2004) and Colombia's Luiz Martinez (2006) all scored from freak clearances.

Jim Stannard has just the one career goal to his credit, which he scored while at Fulham, while Danish Serie 3 striker Jesper Christiansen tried goalkeeping in his spare time and in training. He proved to be so useful that Rangers and FC Copenhagen courted him briefly. Tranmere's Gavin Ward scored from a free-kick inside his own area against Leyton Orient after the ball got caught in a strong wind. They went on to win 3-0. And Necula Raducanu scored seven goals during his career with Rapid Bucharest.

Veteran Mark Crossley scored a last gasp equaliser for Sheffield Wednesday against Southampton at Hillsborough in 2006.

Female 'keepers are equally as effective in front of goal. Millwall Lionesses' Pauline Cope was so bored with the lack of action in her half in their game against Maidstone that she moved up-field to play as an extra sweeper. As soon as she received her first pass she dribbled through the entire opposition line-up and scored one of the 15 her side notched that afternoon!

Just to prove things don't always work out for the goalies though, here are a couple who managed to make a mess of things. Chris Woods and David Seaman both missed important penalties in their careers. Seaman fluffed his chance at the end of Arsenal's shoot-out against Manchester United in the 1993 Charity Shield, while Woods missed his spot kick during a European Cup tie for Rangers.

Outfield 'Keepers

In the days before substitutes were allowed it was not uncommon, if there was an injury to the goalkeeper, for an outfield player to deputise while the patched up goalie would be left to disrupt opposition attacks down one of the flanks. Consequently, there are a number of stories about great performances between the sticks from men alien to that position:

Nat Lofthouse saved a penalty for Bolton against Wolves in the late 1950s after an injury to his 'keeper. He said afterwards that it was one of the finest moments of his distinguished career.

Bobby Moore saved a penalty for West Ham towards the end of his career only to see the rebound drop right at the striker's feet. Sadly Moore couldn't pull off a dramatic double save.

David Webb stepped up to replace Chelsea's Peter Bonetti after the 'keeper was injured against Coventry in 1971. He also played in goal for their match against Ipswich the following week and helped his team to a 2-0 win by keeping a clean sheet.

Former Republic of Ireland manager Mick McCarthy kept a clean sheet for Millwall against Hull in 1991.

Hollywood's Vinny Jones spent some time between the sticks while at Wimbledon.

Belgian midfielder Eric Viscaal took over in goal for Ghent against Lokeren in 1994 after his goalie had been sent off. His first task was to save the resulting penalty, which he did, and then, with only moments left, Ghent were themselves awarded a penalty. Viscaal of course stepped up and knocked it in!

Sunderland striker Niall Quinn ended up between the sticks after Thomas Sorensen was stretchered off with fifteen minutes left of their 1999 clash with Bradford. He kept a clean sheet and they won 1-0, Quinn himself having scored the only goal just minutes earlier. Some years before, the big Irishman, then at Man City, had saved a penalty from Aston Villa's Dean Saunders.

Commentator Speak 3

"He sliced the ball when he had it on a plate"
RON ATKINSON

"I wouldn't be surprised if this game went all the way to the finish"
IAN ST JOHN

"There's no finer sight than when Henry opens his legs and just comes on the ball"
TERRY PAINE

"There's no need for words to describe that goal. Oh, it had speed, power, movement and finishing"
DAVID PLEAT

"The Croatians don't play well without the ball"
BARRY VENISON

"He was in an offside position, but I don't think he was offside"
JIMMY GREAVES

"That's lifted the crowd up into the air"
BARRY DAVIES

"Aston Villa are seventh in the league and that's almost as high as you can get without being one of the top six"
IAN PAYNE

*"He's the man brought on to replace Pavel Nedved, the
irreplaceable Pavel Nedved"*
CLIVE TYLDESLEY

*"The European Cup, almost 17 pounds of silver, is worth its
weight in gold"*
BRIAN MOORE

*"Manchester United could only beat Exeter 2-0, and it was just
1-0 at one point"*
ALAN BRAZIL

*"And some five hundred Italians have made the trip in a crowd of
only four hundred"*
RADIO COMMENTATOR

"Darren Anderton has been repulsed by the Romanian defence"
BRIAN MOORE

"The game was played in Cologne and it stunk"
MARK LAWRENSON

*"Chile have three options. They could win or they could lose. The
tide is in their court now"*
KEVIN KEEGAN

Football Legends: Kevin Keegan

Keegan began his professional career with lowly Scunthorpe having been
dismissed by Doncaster in 1968. Moving to Liverpool under Bill Shankly
in 1970 allowed him display his prodigious talent on the highest club
stage, the European Cup, which he helped win in 1977. This was simply
the culmination of his career at the club however, for he already had
three League titles (1973, 1976 & 1977), two UEFA Cups (1973 & 1976)
and the FA Cup (1974) under his belt. He then moved to SV Hamburg

and was named European footballer of the year twice, in 1978 and 1979, the first Englishman to be so honoured. Having graduated to the England team in 1973, and become captain in 1976, he never quite achieved the international success he craved and Bobby Robson dropped him after England's poor performance at Spain '82. He then had brief stints at Southampton and Newcastle before retiring from playing in 1983. Keegan then took some time away from the game before coming back to manage Newcastle, England and Manchester City, all of which gave us plenty of opportunity to listen to post match interviews containing this gibberish:

"He can't speak Turkish but you can tell he's delighted"

"The 33- or 34-year-olds will be 36 or 37 by the time the next World Cup comes around, if they're not careful"

"The ball was still moving when it hit the back of the net"

"We deserved to win the game after hammering them 0-0 in the first half"

"There'll be no siestas in Madrid tonight"

"The ref was vertically 15 yards away"

"England have the best fans in the world, and Scotland's fans are second to none"

"Football is always easier when you've got the ball"

"Goalkeepers aren't born today until they're in their late twenties or thirties"

"The good news for Nigeria is that they're 2-0 down very early in the game"

"They compare Steve McManaman to Steve Heighway and he's nothing like him, but I can see why. It's because he's a bit different. They're both called Steve"

"Bobby Robson must be thinking of throwing some fresh legs on"

"I'd love to be a mole on the wall in the Liverpool dressing room at halftime"

"I came to Nantes two years ago and it's much the same today, except that it's totally different. The red light district is still the same, though it's a lot bigger and more expensive. I prefer Hamburg. There are these ladies there with fully formed moustaches"

"A tremendous strike which hit the defender full on the arm, and it nearly came off"

"I don't believe there is anybody bigger or smaller than Maradona"

1234567891011

Chants & Songs

It is thought that organised chanting probably began in Mexico where the fans' passion for shouting the team's name gradually evolved into something much more. By the 1960s it was common to hear fans chanting the score-line to bait the losing side, and by the 1980s the Queen song 'We Are The Champions' had become a popular anthem, one of many ditties designed to irk the opposition. Gradually chants such as 'Here we go, here we go, here we go' mutated into songs that mentioned teams and players by name. The number of popular tunes available now means that new words can be adapted to fit almost any structure, though old favourites like 'When The Saints Go Marching In', 'Bread Of Heaven' and Lonnie Donegan's 'My Old Man's A Dustman' remain commonplace.

Some sides will even go so far as to adopt a popular tune as their own, such as Stoke City with Tom Jones's 'Delilah' or Crewe Alexandra with Glen Miller's 'Chatanooga Choo Choo', the latter for more obvious reasons. Strangely, the Crewe squad remains the only one in British Football not to have released a club record. Chris Waddle and Glenn Hoddle did the exact opposite, of course, with 'Diamond Lights' in 1987, a criminal record if ever there was one. Jeff Beck's 'Hi-Ho Silver Lining' used to be associated with both Sheffield clubs, but it has since made its way south to Birmingham, where it is now more commonly used at Molineux by Wolves fans, most recently after their promotion to the Premier League ('And it's Hi-Ho Wol-ver-hampton, and away we go etc').

Let's take a moment now to enjoy some of the popular songs and chants from the terraces in recent years. Some are amusing, while others are downright offensive; hopefully most will tickle the ribs. The list starts with chants that are used universally. The 'insert team' brackets allow you to do just that:

"My old man said be a [insert team] fan and I said 'fuck off, bollocks, you're a cunt!'"

"Build a bonfire, build a bonfire, put [insert team] on the top, put [insert team] in the middle and then burn the fucking lot!"

This next one is usually reserved for when your side is winning comfortably, but some fans wheel it out when they're getting thrashed, just for a giggle:

"Can we play you, can we play you, can we play you every week? Can we play you every week?"

And this chant just begs you to sing along, depending on how your team are playing/what mood you're in:

"We're the best/worst* (delete as applicable) team in the league!"

This can usually be heard during the festive season:

"Away in a manger, a crib for a bed, the little Lord Jesus sat up and he said, 'We hate [team]! We are the [team] haters!'"

While this is usually reserved for the visit of Manchester United, it can be applied to almost any team:

"Who the fuck are [insert team], who the fuck are [team]? Who the fuck are [team] when the [your own team] go marching on!"

As the goalkeeper runs up to take a goal kick, the most common sound from opposing fans is:

"Ooooooooooooooooooooooooh, you're shit aaaaaaaaaaaaaaaaaah!"

This next chant is perhaps the one heard most often. It's simple, effective and, except in Real Madrid's case when they won the first five European Cups, or the Brazilian side that won Mexico '70, absolute rubbish:

"And it's [insert team], [insert team] FC, they're by far the greatest team the world has ever seen!"

And here are a couple of chants commonly heard when one team is assured of cup victory:

"We love you [insert team], we do. We love you [insert team], we do. We love you [insert team], we do. Oh [insert team], we love you!"

This is usually followed by a bout of rhythmic handclapping and the chanting of the team's name. And now for the most popular chant during FA or League Cup fixtures:

"Que sera sera, whatever will be will be, we're going to Wembley, que sera sera!"

The Referee's a Wanker!

The man in charge is always going to take some stick. During the average game he'll make hundreds of decisions, at least half of which will be wrong, or so the fans think. So the very least the ref can expect is a verbal mauling from ten thousand or so angry supporters:

"We know where you live, we know where you live. You fat bastard, you fat bastard, we know where you live!"

"Are you Stevie, are you Stevie, are you Stevie Wonder in disguise? Are you Stevie Wonder in disguise?"
(To Bread Of Heaven.)

This, of course, is to 'My Old Man's A Dustman':

"The referee's a wanker, he wears a wanker's hat, and when he saw his whistle he said I'm blowing that. He books them with the yellow, sends them off with red, but we know he only got the job 'cos the advert said 'brain dead'"

After a particularly bad decision, he's likely to hear this, to the tune 'She'll Be Coming Round The Mountain':

"The ref's got a tenner on the game, the ref's got a tenner on the game, the ref's got a tenner, the ref's got a tenner, the ref's got a tenner on the game!"

Or this:

"You're not fit to ref non-League, you're not fit to ref non-League"

Some even come under fire if they look like they've indulged a little too much over the festive season:

"They had to grease the turnstile just to get the bastard in, they had to grease the turnstile just to get the bastard in, they had to grease the turnstile just to get the bastard in, for he's a big fat bastard!"

And if the fans of one team believe the official is giving them a number of bad decisions, they'll hurl this in the direction of the opposing fans, to the tune 'Blue Moon':

"Twelve men, you've only got twelve men!"

Okay, that's enough abuse for the man in black, green, gold, red, or whatever colour he's allowed to wear these days. Let's crank up the abuse to a different level entirely...

National Anthems

The Gunners

Having been founded in 1886, Arsenal's nickname was acquired around the time they were known as Woolwich Arsenal. Naturally, weapons were stored in an arsenal. Defender Tony Adams, one quarter of an almost impregnable back line, had the unfortunate nickname 'Donkey'. Though it's unclear how he earned the tag, it was probably started by friends ribbing him over his noted lack of pace and occasional clumsiness with the ball. Legend Malcolm Allison endorsed this, saying:

"No footballer of talent should play in the back four"

Whatever, a one time girlfriend of the defender, model Caprice, suggested that there might be an anatomical explanation. Opposition fans delighted him with this taunt as a result:

"Eeeyore, eeeyore!"

They were at the ready again after Adams admitted to alcoholism, this being sung by Middlesbrough supporters to the tune 'Guantanamera':

"One triple vodka, there's only one triple vodka!"

Very helpful. Team-mate Paul Merson also admitted to problems with drink and drugs, prompting some fans to chant:

"Who's got the most expensive handkerchief?"

Adams stepped in to help his mate, trying to silence them with this quote, whatever it means:

"Left alone, with our heads on, we can be pretty mental"

The fans had the last laugh, however, when Adams drove into a wall while drunk and suffered the consequences:

"Jingle bells, jingle bells, jingle all the way, oh what fun it is to see Adams put away!"

Queen's Park Rangers' supporters also managed to come up with a reminder to the defender:

"Who's that driving on the pavement, who's that crashing through the wall? He plays in red and white and he parties every night, Tony Adams is a donkey after all"

Team-mate Emmanuel Petit managed to give his own fans something to chant about on account of his Christian name:

"He's tall, he's quick, his name's a porno flick"

And these chants, to the tune of 'Lord of the Dance', thank the Arsenal manager for bringing a superstar to north London:

"Score, score, wherever we may be, we are the boys from Highbury, and we thank you Wenger, wherever you may be, we thank you Wenger for Thierry Henry!"

"Run, run, whoever you may be, there's no one as fast as our Henry. You'll be seeing red and nothing of the ball, 'cos we are the fucking Arsenal!"

A player helped on his way out of Highbury was Frenchman Nicholas Anelka. He'd angered fans by signing for Manchester City, but his replacement was ready to step in, as this ditty announces:

"Chim-chimeney, chim-chimeney, chim-chim cheroo, who needs Anelka when we've got Kanu?"

Patrick Vieira couldn't escape from Arsenal's denouncers either.

Opposition fans taunted him with this, sung to the tune of Dean Martin's 'Volare':

"Vieira, ooo-oooh! Vieira, ooo-oooh! He comes from Senegal, and his dad's a cannibal"

And the whole team have come under fire since manager Arsène Wenger signed a number of Frenchmen. Opposing fans delight in singing:

"Who let the Frogs out? Who, who, who, who?"

And any team playing boringly is likely to hear this (reminding the side that the north Londoners were famous for eking out dull 1-0 wins in the 1990s):

"Are you Arsenal, are you Arsenal, are you Arsenal in disguise? Are you Arsenal in disguise?"

The Arsenal fans themselves don't mind poking a bit of fun at their own team, especially if they're playing well but not scoring:

"Nil-nil to the Arsenal, nil-nil to the Arsenal"

Yet another Londoner, the Arsenal's Dennis Bergkamp, came in for some abuse over his noted fear of flying. Chelsea fans were the first to get stuck in with:

"There's only one British Airways, one British Airways!"

Of course the Highbury faithful replied with:

"You're just a shit team in Fulham, shit team in Fulham"

'Volare' was also used to let everyone know which team Bin Laden supposedly supported in his youth:

"Osama whoa-oh, Osama whoa-oh, he supports the Arsenal and he's hiding near Kabul"

After the Glazer family's £800 million takeover of Manchester United, the north Londoners were quick to have a dig (at the 2005 FA Cup Final) when they turned up with masks of the American, fake $100 bills and this chant:

"U-S-A, U-S-A!"

The Villains

The club, founded in 1874, gained its nickname from the corruption of the Villa Cross, the name of a church in Aston. Villa fans are noted as some of the most inventive when it comes to penning a catchy chant. Here, most of the team get a look in, to the tune of 'Mambo No. 5':

"A little bit of Villa in our lives, a little bit of Gabby down the sides, a little bit of Petrov's what we need, a little bit of Baros with his speed, a little bit of Mellberg in defence, a little bit of Barry as he's immense, a little bit of singin' from the fans, a little bit of O'Neill 'cos he's our man!"

And this next ditty was sung after victory over arch rivals Birmingham City (to the tune 'Amarillo'):

"1-0 to Aston Villa, Stevie Davis having a thriller, Super Kev just scored the winner, 'cos we're the pride of Birmingham. Sha-la-la-la-la-la-la-la youth-youth, sha-la-la-la-la-la-la-la youth-youth, sha-la-la-la-la-la-la-la youth-youth, we're the pride of Birmingham"

Aston Villa fans don't always have much to cheer about but they're quite happy to remind their local neighbours about their even worse record in all competitions:

"Birmingham City, Birmingham City, a hundred years and won fuck all, Birmingham City"

City had their revenge though with this though, sung to the tune 'Don't Cry For Me, Argentina':

"Don't cry for me, Aston Villa, the truth is we cannot stand you. All through our wild days, our mad existence, we took the Holte End without resistance"

Never likely to shy away from picking on the Liverpool fans, the Holte End faithful rebounded and came up with this, sung to the Liverpool anthem 'You'll Never Walk Alone':

"Sign on, sign on, with your pen in your hand, and you'll never work again, you'll never work again. Sign on, sign on..."

And this was penned just to needle Wolverhampton Wanderers fans:

"You're just a bus stop in Aston!"

City/The Blues

Most Birmingham City chants are directed at their local rivals Aston Villa, West Bromwich Albion and Wolves, mainly because the three have much better records in League and Cup competitions. The Blue trophy cabinet is all but bare in fact, and has been since 1875. This is their theme tune:

"All through life it's a long, long road, there'll be joys and sorrows too, as we journey on, we'll sing this song for the boys in royal blue. We're often partisans, la, la, la, we will journey on, la, la, la, keep right on to the end of the road, keep right on to the end"

Rovers/The Blue & Whites

Before we get into the comedy and abuse, we'll start with a Cup Final chant from Blackburn's 1882 encounter with Old Etonians, a mere seven years after their birth:

"All hail ye gallant Rovers lads, Etonians thought you were but cads, they've found a football game their dads, by meeting Blackburn Rovers!"

They lost the match 1-0 and would have to wait a couple more years before tasting victory in the competition. They actually ended up winning the trophy from 1884 to 1886, thus completing a memorable hat-trick. 1890-91 brought another two successes for five wins in just eight years.

More than a century later, and with a young Alan Shearer up front and manager Kenny Dalglish at the helm, Blackburn Rovers - also known as the Riversiders - won their first Premiership trophy in 1995. Since then they've slipped somewhat and the fans have had precious little to cheer about, so they remind their opponents about those glory days whenever they get the chance:

"All things bright and beautiful, all trophies great and small, Rovers have won the Premiership, while you lot have won fuck all!"

Burnley are the arch-rivals and this is the anthem wheeled out whenever the two meet. The chant was clearly around long before the change in name to the top flight, however. Otherwise it might be construed as a derogatory ditty and used by rival fans if Rovers were to be relegated:

"Now I've followed the Rovers for many a year, and I've spent all my money on football and beer. I've one aim in life before I am gone, and that's to follow Rovers in Division One. And it's no, nay, never, no nay, never no more, will we play the Burnley bastards, no never, no more!"

Here's another dig at their rivals:

"You're town is twinned with hell, you're ugly and you smell!"

Norwegian Stig-Inge Bjornebye was immortalised with this chant during a spell at Ewood Park:

"Bjornebye in my gang, my gang, my gang, Bjornebye in my gang, oh yeah!"

And striker Dwight Yorke had the perfect surname to fit this chant:

"Start spreading the news, he's playing today, I want to see him score again, Dwight Yorke, Dwight Yorke. If he can score from there, he'll score from anywhere, it's up to you, Dwight Yorke, Dwight Yorke"

Random Balls 4

"Ian Baird is dashing around like a steam roller up front"
Martin Tyler

"What will you do when you leave football, Jack? Will you stay in football?"
Stuart Hall

"Well, Clive, football is all about the two Ms: movement and positioning"
Ron Atkinson

"Eighty per cent of teams who score first in matches go on to win them, though they may draw some or occasionally lose"
David Pleat

*"That's bread and butter straight
down the goalkeeper's throat"*
ANDY GRAY

*"Very few of us have any idea of what life is like living in a
goldfish bowl, except, of course, those of us who are goldfish"*
GRAHAM TAYLOR

"This World Cup ball is definitely rounder"
TOMMY SMYTH

"Many supporters won't stand for all-seater stadiums"
GUY MICHELMORE

"The one thing that tackle wasn't was high and dangerous"
ANDY GRAY

"Glenn is putting his head in the frying pan"
OSSIE ARDILES

"I would have to be deaf not to read the allegations"
  BOBBY DOWNES

"For my money, Duff, servicing people from the left with his balls in there, is the best option"
  ANDY GRAY

"I do want to play the short ball and I do want to play the long ball. I think long and short balls is what football is all about"
  BOBBY ROBSON

"England now have three fresh men with three fresh legs"
JIMMY HILL

"And he crosses the line with the ball almost mesmerically tied to his foot with a ball of string"
  IAN DARKE

"Ian Wright's an excellent player but he does have a black side"
  GARY LINEKER

"I watched the game and saw an awful lot of it"
  ANDY GRAY

The Trotters

This nickname developed from the old word 'trotter' meaning a traveller or wanderer in about 1874. The Bolton fans are known for coming up with a decent tune occasionally. This was aimed at their local northwest rivals in 2000:

"This is what it's like to be Blackburn, this is what it's like to be sad, this is what it's like when your sister's shagging your dad!"

And don't believe 'Lord Of The Dance' can only be used by certain clubs. Here's Bolton's version of the tune:

"Run, run, wherever you may be, we are Bolton Wanderers FC, and we'll beat you up whoever you may be, and we'll put you in the infirmary"

The Pilgrims

The Pilgrim Fathers left Boston on their way to the New World in 1620, though the club wasn't founded for another 313 years. Boston fans delighted in taking the piss out of their own board with this tune after the club had been docked points and fined following an investigation into their finances at the end of the 2002 season:

"We're cheats and we know we are, we're cheats and we know we are!"

The Bantams

Bradford City got their nickname from their team colours, which were said to resemble a bantam chicken, around the time they came into being in 1903. Their theme song has a dig at their strongest local rivals, while celebrating their penchant for a drop of alcohol:

"We're Bradford City, the pride of the north, we hate Newcastle and Leeds of course. We drink our whisky and bottles of brown, the Bradford boys are in town, na, na, na, na, na, na, na!"

Their fans didn't even bother saving the abuse for their opponents towards the end of their disastrous 2000-01 season. Their first year (1999-2000) in the top flight for 77 years had been a struggle, but they'd survived with a 1-0 win over Liverpool on the last day of the season. The following year they were definitely on the slide. Everton condemned them to life back in the First Division with a 2-1 victory on the final day, and the crowd responded well with:

"We're going down in a minute, down in a minute!"

Their rivalry with Leeds became much more fierce after old enemies Bradford Park Avenue folded in 1974. Older fans of the now defunct club will know that a certain Bill Shankly's application to manage them was rejected in 1953. Who knows how differently their history would have been written had he got the job instead of Norman Kirkman. There can't be many left, however, who watched Bradford Park Avenue suffer the indignity of being the first club to be relegated in consecutive seasons in 1922 and 1923.

The Seagulls

Brighton and Hove Albion has been around since 1900. Their players and fans tend to take a fair amount abuse on behalf of the gay community in the area. 'Bread Of Heaven' is the preferred method of delivery:

"Does your boyfriend, does your boyfriend, does your boyfriend know you're here? Does your boyfriend know you're here?"

There's also a landmark that opposing fans believe mirror Brighton's fortunes:

"Down with the pier, you're going down with the pier"

As a brief statistical aside, Ernie Wilson played more than 500 matches for the club, and, on two occasions, had the chance to play 100 times in succession. Sadly, injury ruled him out of this record-breaking feat both times, stranding him on 99.

The Robins

Founded in 1894, Bristol City's nickname derives from their red shirts. They have a number of chants but the most commonly used alludes to their west-country love of a good drop of apple juice and their pleasure at baiting the local rivals:

"Drink up thee cider, drink up thee cider, for tonight we'll merry, merry be. We went down to the Rovers, to do the bastards over, so drink up thee cider in a jar!"

The Bluebirds

Cardiff's nickname also derives from the colour of the side's shirts, which have remained largely unchanged since their founding in 1899. City were responsible for taking the FA Cup out of England for the only time in its history in 1927 after their 1-0 victory over Arsenal. They've saved their best chants for their local rivals, however:

"Who's that team they call the Cardiff? Who's that team they all adore? We're the boys in blue and white, pissed and looking for a fight, and we'll hate the Swansea bastards evermore!"

And this is to the tune of 'My Liverpool Home':

"He's a Swansea Jack, he wears black and white like he's some sort of queer, he can't handle women and he can't handle beer,

he's a Swansea Jack"

Celtic

The Catholic Bhoys make up one half of perhaps the fiercest domestic football rivalry (they were founded in 1888), and most of their chants are reserved for arch rivals, the predominantly Protestant, Rangers:

"Sure it's a grand old team to play for, and it's a grand old team to see, and if you know your history it's enough to make your heart go oh-oh! We don't care what the Rangers say, what the hell do they know? We only know that there's going to be a show and the Glasgow Celtic will be there"

Here's another tune, popular amongst supporters in the 1970s when their alliance with the revolutionary Irish threatened to destabilise the English presence in the country:

"I am a merry ploughboy and I plough the fields by day, until a certain thought came to my mind that I should run away. Now I've always hated slavery since the day that I was born, so I'm off to join the IRA and I'm off tomorrow morn"

All Catholic sides refer to the Protestants as Huns, though it's not immediately clear why. Some say the word, which is more commonly associated with the Germans during the Second World War, has its roots in the Glorious Revolution in 1688, when the Catholic James II was ousted by the Protestant William of Orange. Whatever the origin, the word now crops up in the occasional abusive chant:

"Can you see a happy Hun? No, no! Can you see a happy Hun? No, no! Can you see a happy Hun? I can't see a fucking one!"

The Addicks or sometimes Valiants

Charlton's nickname is thought to be a corruption of the word athletic, but the name could also derive from the local fish shop workers shouting 'Haddocks!'. Indeed the owner of the shop repeatedly turned up to matches with a haddock nailed to a piece of wood. The Londoners, founded in 1905, love reminding their neighbours about the state of their ground:

"Selhurst Park is falling down, falling down, falling down. Selhurst Park is falling down. We hate Palace"

Home favourite Claus Jensen endeared himself to the fans and was rewarded with his own tune:

"You'd better watch out, you'd better not cry, you'd better not shout, I'm telling you why. Santa Claus is coming to town. He's making a run and checking inside, he and JJ are gonna score twice. Santa Claus is coming to town"

Striker Andy Hunt was also immortalised in song:

"Oh Andy Hunt, Andy Hunt, Andy Andy Hunt, he plays up front, he's got a name like a fanny, Andy Andy Hunt!"

The travelling support likes to remind the home fans that Charlton are the pride of the south with this offering:

"We are the pride of all London, the kings of the south, we hate the Palace 'cos they are all mouth. The Addicks will rise and the Eagles will fall, 'cos we are the Charlton, the greatest of all"

It's Going to be a Blue Day

Chelsea FC was founded in 1905. This is the chorus to the 1972 Top Five hit for their fans. It has stood the test of time remarkably well considering the relatively short shelf-life of most football related efforts.

"Blue is the colour, football is the game, we're all together and winning is our aim, so cheer us on through the sun and rain, 'cos Chelsea-Chelsea is our name"

Survival at Stamford Bridge's Shed End was often a priority during the troubled 1970s and '80s. In fact crowd trouble led to the ground being equipped with electrified security fencing! This song became increasingly popular at the time (Tune - 'Those Were The Days'):

"We are the Shed, my friend, we took the Stretford End, we'll sing and dance and do it all again, we live the life we choose, we fight and never lose, for we're the Shed, oh yes, we are the Shed"

Chelsea are also known as the 'Pensioners' on account of the veterans' hospital nearby. Their fans have had a great deal more to cheer about since Russian billionaire Roman Abramovich bought the club and invested heavily in new players. Here they pay tribute to the new era with music from the 'Only Fools and Horses' theme:

"He's got Drogba in his pocket, he signed Shevchenko from Milan. Well if you want the best ones and you don't ask questions, then Roman is your man. Where it all comes from is a mystery. Is it from the drugs or the steel or the oil in the sea? So come on Chelsea throw your celery, 'cos we are the famous CFC. La-la-la-la-la, la-la-la-la-la"

You may be wondering about the significance of the celery line, and if you are, here is an explanation of sorts. Brighton fans supposedly underwent an initiation ceremony on the pier which involved celery sticks, quite why is not known, however. It is thought that Chelsea fans witnessed the ritual and brought the celery chant to Stamford Bridge. In the 1980s it was common for thousands of fans to turn up to matches with the vegetable though police, worried about the impact this would have on hooliganism, started arresting fans brandishing the sticks in case there was too much salad tossing.

Here's their take on 'Mambo No.5':

"A little bit of Sheva in our lives, a little bit of Ballack down the sides, a little bit of Terry's what we need, a little bit of Shauny with his speed, a little bit of Ashley in defence, a little bit of Drogba as he's immense, a little bit of singing from the fans and a little bit of Jose 'cos he's our man"

Former manager Claudio Ranieri was less than impressed with the Russian's football brain though, this quote coming towards the end of the 2003-04 season:

"Abramovich knows nothing about football"

The Chelsea faithful don't mind though. The extra cash bought them back to back Premiership titles:

"Debt free wherever you may be, we're going to buy everyone we see, and we don't give a fuck about the transfer fee, 'cos we are the wealthy CFC!"

Arsenal's Jose Antonio Reyes has always taken a bit of stick from the Chelsea faithful because they believe his dark skin hints at a traveller's background, hence this slight change to the original song:

"The wheels on your house go round and round, round and round, round and round. The wheels on your house go round and round, all day long"

And the Addams family theme gets another reworking in honour of Chelsea's midfield maestro:

> *"He's in our midfield foursome, he's absolutely awesome, and
> when he wants he'll score some, it's Franky Lampard"*

New signing, Dutchman, Arjen Robben, got his praises sung to the
'Hokey Cokey':

> *"Do the Arjen Robben, do the Arjen Robben, you do the Arjen
> Robben 'cos that's what it's all about. You put your left leg in,
> your right leg out, in-out in-out you shake it all about. You do
> the Arjen Robben and you turn around 'cos that's what it's all
> about"*

Chelsea were quick on the uptake after Paul Gascoigne was held on
suspicion of beating partner Sheryl in 1996. They sang this to the tune of
the Pet Shop Boys' hit 'Go West':

> *"He's fat and he beats his wife, he's fat and he beats his wife"*

The fans were also quick to rib England's Peter Shilton after he was
disturbed with a woman in a county lane in 1980. Apparently the woman's
husband turned up expecting an explanation, so Shilton jumped into his
car and sped off, into the nearest lamp-post as it happens:

> *"Peter Shilton, Peter Shilton, does your missus know you're
> here?"*

During a Chelsea - Galatasaray fixture the Blues' fans came up with
these alternative lyrics to 'Go West' and it's other, arguably better known,
variant:

> *"You're Shish and you know you are!"*

Ray Parlour went through one of the most expensive divorce cases in
football history in 2004. Judges ordered that his wife was entitled to one
third of his future earnings, a substantial sum, thought to be in the region
of £400,000 a year. Chelsea fans were waiting for the ginger midfielder

when he arrived at Stamford Bridge for a League encounter:

"She's got all your cash, she's gone and got all your cash"

And (to the tune 'Go West') as any footballer hears if they've suffered marital difficulties:

"Stand up if you've shagged his wife, stand up if you've shagged his wife…"

They also came up with this when Cristiano was struggling in his first Premiership season:

"The wrong Ronaldo, you've bought the wrong Ronaldo!"

The Exiles, Cestrians or Blues

The colour of their shirts is responsible for Chester (founded 1884)'s commonly used nickname. City seem to come under fire for all sorts of reasons, the main one appearing to be their proximity to the Welsh border. Opposition fans delight in taunting them with (sung to the Pet Shop Boys' tune 'Go West'):

"You're Welsh and you know you are, you're Welsh and you know you are"

The Addams family theme can also be employed to give:

"Your mother is your sister, your father is your brother, you like to fuck each other, the Chester family!"

Sky Blues

Coventry's main football club was founded in 1883. Portly City man

Micky Quinn was nicknamed 'Sumo', a name that stuck with him even after his career as a player had ended. Aston Villa fans were probably the first of many to use this ditty:

"Who ate all the pies? Who ate all the pies? You fat bastard, you fat bastard, you ate all the pies!"

And Portsmouth fans cheered him on with this after he'd been transferred for a pretty hefty sum:

"He's fat, he's round, he's worth a million pounds"

Former Reading manager Mark McGhee was on the receiving end of the same tune when he allowed the Lions to freefall towards a lower division:

"He's fat, he's round, he's taking Millwall down! Mark McGhee! Mark McGhee!"

But back to Sumo briefly. The player himself once made a pass at Miss World, little realising that she didn't speak any English:

"You look wonderful; I was just wondering whether you fancied a shag"

The Eagles

Founded in 1861, Crystal Palace's nickname derives from a former ground called The Nest. Here's a fantastic bit of abuse hurled in manager Steve Bruce's direction after he left the club for Birmingham City, a club run by adult industry giant David Sullivan. The theme tune is fairly obvious:

"Brucie the elephant packed his bags and said goodbye to the Palace, off he went like a greedy fat lump, cunt cunt cunt. Brucie the elephant packed his bags and trundled off to the porn shop,

off he went to the Birmingham scum, cunt cunt cunt!"

And here's their tribute to the Brighton players having just scored their fifth during a comprehensive home win:

"We've scored five, they've scored none, Brighton take it up the bum, with a nick-nack paddy-whack give the dog a bone, why don't Brighton fuck off home!"

Challenged in the looks department, as in the ugly tree was probably felled on top of him, Iain Dowie then had to endure this chant from the *home* fans:

"He's ugly as fuck but he's gonna take us up!"

The Toffees

The sweet shop next to the ground used to give away toffees after a good result, though Everton (1878) are also sometimes known as the Moonlight Dribblers on account of the team's reputation for training after dark in their early years to try and improve their awareness. Their fans, of course, save their best for arch rivals Liverpool, this being sung to the tune of 'The Halls Of Montezuma':

"We hate Bill Shankly and we hate St John, but most of all we hate Big Ron, and we'll hang the Kopites one by one on the banks of the Royal Blue Mersey. To hell with Liverpool and Rangers too, we'll throw them all in the Mersey, and we'll fight, fight, fight, with all our might for the lads in the Royal Blue jersey!"

The fans were quick to pen a ditty in honour of volatile striker Duncan Ferguson after their cult hero was found guilty of drink driving (tune - 'Lord Of The Dance'):

"Drink, drink, wherever we may be, he is the Dunc and disorderly, and he will drink wherever he may be, 'cos he is the Dunc and disorderly.

"I felt like Dunc yesterday, and I felt like Dunc the day before, and I'm gonna be like Dunc like I've never been before, then we're going to be as happy as we can be, for he is the Dunc and disorderly!"

(Big Dunc didn't just get into trouble for his off-field antics though. Though he was repeatedly warned about his habit of head-butting opponents, he made the mistake of launching himself at Raith Rovers player Jock McStay during a match at Ibrox. The referee somehow missed the assault and didn't even book the striker, but Ferguson had allowed people to see the side of him that should have been contained. Perhaps it was partly because of his reputation for this kind of attack that he ended up doing three months in Barlinnie prison for a similar incident a year later. He then wasn't allowed to play for the prison team and had to keep fit for new club Everton by working out for an hour a day in the exercise yard. Everton fans gave him a not very well deserved standing ovation upon his release. He then hospitalised a burglar who, rather unwisely, chose to break into his house.)

Birmingham fans were less than complimentary about the Toffees though, this to the tune 'Hey Baby':

"Hey Scousers, oooh-aaah, I want to know, where's my video?"

The Cottagers

Fulham was formed in 1879. Their fans, known after their Craven Cottage ground, had little to cheer about until the arrival of Mohamed Al-Fayed. It was thought, mistakenly perhaps, that his money would guarantee instant success through the acquisition of top quality players:

"We're so rich it's unbelievable"

Of course opposing fans had other ideas, this mocking the Egyptian's attempts to become English:

"If your chairman's got a passport clap your hands, if your chairman's got a passport clap your hands!"

And here's a tune popular during the 1970s when a certain England captain joined the squad (tune - 'Y Viva Espana):

"Oh this year we're going to win the cup, hey viva El Fulham. Then next year you know we're going up, hey viva El Fulham. Alan M is a wonder that's for sure, hey viva El Fulham. And Bobby? Well do we need say more? It's Fulham por favor!"

The Gills (1893)

This is a tune from the 1970s, Gillingham supporters being among the most vocal in the lower leagues (tune - 'Just One Of Those Songs'):

"We ain't Jack and Jill, we ain't Bill and Ben, we ain't Ken Dodd or his Diddy Men, we ain't Looby Loo with all her toys, we are the Gillingham Boot Boys!"

The Mariners

Founded in 1878, Grimsby are known as the Mariners because of the important local industry Here's a classic chant delivered to the north-easterners by opposing fans, commenting beautifully on the town's best known feature:

"You only sing when you're fishing, sing when you're fishing!"

A variation on this is usually aimed at Norway whenever they meet a British side incidentally:

"Sing when you're whaling, you only sing when you're whaling"

Grimsby's Blundell Park ground is unusual in that it's actually in neighbouring Cleethorpes. It has been used by the Mariners since 1899 and boasts the oldest stand in the Football League. One of the others is known as the Findus Stand because the frozen food specialists are particularly associated with the town. Fans in the 1980s adopted the inflatable fish 'Harry the Haddock' as yet another nautical team mascot. Soon thousands were seen at the ground.

Pool

Hartlepool United have had precious little to cheer about in their hundred years. The Victoria ground, formerly a rubbish tip - and some would say it still is - was the first to be bombed by German Zeppelins in 1916, and the club remained largely in the bottom flight. Four times in the late 1920s they were knocked out of the FA Cup by non-League opposition and they battled for financial security on a day-to-day basis. They have also been forced to reapply to the League on the most occasions. There was the occasional upswing in their fortunes however. They almost beat the Busby Babes in their championship year (1957), only going down 4-3, and in 1968 they gained promotion to Division Three, albeit for a single season. Recent times have brought some success though. Under Mike Newell they were promoted in 2002, the year that their mascot H'Angus the Monkey was elected mayor of the town under the slogan 'Free Bananas For Schoolchildren'. And in 2007 they enjoyed an astonishing 22-game unbeaten streak that saw them promoted and challenging for the top spot once again. Their fans don't mind having a poke at themselves too, perhaps because of their many years of misfortune:

"My brother's in borstal, my sister's got pox, my mother's a whore

down Hartlepool docks. My uncle's a pervert, my aunty's gone
mad, and Jack the Ripper is my dad, la la la, la la la..."

Hibs (1875)

Hibernian fans were immediately in full voice when Dutchman Frank de Boer missed a penalty for Rangers in the Scottish Cup. Even his brother didn't manage to avoid a decent helping of abuse:

"One's called Ronald and one's called Frank. One's missed a
penalty and the other one's wank"

The Tractor Boys

This nickname is really only a recent addition to the list of alternative names, and it derives from the agricultural industry that thrives in the area. Since their formation in 1878, Ipswich's rivalry with local enemies Norwich has been well documented, and most of their songs hurl the abuse up the coast at the Canaries. Here's a clean song for now, however, though it does make the fans sound awfully posh:

"My name is Edward Ebenezer Jeremiah Brown, I'm a football
supporter of Ipswich Town. Wherever they play you'll find me,
I haven't missed a game since I was three, with my scarf and
rattle and big rosette, singing, 'Where was the goalie when the
ball was in the net?' Follow the Town, up or down, my name is
Edward Ebenezer Jeremiah Brown, but everyone calls me Ted!"

Killie

Kilmarnock, formed in 1869, is the second oldest club in Scotland. In their first game in the Scottish Cup in 1873 they turned up against Renton expecting to play rugby. During the course of their 3-0 defeat it was also noticed that along with not knowing the rules, they were also a man short! Here's their most famous supporters' song:

"As he lay on the battlefield dying, with blood pouring out of his head, he propped himself up on one elbow, and these are the words that he said: Kilmarnock! Kilmarnock! We are the champions!"

The fans are also particularly fond of berating Ayr United's following over the state of Somerset Park:

"Who's the clown who built your stand? Lego, Lego! Who's the clown who built your stand? Lego, Legoland!"

Random Balls 5

"I never make forecasts, but whoever wins that game will win the final"
KEN BATES

"The first two-syllable word I learned when I was growing up was discretion"
EAMON DUNPHY

"You don't score 64 goals in 86 games at the highest level without being able to score goals"
ALAN GREEN

"They're two points behind us so we're neck and neck"
BOBBY ROBSON

"It looks to me as though Carragher has cramp in both groins"
ANDY TOWNSEND

"Martin Keown is up everyone's backside"
TREVOR BROOKING

"Real Madrid are like a rabbit in the glare of the headlights in the face of Manchester United's attacks, but this rabbit comes with a suit of armour in the shape of two precious away goals"
GEORGE HAMILTON

"In some ways cramp is worse than having a broken leg but leukaemia is worse still. Probably"
KEVIN KEEGAN

"Lampard fired straight through the middle of a non-existent wall"
PAUL MCKENNA

"Well Celtic were nine points ahead, but somewhere along the road their ship went off the rails"
RICHARD PARK

"That's football, Mike. Northern Ireland have had several chances and haven't scored while England have had no chances and scored twice"
TREVOR BROOKING

"Either side of the post and that would have been a goal"
DAVE BASSETT

"That's what I call one of those indefensible ones and you can't defend against them"
ANDY GRAY

"The lad got over excited when he saw the whites of the goalpost's eyes"
STEVE COPPELL

"Gary always weighed up his options, especially when he had no choice"
KEVIN KEEGAN

"Unfortunately we keep kicking ourselves in the foot"
RAY WILKINS

"Well we scored nine, and you can't get more than that"
BOBBY ROBSON

"1-0 is usually enough to win in the group games"
MARCELLO BALBOA

"He had an eternity to play that ball but he took too long over it"
MARTIN TYLER

The Peacocks

Though Leeds (1919) are more commonly called United, this nickname is unusual. It is supposed to derive from an early colourful strip, though this remains unclear. Their all-white strip was introduced by Don Revie because it made the team look like Spanish giants Real Madrid. This is one of their most famous songs, the accompanying music being 'Que Sera, Sera':

"When I was just a little boy, I asked my mother, 'What should I be?' Should I be Chelsea, should I be Leeds? Here's what she said to me: 'Wash your mouth out son and go get your father's

gun, and shoot all the Chelsea scum, Leeds are the number one!'"

And here's another Leeds anthem, this one made famous as a pop song in 1972:

"Here we go with Leeds United, we're gonna give the boys a hand, stand up and sing for Leeds United, they are the finest in the land! Marching on together, we're gona see you win, la-la-la, la-la-la, we are so proud, we shout it out loud, we love you Leeds-Leeds-Leeds!"

This next line is sung to Coventry fans who were disappointed to lose two of their best players. The tune is, of course, from the Righteous Brothers:

"You've lost Ndlovu and Whelan, you've lost Ndlovu and Whelan, you've lost Ndlovu and Whelan, now they're gone, gone, gone, and you can't go on..."

A tally of just 28 goals in 38 matches during the 1996-97 season prompted some fans to bring out the Dame Vera Lynn:

"We'll score again, don't know where don't know when, but I know we'll score again some sunny day"

The Imps

The imp was a mythical creature sent by Satan to cause havoc on earth. An angel prevented disaster in Lincoln and the imp became the city's symbol. Though the club was founded in 1883, they have had mixed fortunes over the years, promotion usually following relegation. In 1987 they became the first side to be automatically relegated to the Conference but they returned to the Fourth Division at their first attempt. A quick spell in the dizzy heights of the Third Division was followed, yet again, by relegation, as this tune proudly announces:

"Division Three, kiss my arse! Division Four, we're home at last!"

Kop a Load of This

Formed in 1892, Liverpool has its signature tune, just as most of the other national sides have theirs, though this Gerry and the Pacemakers hit from 1963 (shared with Celtic north of the border) is one of football's most famous and rousing anthems:

"As you walk through the storm, hold your head up high and don't be afraid of the dark. At the end of the storm is a golden sky, and the sweet silver song of the lark. Walk on through the wind, walk on through the rain, though your dreams be tossed and blown. Walk on! Walk on! With hope in your hearts, and you'll never walk alone, you'll never walk alone!"

The club's fans are always ready to dish out a good helping of abuse to their red counterparts in the northwest. This is sung to the tune of 'In My Liverpool Home':

"In your Manchester scrubs, you speak with accents that no one can stand, you're fat, ugly bastards with shit on your hands, in your Manchester scrubs"

Now let's give Liverpool some abuse. This tune, which is the same as the one above, is sung repeatedly to the Kop by away fans, most notably those supporting United:

"In your Liverpool slums, in your Liverpool slums, your mum's on the game and your dad's in the nick, you can't get a job 'cos you're so fucking thick, in your Liverpool slums.

"In your Liverpool slums, you look in the dustbin for something

to eat, you find a dead dog and you think it's a treat, there's piss on the pavements and shit in the street, in your Liverpool slums"

Celtic fans, incidentally, with whom they share many chants, resurrected this tune while watching their side play in the south of France in a Champions' League tie recently. Of course they delighted in changing the words, with some irony, to:

"In your Monaco slums, you look through the window for something to eat, you see a live lobster and think it's a treat, in your Monaco slums"

This is perhaps the best-known supporters' song:

"Oh I am a Liverpudlian, from the Spion Kop, I like to sing, I like to shout, I go there quite a lot. I support the team that play in red, a team that you all know, a team that we call Liverpool, to glory we will go"

Manchester United fans came up with this line to Liverpool goalkeeper David James after the latter had performed poorly during United's victory in 1997 (It has to be said that James then earned the rather unfortunate nickname 'Calamity' after a series of high-profile blunders cost both club and country vital matches):

"David James, superstar, drops more bollocks than Grobbelaar"

Another ex-Liverpool man on the end of some abuse was Emile Heskey. The big striker never quite lived up to his early promise, though he was repeatedly, if somewhat curiously, selected to play for his country. In 2004 Birmingham City's fans reminded him of his shortcomings, this being sung to the tune of 'She'll be coming round the mountain':

"If Heskey plays for England so can I, if Heskey plays for England so can I, if Heskey plays for England, Heskey plays for

England, Heskey plays for England so can I!"*

Even assistant manager Phil Thompson couldn't escape, partly due to the size of his nose, which earned him the nickname Pinocchio. Fans were quick to pounce with:

"Get your nostrils, get your nostrils, get your nostrils off the pitch, get your nostrils off the pitch"

Or the alternative:

"It's long, it's thick, it's bigger than his dick, Thompson's nose, Thompson's nose!"

Or even:

"He's got the whole world in his nose, he's got the whole world in his nose"

Okay, one more, this from Newcastle fans and sung to the tune 'Let It Snow':

"The shadow outside is frightening, and it's so big it don't let the light in, you can see it wherever you go: Thompson's nose, Thompson's nose, Thompson's nose!"

Inspirational captain Steven Gerrard has had a number of tunes penned in his honour but this is perhaps the best, sung to the theme 'Can't Take My Eyes Off You':

"You're just too good to be blue, can't take the ball off you, you've got a heavenly touch, you pass like Souness to Rush, and when we're drunk in the bars, we thank the Lord that you're ours, you're just too good to be true, can't take the ball off you. Na-na na-na…"

Danish import Jan Molby came under fire because of his physique - in that he carried a little extra weight around the middle - prompting some fans to shout (to 'Bread of Heaven'):

"Have you ever, have you ever, have you ever seen your feet?
  Have you ever seen your feet?"

And he found himself on the receiving end again with this, sung to the tune 'Amazing Grace':

"Slim-fast no chance, slim-fast no chance, slim-fast no chance, no
  chance!"

This next ditty was quickly penned in response to Michael Owen's two late goals against Arsenal in the 2001 FA Cup Final at the Millennium Stadium in Cardiff. A slide-rule pass from Danny Murphy, an Englishman as it happens, provided Owen with the winner:

"One-nil down, then two-one up, Michael Owen won the cup,
  a world-class paddy-pass gave the lad the ball, and poor old
  Arsenal have won fuck all"

Devastated Arsenal fans couldn't think of anything other than to give Owen some stick over his baby-faced looks:

"Back to school on Monday, you're going back to school on
  Monday"

The Stones

Maidstone were a professional outfit from 1897 until 1927, but hard times and not much in the way of good fortune meant they played as amateurs for the next half century. Having joined the Southern League, they won the Conference and finally achieved full League status in 1989. Sadly they were overcome by financial difficulties in the early 1990s and had to fold. Their supporters were reasonably vocal given that four figure crowds were the exception rather than the norm, this being sung to Rod Stewart's 'Sailing':

"We are Maidstone, we are Maidstone, Super Maidstone from nowhere. We are Maidstone, we are Maidstone, Super Maidstone from nowhere. No one likes us, no one likes us, the council hate us, we don't care. We are Maidstone from nowhere!"

The Light/Sky Blues

The Rodgers and Hart song 'Blue Moon' remains the Manchester City (1887) anthem. Different versions exist of course, but here is the most widely used:

"Blue Moon, you saw me standing alone, without a dream in my heart, without a love of my own. Blue Moon, you knew just what I was there for, you heard me saying a prayer for someone I could really care for. Then suddenly they'll appear before me, the only one my arms could ever hold, I heard someone whisper, 'Please adore me', and when I looked my moon had turned to gold. Blue Moon, now I'm no longer alone, I have a dream in my heart, I have a love of my own. Blue Moon, you started singing our tune, you won't be singing for long because we beat you 5-1"

Any manager not delivering results is bound to be made to suffer by the home supporters, as Alan Ball, who sadly died in April 2007, found out while at Manchester City:

"Alan Ball, Alan Ball, he's a squeaky ginger bastard only three feet tall!"

Legend has it that the father of City striker and cult hero Uwe Rosler was in an aircraft that bombed Manchester during the Second World War.

Fans were quick to suggest where the ordnance might have fallen:

"Rosler's dad's a German, he wears a German hat, he dropped a bomb on Old Trafford, and don't we love him for that"

This next chant is wheeled out to the tune of 'Always Look On The Bright Side Of Life', though it is a dig in extremely bad taste at United:

"Always look on the runway for ice"

Equally base is their reminder to Leeds supporters that two were killed at a UEFA Cup match on the continent:

"Always look out for Turks carrying knives, kebab, kebab, kebab, kebab"

United's outstanding midfielder Roy Keane was hated by City fans, but he did give them the chance to chant his name on occasion, this coming after the player scored the own goal that put the Reds out of the 2000 Champions' League:

"Who's that twat they call the Keano? Who's that twat they all adore? Give him fifty thousand quid and he'll score for Real Madrid and they won't have the treble any more!"

Leeds United rejected the transfer of Scottish international Asa Hartford because the medical showed he had a tiny hole in his heart. The condition merely allows a small quantity of oxygenated and deoxygenated blood to mix inside the heart, which, though rarely life-threatening can cause minor health problems. Of course the fans were quick to seize on an opportunity:

"There's a hole in your heart, dear Asa, dear Asa. There's a hole in your heart, dear Asa, a hole!"

Commentator David Coleman, of course, was bound to chip in with a load of balls about this story, as he proved, albeit accidentally, during Scotland's match against Peru at the World Cup in Argentina in 1978:

"He really is a whole-hearted player"

Coleman's immediate apology prevented the BBC's switchboard from melting down.

Manager Speak 3 – What are they on about now?

"A goalkeeper is a goalkeeper because he can't play football"
RUUD GULLIT

"No team won anything without a dodgy 'keeper"
BOBBY ROBSON

"I was in Holland once and there were five coaches to seven kids. You don't get that one on one training over here"
LAWRIE SANCHEZ

"In football, time and space are the same thing"
GRAHAM TAYLOR, SPEAKING RELATIVELY OF COURSE...

"History is today and tomorrow"
EAMON DUNPHY

"It's a love-hate relationship, and he loves me"
GRAHAM TAYLOR

"Sol Campbell using his strength there, and that is his strength, his strength. You could say that's his strong point"
KEVIN KEEGAN

"One of his strengths is not heading"
KEVIN KEEGAN

"I left a couple of my foreign players out last week and they started talking in foreign. I knew what they were saying though"
HARRY REDKNAPP

"He's captain of Rangers and that's one of the reasons he's captain"
WALTER SMITH

"As I've said before and I've said in the past"
KENNY DALGLISH

"He's not fast but he's quick"
TOMMY SMYTH

"There's no point practicing penalties. Di Biaggio of Italy took 17 in practice and scored every time. But the next day he missed against France which proves it doesn't work"
RAY CLEMENCE

"And we all know that if you stand still in football you go backwards"
PETER REID

"It's our Achilles heel that has been stabbing us in the back all season"
DAVID O'LEARY

The Red Devils (1878)

Here's Manchester United's signature tune, penned during their recent purple patch when everything seemed to go right. Of course it also has a dig at their arch rivals in the city:

"Since City beat United my true love sent to me: European Champions, eleven years of glory, ten years in Europe, nine past Ipswich, eight-one at Forest, seven past the Cockneys, six title trophies, five-nil wins, four FA Cups, treble in '99, two doubles and an Eric Cantona!"

Of course with each success this tune gets updated, so it now includes their recent League and Champions' League victories. Manchester United defender Rio Ferdinand famously missed a drugs test in 2003 and was handed an eight-month ban by the FA. Opposing fans quickly came up with this, sung to the tune of Afroman's 'Cos I Got High':

"He's out of the England squad and we know why. 'Cos Rio got high, Rio got high, Rio got high. La-la-la, la-la-la!"

Wolves' fans were also quick on the uptake (tune - 'Blue Moon'):

"Rio, you should have pissed in the cup, should have pissed in the cup, you should have pissed in the cup"

Journalist and broadcaster Michael Parkinson was equally scathing in his Daily Telegraph column:

"We're near the end of another football season of spitting, punching, diving, effing and blinding and various other sporting pastimes like financial skulduggery and forgetting to pee in bottles"

Another defender was immortalised after his performances helped United win the famous treble (League, FA Cup and European Cup) in 1999:

"Jaap Stam is a big Dutchman, get past him if you fucking can, try and do a trick and he'll make you look like a dick, Jip-Jap, Jaap Stam"

The Neville brothers also get a look in (tune - 'Rebel, Rebel'), as does their father:

"Neville Neville, your future's immense, Neville Neville, you play in defence, Neville Neville, like Jacko you're bad, Neville Neville is the name of your dad"

Oldham fans wrote this for goalkeeper and World Cup winner Fabien Barthez:

"He's French, he's shit, his head's a fucking tit"

Another 'keeper who was bound to take some shit from the fans was American Tim Howard, on account of his slight verbal affliction (tune - 'Go West'):

"Fuck off, he's got Tourette's, fuck off, he's got Tourette's…"

Perhaps the most famous United player of all was also one of the most vulnerable when it came to chants. He hardly helped himself with his off-field antics, but did George Best really deserve this (sung to the tune of 'She'll Be Coming Round The Mountain')?:

"Would you like another Stella, Georgie Best? Would you like another Stella, Georgie Best? Would you like another Stella, 'cos your face is turning yella, would you like another Stella, Georgie Best?"

Believe it or not there are another five verses to this, all of which offer the beleaguered George a different beverage. The last verse must have been penned before his death, however, and is not printable here.

Eric Cantona set himself up for some chanting with his infamous kung-fu kick into the crowd at Crystal Palace in 1995. West Ham fans were the first to react with:

"Ooooh-aaaaah, French wankaaa!"

Wayne Rooney was never going to escape from the fans after wearing a vest under his then Everton shirt saying:

"Once a blue, always a blue"

Of course he was off to Manchester United for £20-odd million shortly afterwards, and fans don't forgive or forget U-turns like that very quickly. Soon after his arrival a series of on-pitch misdemeanours usually saw him getting sent from it, to this chorus from visiting fans:

"He's fat, he's Scouse, he'll rob your fuckin' 'ouse!"

And Charlton fans liked to remind him that he carried a bit of extra weight early in his career with:

"You've got bigger tits than Jordan, bigger tits than Jordan!"

Not even a stunning hat-trick soon after his arrival in Manchester could silence the critics:

"What a waste of money, what a waste of money!"

One of Rooney's predecessors had a name ideally suited to a good chant:

"Andy Cole, Andy Cole, Andy Andy Cole, he gets the ball, he scores a goal, Andy Andy Cole"

Of course opposition fans were quick to remind the striker what they thought of him whenever he scuffed another shot or blasted wide from twelve inches out:

"Andy Cole, Andy Cole, Andy Andy Cole, he gets the ball, he does fuck all, Andy Andy Cole!"

Team-mate Ole Gunnar Solskjaer, known as the baby-faced assassin on account of his looks and knack of coming on as a substitute and scoring vital goals, was immortalised in this ditty, sung to the tune of 'You Are My Sunshine':

"You are my Solskjaer, my Ole Solskjaer, you make me happy when skies are grey, and Alan Shearer was fucking dearer, so please don't take my Solskjaer away"

United's fans have a long standing rivalry with their old enemy across the Pennines, who, when they began their slide down the divisions and began shedding players, were bound to be singled out. In fact the Reds started singing this, particularly after cult hero Eric Cantona's departure:

"Leeds are our feeder club"

This was another favourite, highlighting the same club's financial worries:

"Bust in a minute, you're going bust in a minute!"

And here's another City-baiting ditty, this time to the tune of 'Living Next Door To Alice':

"Twenty-four years waiting for a chance, to win a major trophy and give silverware a glance, but for twenty-four years we've been living next door to City, City, who the fuck are City?"

In her autobiography, Victoria Beckham revealed that she'd been targeted by fans with this, to the tune 'Go West':

"Posh Spice takes it up the arse, Posh Spice takes it up the arse!"

Of course when Manchester United next played the Arsenal, the fans were waiting for a sight of Mrs Beckham:

"Does she take it, does she take it, does she take it up the Arsenal? Does she take it up the Arsenal?"

New acquisition, Korean Park Ji-Sung, has been accepted into the fan base already judging by this ditty:

"Park, Park, wherever you may be, you eat dogs in your home country. It could be worse, you could be Scouse, eating rats in your council house"

And here's a different set of lyrics set to John Fogerty's 'Bad Moon Rising':

"I see the Stretford End rising, I see the treble all the way, I see us beating Bayern, I see wins home and away. Don't go out tonight unless you're wearing red and white, I see the treble all the way"

Now that Chelsea have had something to cheer about, United fans were quick to remind them that their success was short-lived, and that the 2006-07 season put the Mancunians back on track:

"Mourinho, are you listening? Will you keep our trophy glistening? We'll be there in May to take it away, walking in our Fergie wonderland!"

While 6-0 up against Roma in the 2007 Champions' League, the Old Trafford faithful started belting out:

"Are you City, are you City, are you City in disguise? Are you City in disguise?"

Let's leave the last word on the Reds to York fans though. Their team somehow managed to beat the giants 3-0 in a League Cup tie in 1995, even though Alex Ferguson had played a strong side (some of the top clubs seek to devalue the competition by fielding under strength sides so they can concentrate on League or Champions' League fixtures):

"The grand old duke of York, he had eleven men and he marched them up to Old Trafford and shat on Ferguson. And when there was one there was one, and then there were two there were two, and when they banged the third one in they knew they'd fucked Man U!"

Boro (1876)

Middlesbrough striker Joseph Desiree Job was honoured in this ditty with a double meaning:

"One Job on Teesside, there's only one Job on Teesside!"

And here's a nice chant involving the pontiff:

"All the Geordies went to Rome to see the pope, all the Geordies went to Rome to see the pope, all the Geordies went to Rome to see the pope! And this is what he said: 'Who's that team they call the Boro, who's that team they all adore? They play in red and white, and they're fucking dynamite, and I'll support the Boro ever more!'"

The Lions

Named after their stadium, The Den, the Millwall Lions were founded in 1885. Their fans have been known to cause a ruckus or two in their time, but they're quite happy to bait the opposition with a good chant too. This was heard being sung to the more rural teams during the nationwide cattle scare a few years ago:

"Head, shoulders, foot and mouth, foot and mouth. Head,
shoulders, foot and mouth, foot and mouth!"

A few years earlier they'd penned a chant to celebrate the achievements of legendary hard-man Harry Cripps, a player with the distinction of having broken more opponents' legs than anyone else in League history (the tune is 'Danny Boy'):

"Oh 'Arry Boy, the fans, the fans are calling, from end to end
and down the Cold Blow Lane. We want a goal, we need your
inspiration, oh 'Arry Boy, you know we love you so. Throughout
the years you've given us your everything, now in return we
give this song to you, for what you've done is something quite
exceptional, we pledge ourselves to you our 'Arry Boy"

Motherwell (1886)

Here's a nice chant from north of the border, sung to the tune of the 'Wild Rover'. It's not aimed at another side and barely seems to celebrate the home side either, but the lyrics are interesting for other reasons:

"Well I've been a muff diver for many a year and I've spent all
my money on muff diving gear. From goggles to flippers and an
oxygen tank, if I can't have a muff dive I'd better have a wank.
And it's Motherwell, Motherwell FC, they're by far the greatest
team the world has ever seen"

The Magpies

The nickname obviously stems from the black and white stripes on the home kit, though it hasn't actually been in use from the club's inception in 1881. Newcastle's Toon Army's theme song is 'Blaydon Races', a traditional English ballad. Of course there are a number of versions but this is perhaps the most popular:

"We went to Blaydon Races, 'twas on the ninth of June, eighteen hundred and sixty-two. On a summer's afternoon, we took the bus from Bamburghs and she was heavily laden. Away we went along Collingwood Road, that's on the road to Blaydon!

"Oh, me lads, you should have seen us gannin', passing the folks along the road. Just as they were standin', all the lads and lasses there, all with smiling faces, gannin' along the Scotswood Road to see the Blaydon Races!"

While he was at the club, Lee Bowyer was always likely to get some stick after revealing that he occasionally liked to go out without wearing underpants:

"He's here, he's there, he wears no underwear"

And he was going to get a load more after becoming involved in an alleged assault on an Asian man in 2000. This from the Chelsea song-smiths:

"Down with the Ripper! You're going down with the Ripper!"

Charlton fans too had their own opinion on the incident, this being sung to the tune 'Hey Baby':

"Hey, Lee Bowyer, Ooooh-aaaah, I want to know why you're not in jail!"

Middlesbrough fans co-wrote these lyrics (tune: 'Yellow Submarine') with the Toon Army to celebrate Sunderland manager Peter Reid's achievements just up the road:

"In the town of Sunderland, there lived a man called Peter Reid,

*and he had a monkey's head, peeled bananas with his feet. Peter
Reid's got a fucking monkey's head, a fucking monkey's head, a
fucking monkey's head. Peter Reid's..."*

The Canaries

Again, the name is taken from the team's colours, which were first
employed around 1902. Written by Albert Smith in 1890, Norwich City's
official song claims to be the oldest football song in the world still in
regular use. It's called 'On The Ball City' and though it has a number of
verses, only the first is normally sung:

*"Kick it off, throw it in, have a little scrimmage, keep it low,
splendid rush, bravo win or die. On the ball City, never mind
the danger, steady on, now's your chance, oohhh, we've scored a
goal. City (clap clap clap), City (clap clap clap), City (clap clap
clap)"*

The fans also penned this tune, a real crowd pleaser, for North African
import Youssef Safri, and it's sung to Status Quo's 'Rocking All Over The
World':

*"Well here we are and here we are and here we go, Youssef's
better than Juninho, here we go, Moroccan all over the world!"*

Another favourite involves the diminutive Paul McVeigh, who, at only
5-foot-4, was the joint shortest player in the Premier League for the
2004-05 season (Paul Dickov was the other of little stature.) This is sung
to the chorus of Frankie Valli's 'Can't Take My Eyes Off You':

*"We love you Paul McVeigh, and if it's quite alright we love you
Paul McVeigh, despite your lack of height we love you Paul
McVeigh. Cross the ball and he'll score"*

It's worth noting that McVeigh is currently on loan at Burnley (although

Charlton are interested), so the wee fella may not be a mighty Canary for much longer. Arsenal fans, incidentally, used the same tune to salute the different haircuts of cult hero Freddy Ljungberg:

"We love you Freddy because you've got red hair, we love you Freddy because you're everywhere, we love you Freddy. Cross the ball and he'll score"

In their 2000 clash with rivals Walsall, Norwich fans delighted in telling a rather large woman who wandered onto the pitch to:

"Keep your tits in, keep your tits in, keep your tits in for the lads. Keep your tits in for the lads!!"

Chairwoman - and celebrity chef - Delia Smith launched into a halftime rallying call to players and fans alike in their 2005 match against Manchester City, even though she was clearly under the affluence of incohol. Norwich then threw away a two-goal lead and eventually lost 3-2. Recipes for 'laughing stock' abounded the next morning of course. Chelsea fans were the next visitors to Carrow Road and they gleefully baited the Canaries with:

"We've got Abramovich, you've got a drunken bitch!"

Of course the Norwich fans were quick to reply with:

"We've got a brilliant cook, you've got a Russian crook"

And keeping with the culinary theme, the fans are well versed in this tune:

"Delia Smith's a cracking cook, she feeds our whole team porridge, she also likes her steak au poivre, but that doesn't rhyme with Norwich!"

Forest (1865)

The fans in Nottingham are particularly vocal, especially when it comes to giving their local rivals a healthy dose of abuse:

"We'd rather be bombing Derby than Iraq, rather be bombing Derby than Iraq, we'd rather bomb Derby, rather bomb Derby, we'd rather bomb Derby than Iraq"

This chant is likely to come straight back at them from the Rams:

"Robin Hood, Robin Hood riding through the glen, Robin Hood, Robin Hood with his band of men. He steals from the rich, gives to the poor...silly cunt, silly cunt, silly cunt!"

This banner was seen at an FA Cup match between Chelsea and Forest, a gentle reminder to Jose Mourinho that a certain someone had managed to win a couple of highly prized trophies while manager at the City Ground:

Shaun Wright-Phillips - £21m
Andriy Shevchenko - £30m
2 European Cups - priceless
Money can buy you duff players
For everything else there's Cloughie

County

Formed in 1864, Notts County have entered every single FA Cup competition since 1877. When they captured the trophy in 1894, they became the first Second Division side to win it. It's quite a well-known snippet of trivia that Italian giants Juventus took their strip from Notts County, hence the popular chant at Meadow lane when the team are playing well:

"Juve, it's just like watching Juve!"

Pompey

Founded in 1898, the team is named after a pub that stands by the main entrance to the ground. Here's a nice tune penned for Portsmouth striker Aiyegbeni Yakubu, sung to the tune 'Agadoo':

"Ya-ka-bu-bu-bu, feed the Yak and he will score, to the left and to the right, feed the Yak and he will score"

Of course the side also boasts the unique chant to the Pompey Chimes, sung in time with a chiming clock:

"Play up, Pompey, Pompey, play up"

Random Balls 6

"And with four minutes gone the score is already 0-0"
Ian Darke

"The ball stuck to his foot like a magnet attracting a piece of steel, or metal rather"
Tom Tyrrell

"The Gillingham players have slumped to their feet"
Mick Quinn

"And Lineker scored the equaliser thirteen minutes from the end; talk about a last-minute goal"
SIMON MAYO

"I played cricket for my local village. It was 40 overs per side and the team that had the most runs won. It was that sort of football"
BOBBY ROBSON

"Davie Hay still has a fresh pair of legs up his sleeves"
JOHN GREIG

"We're flying on Concorde and that will shorten the distance. It's self explanatory"
BOBBY ROBSON

"They didn't lay a glove on the chin of the goal in the second half"
RAY WILKINS

"That decision, for me, was almost certainly definitely wrong"
KEVIN KEEGAN

"I'd say he's the best in Europe if you put me on the fence"
BOBBY ROBSON

"If you gave Arsène Wenger eleven players and told him to pick his team, this would be it"
ANDY GRAY

"Had we not got that second goal, I think the score might have been different, but I'm not sure"
DAVID PLEAT

"Liverpool don't do very well in Italy, especially against Italian teams"
TOMMY SMYTH

"Barnsley have started off the way they mean to begin"
CHRIS KAMARA

"If you don't score goals you're not going to win the match"
BOBBY ROBSON

"And Ritchie has now scored eleven goals, exactly double the number he scored last season"
ALAN PARRY

"Spurs are 2-0 up. If they score again before the end of half time, they win it, don't they?"
RICHARD KEYS

"It's 1-1 here, and if there are no more goals it'll be a draw"
TOMMY SMYTH

"Preki quite literally only has the one foot"
DAVID PLEAT

Preki, incidentally, plays for the Kansas City Wizards, a team in the North American League. He once scored a beautiful twenty-five yard free-kick and while he and his team-mates were celebrating, the opposition scored from the kick-off. The celebrations then died down pretty quickly, as you can imagine.

"McCarthy shakes his head in agreement with the referee"
MARTIN TYLER

The Gers (1873)

Rangers' fans, most of them fiercely Protestant, can lay claim to a number of patriotic songs and chants, these two in particular. The first is to the tune 'Wandering Star', the second to 'We're no awa' to bide awa'':

"Do you know where hell is? Hell is in the Falls. Heaven is the Shankhill Road and we'll guard old Derry's walls. I was born under a Union Jack, a Union, a Union Jack"

"As I was walking down Copland Road I met a crowd of strangers. They said to me, 'Where can we see the famous Glasgow Rangers?' So I took them off to Ibrox Park to see a great eleven. Said I, 'It isn't paradise but, man, it's my blue heaven!'"

Here's another anti-Celtic favourite, the 'teuchter' being a native highlander:

"I once met a poor little teuchter, his face was all battered and torn, he made me feel sick so I hit him with a brick and he won't be able to sing anymore"

Former goalkeeper Andy Goram was diagnosed with a mild form schizophrenia. Kilmarnock fans grabbed the opportunity to taunt him with:

"There's only two Andy Gorams, two Andy Gorams…"

Goram then pulled out of Scotland's 1998 World Cup squad because he was mentally unprepared for the tournament. (Back in 1988, incidentally, he scored a goal for Hibs against Morton.) In 2001 the 'keeper was targeted as a loan signing by Manchester United as Sir Alex Ferguson felt he was short on cover between the sticks. This is Goram's alleged reply to Ferguson's approach (by phone), because he mistakenly believed it was a crank call from former team-mate and practical joker Ally McCoist:

"Look, just fuck off, will you. I've got a pub to run and goats to feed"

(How his second personality reacted is not recorded.)

Dundee fans delight in giving both Rangers and Celtic a good ribbing with this (sung to the tune of 'You Are My Sunshine'):

"You are a weegie, a stinking weegie, you're only happy on giro day, your mum's a stealer, your dad's a dealer, please don't take my hubcaps away!"

The Blades

Named after the steel industry that made the city famous, Sheffield United (1889) save a certain amount of personal hatred for their city rivals Sheffield Wednesday. The clubs even used to share the Bramall Lane ground, which once hosted a Test match between England and Australia. Neither side has had much to sing about recently so they might as well keep sending the abuse laterally:

"Wednesday, whatever will you do? You're going down to Division Two. You can take your trumpet and you can take your drum and go and play with the [select lower league side] scum!"

Of course this is likely to elicit the response:

"Neil Warnock has a farm E-I-E-I-O and on that farm he has some pigs E-I-E-I-O. With a [select crap player] here and a [player] there, here a [player], there a [player], everywhere a [player]. Neil Warnock has a farm E-I-E-I-O"

And there's always likely to be some 'praise' for their striker:

"Gilles de Bilde, can he fix it? Gilles de Bilde, can he fuck!"

In the club's early years their nickname was so popular that Wednesday adopted it. Of course this meant the number of abusive chants dropped considerably and the idea of having both clubs with the same nickname was immediately abandoned. Wednesday are now known as The Owls, because of their venue in Owlerton, instead.

Here's a final tune from the Blades to the sound of John Denver's 'Annie's Song':

"You light up my senses like a gallon of Magnet, like a packet of Woodbines, like a good pinch of snuff, like a night out in Sheffield, like a greasy chip butty, oh Sheffield United, come thrill me again!"

The Saints

The first president of the club, a curate of St Mary's, led to the Southampton team acquiring its nickname in 1885. Their finest hour came in the 1976 FA Cup Final when they beat Manchester United, immediately spawning this song to the tune of 'The Wild Rover':

"Twas back in 1976 on the first of May, we all went to Wembley to watch Southampton play, and we showed them how to drink the beer and we showed them how to sup, then we even showed

United how to win the Cup!"

The Shrimpers

Named after the local industry, and founded around 1906, Southend's favourite chant is reserved for local rivals Colchester United, particularly targeting their opponent's ground:

"Layer Road is falling down, falling down, falling down, Layer Road is falling down, poor old Col U. Shall we kick it down some more, down some more, down some more, shall we kick it down some more? Poor old Col U!"

They also like to celebrate their proximity to the coast, though why the military ordnance is included is not clear:

"Oh we do like to be beside the seaside, we do like to be beside the sea, with a bucket and spade and a fucking hand grenade, beside the seaside, beside the sea"

The Hatters (1883)

Named after their traditional hat-making industry, Stockport County were on the receiving end of this particularly gruesome chant. The words were applied to the Welsh anthem 'Bread of Heaven':

"Did the doctor, did the doctor, did the doctor kill your mum? Did the doctor kill your mum?"

The reference, of course, is to Britain's worst serial killer, local GP Harold Shipman.

The Black Cats

Formed in 1879, Sunderland FC was named after a gun battery on the River Wear, which was itself named after a stray black cat that was found there in 1805. One of the most famous songs from the northeast focuses on the financial scandal involving Swindon manager Lou Macari in 1990. The southerners should have been promoted to the top flight but Macari's dealings ensured they stayed down, as this Sunderland ditty announces:

"We went to Wembley Stadium on the twenty-eighth of May, heading for the play-offs with Swindon Town to play. We didn't win a trophy and we didn't win a cup but what really riles the Geordies is that we lost and still went up"

The Gulls

Torquay United (1898) have enjoyed precious little success throughout their history. The one title they did earn though was for supposedly having the 'Best Behaved Supporters' in 1968. That prompted this ditty, to the tune of 'She'll Be Coming Round The Mountain':

"We're the best behaved supporters in the land, the best behaved supporters in the land, we're the best behaved supporters, best behaved supporters, the best behaved supporters in the land.

"Singing I threw a bottle at the ref, I threw a bottle at the ref. I threw a bottle, I threw a bottle, I threw a bottle at the ref!"

Spurs

Shakespeare's character Harry Hotspur hailed from Northumberland, the name of Tottenham's first ground in 1882. Tottenham fans have had little to cheer about in recent times, their last meaningful achievements being winning the League Cup in 1999 and 2008, the former under new manager George Graham. Before he arrived at White Hart Lane, the home fans delighted in taunting the ex-Arsenal boss about his alleged illegal acceptance of money to grease the wheels during player transfers:

"Georgie Graham's magic, he wears a magic hat, and when he saw the agent's bung, he said, 'I'm having that'"

Some fans of course could never forgive Graham for coming to Spurs having had great success with their bitter rivals only a few seasons earlier. Hence they referred to themselves as the:

"Man in the raincoat's blue and white army"

They were less compassionate towards a certain Charlton defender:

"Rufus is a dog's name, Rufus is a dog's name, la-la-la-la (woof!) la-la-la-la (woof)"

How the fans long to return to the glory days with:

"Spurs are on their way to Wembley, Tottenham's going to do it again. We don't give a fuck, we're going to bring the Cup back home to White Hart Lane"

And:

"Glory, glory Tottenham Hotspur. Glory, glory Tottenham Hotspur. Glory, glory Tottenham Hotspur, when the Spurs go marching on on on! Tottenham are the greatest team the world has ever seen, Tottenham are the greatest team the world has ever seen, Tottenham are the greatest team the world has ever seen, and the Spurs go marching on on on!"
(Chorus)
"We're the pride of north of London, we're the kings of White Hart Lane, we're the pride of north of London, we're the kings

of White Hart Lane, we're the pride of north of London, we're the kings of White Hart Lane, and the Spurs go marching on on on!"

One man in particular seemed destined to bring some silverware back to the white half of north London, and his self-deprecating dive after his first goal for the club ensured immediate cult-hero status:

"Chim-chimenee, chim-chimenee, chim-chim cheroo, Jurgen was a German but now he's a Jew!"

Okay, one for the festive season at Arsenal's expense:

"Hark now hear, the Tottenham sing, the Arsenal run away, and we will fight forever more because of Boxing Day"

Tranmere (1884)

The Prenton Park faithful are mostly keen to point out that they shouldn't be confused with the other local teams, this being sung to the tune of 'The Wild Rover':

"Don't be mistaken and don't be misled, we're not Scousers but we're from Birkenhead. You can shove your cathedrals and shove your pier-head, 'cos we all follow Tranmere and that's in Birkenhead"

The Saddlers

Named after the local leather industry in 1888, Walsall fans are usually on the receiving end of chants on account of their club's name:

"Small town in Poland, you're just a small town in Poland"

Despite the fact that the team has never made an appearance in the top echelon of English football, the fans certainly seem to think they know where they belong:

"We are the pride of the Midlands, the Villa are scum, we hate the Baggies, the Wanderers and Brum. We are the Walsall, and we are the best, you know we're the Saddlers, so fuck all the rest"

The Baggies

Though the side was formed in 1879, West Brom's nickname probably derives from the fact that the team wore huge shorts just after the war. Their fans always like to welcome a new team or manager to The Hawthorns. This is sung to the tune 'Da Do Ron Ron'; you can guess to whom they are referring:

"Who's the fattest bastard in Division One? It's you Ron Ron Ron, it's you Ron Ron!"

And this is always reserved for the visit of former England and Aston Villa head coach Graham Taylor ('My Old Man's a Dustman'):

"Taylor is a turnip, he's got a turnip's head, he took a job at Villa so he must have been brain dead. He said, 'Do I not like this, do I not like that?', while everyone in England knows that he's a fucking twat!"

The Hammers

From 1895 the team was known as Thames Ironworks, and West Ham are sometimes still called the Irons. Their fans are among the most vocal in the league. Here's their signature tune (adopted on the occasion of the 1923 FA Cup Final), a recording of which reached number 31 in the 1975 music charts:

*"I'm forever blowing bubbles, pretty bubbles in the air, they fly
so high, nearly touch the sky, then like my dreams they fade
and die. Fortune's always hiding, I've looked everywhere, I'm
forever blowing bubbles, pretty bubbles in the air!"*

It's perhaps not as well-known but this tune didn't become the Hammers' theme until it had been tried and tested by Cardiff City, among others. In fact the Welsh side used it as a rousing chorus in honour of their team reaching the 1927 FA Cup Final. You can, of course, swap the 'Fortune' line for this instead, just to make the chant a bit more personal:

"[insert team]'s always running"

The Monkees' 'Daydream Believer' was wheeled out with new lyrics during a match with Leeds just after Peter Reid had taken over, his previous charge having been relegated (the original verse, incidentally, actually celebrated Reid's achievements with the Black Cats):

*"Cheer up Peter Reid, oh what can it mean? He took Sunderland
down, and now he's trying with Leeds"*

Joe Cole was the inspiration for this chant, to the tune of Spandau Ballet's 'Gold':

*"Cole! Always believe in your soul, you've got the power to know
that you're indestructible. Always believe in Cole!"*

Barnsley fans came up with this derogatory chant for a West Ham cult figure, sung to the tune 'D-I-S-C-O':

"D-I-WAN-KEY-O"

(Di Canio himself is probably best remembered for his volatile temper. While at Sheffield Wednesday in 1998 he shoved referee Paul Alcock to the ground after being red carded for fighting with Arsenal's Martin Keown. The official clearly couldn't believe what was happening to him and couldn't decide if he was going to take the push like an official and stand his ground or act like a player and make a meal of it. He staggered back theatrically and fell over... On his way off the pitch Nigel Winterburn charged over and gave the volatile Italian, who was still spitting and fuming, another shove. Di Canio turned round and raised his fist as if to smack the little upstart but he needn't have bothered. Winterburn cowered away at the first sign of trouble, flinching like a Mike Tyson victim. Di Canio was fined £10,000 and banned for eleven games.)

For a while in East London the fans were able to give their humorous take on an age old chant, that is until both the men, one the coach, the other a player, left in rather acrimonious circumstances. The fans were particularly boisterous when the older of the two appeared on the big screen:

"There's only one Frankie Lamp... There's only two Frankie Lampards, two Frankie Lampards!"

Hammers' fans like to taunt their local rivals too. Here's their take on 'My Bonnie Lies Over The Ocean' in honour of Tottenham Hotspur, who boast a large Jewish following:

"My one skin goes over my two skin, my two skin goes over my three. My three skin goes over my foreskin, oh bring back my foreskin to me. Bring back, bring back, bring back my foreskin to me!"

This was the east London reply to the Newcastle taunts towards the end of the 2006-07 season when it became increasingly clear that the Hammers would be relegated. Newcastle actually weren't that far above them in the League so the chant is especially apt:

Toon Army: *"Going down, going down, going down!"*

West Ham reply: *"So are we, so are we, so are we!"*

As it turned out, manager Alan Curbishley, with the slightly illegal help from an Argentinean, engineered a remarkable escape and the Hammers survived in the top flight.

The Hammers' fans were also quick to latch onto the fact that Jose Mourinho was supposedly having problems with Chelsea owner Roman Abramovich. The Blues were 2-1 up in their April 2007 clash at Upton Park at the time when the home fans started chanting:

"Sacked in the summer, you're getting sacked in the summer!"

Unfortunately for the Hammers their troubles continued when Chelsea netted twice more. At the end of April it emerged that the supposed rift between manager and owner had been healed. Chief executive Peter Kenyon assured fans that Mourinho would be staying for the 2007-08 season. Given his record, it's difficult to see why they'd want to dismiss him in the first place. How quickly times change...

The Crazy Gang

Founded in 1889, Wimbledon only acquired their current nickname after the riotous behaviour of the players under a certain Jones, V. c1989. Their meteoric rise up the divisions, from Fourth to First in just nine years, meant that the players had no one to wash their kit or clean their boots until they reached the top flight. Visiting Plymouth Argyle fans were delighted when a certain Wimbledon manager collapsed in the middle of the 1988-89 season. He'd made a few less than complimentary comments about their club and they repaid the ailing man with this ditty:

"He's big, he's fat, he's had a heart attack! Joe Kinnear! Joe Kinnear!"

I knew there was going to be a joke in here somewhere....

Wolves

For nearly 130 years their best chants have been reserved for their nearest rivals, namely West Brom, Birmingham City and Villa:

"Oh I do like to be beside the seaside, oh I do like to be beside the sea, oh I do like to stroll along the prom-prom-prom, where the brass bands play 'fuck off West Brom'"

The Baggies' home strip bears more than a passing resemblance to a Tesco bag, as this ditty, to the tune 'Always Look On The Bright Side Of Life', proudly announces:

"Always shit in a Tesco carrier bag, di-dum, di-dum di-dum di-dum"

The home fans were particularly delighted when Cardiff fans weren't allowed to turn up to a match at Molineux in 2007 and they aimed this at the empty stand:

"You're not singing anymore!"

The club's greatest striker of the current generation was Steve Bull, the Tipton Terror, who, despite an outstanding career at club level, never quite transferred his talent to the international stage:

"Hark now hear the West Bank sing, a new king's born today, his name is Stevie Bull, and he's better than Andy Gray"

Commentator Speak 4

"Arsène Wenger's lips are firmly sealed on Sir Alex Ferguson"
CHRIS SKUDDER

"They've won 66 games, and they've scored in all of them"
BRIAN MOORE

"David O'Leary's poker face betrays his emotions"
CLIVE TYLDESLEY

"The sponsors will want to give the man-of-the-match award to Cristiano Ronaldo, but they should give it individually to the whole team"
DAVID PLEAT

"Gary Neville is in hospital, where Manchester United fear he may have broken his foot"
CLIVE TYLDESLEY

"The crowd think that Todd handled the ball. Well they must have seen something that nobody else did"
BARRY DAVIES

"It's 1-1 now, an exact reversal of the score on Saturday"
RADIO 5 LIVE

"He wasn't just facing one defender; he was facing one at the front and one and the back as well"
TREVOR STEVEN

"That's twice now that he's got between himself and the goal"
BRIAN MARWOOD

"I saw him walking off at halftime rubbing his groin, and I think that was some kind of statement"
DAVID PLEAT

"To be really happy, we must throw our hearts over the bar and hope that our bodies will follow"
GRAHAM TAYLOR

"Maldini has really regurgitated his career at left back"
DAMIEN RICHARDSON

"What a goal! It went straight through the legs of Adams and flew towards the roof of the net like a Wurlitzer!"
GEORGE HAMILTON

"It definitely hit him on the hand but he didn't raise his ball"
MICK MCCARTHY

"Holland are playing a 4-4-2 with three forwards"
J DELLACAMERA

International Abuse

As most of the chants heard at big international fixtures are likely to incite racial hatred, I've had to be particularly careful about what I can include in this section. Here is a tame example: Dutch fans are not likely to forget the occupation of their country by German forces during the Second World War. The invading army systematically confiscated their older relatives' most prized possessions, as this one liner bluntly announces:

"My grandfather wants his bicycle back!"

Here, now, are a few songs that should amuse rather than offend, most of which are aimed at one or more of the home unions.

Scotland

The Scottish national side has taken a fair amount of stick recently. In fact some would say their last major contribution to world football was beating the Dutch in 1978, a wonder goal from wee Archie Gemmill helping to separate the two. So desperate have they been to watch at times that other teams playing poorly get to hear this ditty, to the tune 'Bread Of Heaven':

"Are you Scotland, are you Scotland, are you Scotland in
disguise? Are you Scotland in disguise?"

Their fans did have something to cheer about having beaten England at Wembley the previous year, however. Thousands of fans invaded the pitch at the final whistle and began demolishing the uprights singing:

"We stole your goalposts, your lovely goalposts, you made us
happy when skies were grey. You never knew how much you'd
miss them, 'til we took your goalposts away!"

Since then, any English misfortune has been enough to get the Scots chanting. Even though England almost ensured Scotland's qualification for the later rounds at Euro '96 (a four goal victory over the Dutch would have secured it but Bergkamp pulled one back in the dying seconds), their fans still blasted the English for their loss to Germany in the semis, using a popular song at the time for their backing:

"England's going home, they're going home, they're going. Three
lions on the shirt, but two goals flew past Seaman. After fifteen
pints last night, Gascoigne's fucking steaming. England's going
home, they're going home, they're going"

It was clearly lost on the chanters that England were already home…

There are four or five verses to this next one - all cheering England's failures in major tournaments - but you'll get the flavour from the first instalment, a celebration of a certain South American's 'goal' at Mexico '86:

> *"You put your left hand in, your right hand out, in out in out then shake it all about, you do the Maradona and you turn around, he put the English out out out! Oh Maradona, oh Maradona, oh Maradona, he put the English out out out!"*

Verse two celebrates Chris Waddle's penalty miss at Italia '90 (some say the Hubble Space Telescope has now been recruited to search for the ball, near-earth satellites having found no trace of it), then comes Swede Thomas Brolin's moment, Ronaldinho gets a look in from 2002, and then it's the Portuguese from the last World Cup.

A sense of humour towards their own team was restored when a dispute over a rescheduled kick-off time meant that the Estonian side failed to turn up to play the Scots in a qualifying match for the 2006 World Cup:

> *"There's only one team in Tallinn, one team in Tallinn"*

There is more to this story than meets the eye though. Scotland were high on confidence having just dispatched Latvia 2-0 and they arrived to a friendly welcome in the Estonian capital. The problems began when the Scottish side saw the floodlights at the Kadriorg ground. They were so low that the goalkeepers would not be able to pick the ball up visually from corners or close free-kicks. FIFA solved the problem by moving the kick-off time from 6.45 pm to 3.00 pm. The Scots officials did their best to spread the word throughout the city but the Estonians were having none of it. The TV schedules had been agreed, the team buses organised, the security arrangements made. They could not be altered at such short notice.

At 3.00 pm John Collins led the Scots out but there was no sign of the home side. Up went the chant. Referee Radoman blew his whistle to start the contest and then immediately blew for the end of it. The Estonians turned up two hours later and the tie was awarded, albeit briefly, to Scotland. FIFA eventually ruled that the match should be replayed in Monaco four months later. It was a pretty dull 0-0 draw, much the same as the first encounter…

England

When England arrived at the Olympic Stadium in Barcelona to play lowly Andorra in the Euro 2008 qualifiers, they hadn't scored a goal in more than 270 minutes of football. Israel and Macedonia had somehow held them to a draw in the weeks before, and England were in danger of not qualifying. By halftime of another dire performance the fans were getting pretty agitated, chanting such lines as these to manager Steve McLaren:

"You're not fit to manage non-League"

"Bring back, bring back, bring back my Beckham to me, to me, oh bring back my Beckham to me!"

"What a load of rubbish!"

"You're getting sacked in the morning, sacked in the morning!"

"Borat for manager, Borat for manager"

The abuse here is fairly standard, except for the last line, which asks actor Sacha Baron Cohen to have his alter-ego step off the film set and take charge of the Mickey Mouse outfit that was England in 2007. The question that has long divided England fans asks whether or not the highly paid 'superstars' of the Premiership are actually any good. Our TV stations proudly proclaim our League as the best in the world, producing the best players. Recent form at major championships suggests one of two things is actually happening. Either we have a group of fabulous players who are being undermined by their manager asking them to play out of position or in inappropriate experimental formations and employing the wrong tactics, or, sadly, they are just not much good. The fact that English clubs occupied three of the last four positions in the

2007 Champions' League should tell you something. You decide...

A Steven Gerrard goal finally gave England some hope in Bareclona after more than six hours without finding the net, Peter Crouch's strike in Skopje being the previous time they'd netted. He notched again twenty minutes later and then Preston striker David Nugent scored in the last minute to secure the win. It didn't stop the crowd of 10,000 giving the team and McLaren a huge helping of abuse at the final whistle of this ill-tempered match though (both sides were guilty of some terrible tackling and on another day they might have been down to eight or nine men each). Shall I mention that even though Gerrard will take the plaudits for saving England and McLaren here, he also managed to set himself up for ridicule by shamefully diving while in the Andorran box.

It would cost £2.5 million to sack the manager before his contract expires in 2010, which amounts to one year's salary. If the national side failed to qualify for the Euros though, the national game would lose an estimated £100 million...

At least the England fans can dish out a tune occasionally, when they're not wrecking the town they're in, or ending up behind bars (of the metal variety), that is. This is usually directed at Scotland but it can be equally applied to any of the home unions:

"Shit part of England, you're just the shit part of England!"

Football Legends: Sir Bobby Robson

Sir Bobby is one of the best loved figures in English sport. He won 20 caps for England in the 1960s, having played at both West Brom and Fulham, but then retired in 1967. Two years later he moved to lowly Ipswich to try his hand at management. He achieved fame with the side, though it was by no means instant, when he guided them to FA Cup glory in 1978 and the UEFA Cup in 1981, and then he took them to second place in the top division twice. The following year he was offered the national job, which he accepted, but a poor run initially saw him crucified in the press. A peak was reached in early 1986, however, when England went to South America and beat Brazil, but a World Cup exit the same year at the 'hands' of Maradona and co. saw him come under fire yet again. This continued after the disastrous European Championships in 1988. But Robson fought back, taking the national side to the brink of World Cup glory at Italia '90. Having stepped down with his reputation restored, Robson moved from PSV to Barcelona and then back home. Having taken over as manager at Newcastle in 1999 he began to dominate the weekly gaffes columns, some of which are listed below:

"Eighteen months ago they were one of the best three teams in Europe, and that would include Germany, Holland, Russia and anybody else you like"

"He's very fast and if he gets a yard ahead of himself nobody will catch him"

"We've introduced some movement into Shearer's game now. Last season he played with one leg, this season he's got two"

"Robert said I was picking the wrong team, and I was because he was in it"

"Home advantage gives you an advantage"

"If you're a painter you don't get rich until you're dead. The same happens with managers"

"What can I say about Peter Shilton? Peter Shilton is Peter Shilton. He has been Peter Shilton since the year dot"

"When he was dribbling he used to go through a minefield with his arm. A bit like you go through a supermarket"

"They can't be monks. We don't want them to be monks. We want them to be football players because a monk doesn't play football at this level"

"I'm not going to look beyond the semi-final, but I would love to lead Newcastle out at the final"

"Tottenham have impressed me. They haven't thrown in the towel even though they've been under the gun"

"If we start counting our chickens before they hatch, they won't lay any eggs in the basket"

"I would have given my right arm to be a pianist"

"Their football was exceptionally good and they played some good football"

"Look at those olive trees. They're two hundred years old, from before the time of Christ!"

"Players never know why they're taken off or substituted until they become managers"

"For a player to ask for a transfer has opened everybody's eyebrows"

Who Said This?

"Barcelona: a club with a stadium that seats 120,000 people. And they're all here in Newcastle tonight!"

"Ronaldo is always very close to being either onside or offside"

"We were a little bit outnumbered there. It was two against two"

"You British think I know damn nothing about this game! Well let me tell you, I know damn all!"

"Dunfermline have a difficult month ahead over the next two or three weeks"

"Julian Dicks is everywhere. It's like they've got eleven Dicks on the field"

"If England are going to win this match they are going to have to score a goal"

"You weigh up the pros and cons and then try to put them in chronological order"

"Italy were expecting a cat walk against the USA"

"Robert Lee was able to do some running on his groin for the first time"

"Zidane could be a champion sumo wrestler as he can run like a crab or a gazelle"

Answers

1. Do you know? Please help...
2. Ray Wilkins
3. Ron Atkinson
4. ESPN commentator
5. Dick Campbell
6. Metro Radio
7. Jimmy Hill
8. Dave Bassett
9. Tony Cascarino
10. Glen Hoddle
11. Howard Wilkinson

Money Talks

David Beckham's Real Madrid career looked like coming to an end in the summer of 2007 after he agreed a five-year £127.4 million deal to move to American side Los Angeles Galaxy, an amount that equates to a staggering half million pounds a week! Directors of the club believe the forecast move might already be paying for itself though. LA Galaxy have just sold an extra 7000 season tickets, and with shirt sales also booming, revenue has increased by more than $13 million. Beckham's cut from the shirts, other merchandising and ticket sales could be as much as $250 million if he stays in America for the full five years. He's also likely to be offered film and television roles in his spare time which will further boost his earnings, something he might need if he buys the £11 million Hollywood mansion the couple have their eyes on. Of course he couldn't get away from a certain someone though, ex-Wimbledon hard-man and local C-list celeb Vinny Jones chipping in with:

"He'll spend most of his time carrying Posh's handbags"

Of course this kind of money hasn't always been available in football. Once upon a time players earned what they were paid...

William Shurlock and friend Hugh Case were fined two shillings for playing football in Chester on the Sabbath in 1589. Twenty years later more players were fined for playing in Bedford. Cromwell would try and stamp out the game altogether half a century later.

Having reportedly watched a game of Calcio in Florence in the mid-1660s, Count Albemarle formed a team and challenged King Charles II of England to a game of football. Charles put together his own side and wagered ten gold sovereigns on the outcome, probably the first recorded instance of the gambler losing heavily. The Royal team may have been soundly beaten but the king enjoyed the game so much that he lifted Cromwell's ban on playing it.

The Highways Act of 1835 imposed heavy fines (40 shillings) on anyone caught playing street football, a variation on the game that involved kicking and carrying a ball through the town centres. London was particularly badly affected by such games, indeed Samuel Pepys, the great 17th century author, noted that travel across the capital was often hampered because of the number of people playing.

Before the rules revoking hacking and other dangerous forms of tackling in the 1860s, there was some concern that serious injuries could end the playing careers of young men before they'd really started. The publisher of 'Jack Harkaway's Journal For Boys', Edwin Brett, was less sure about the dangers of the modern game and offered the sum of £20 to be paid to the next of kin if any boy was killed in action, a considerable amount of money in the mid-Victorian era.

The first FA Cup was made by Hall and Company in 1871 at a cost of just £20. It became known as the Little Tin Idol and was presented for the next quarter of a century until it was stolen. Not even a £10 reward and extensive investigations managed to turn anything up and the trophy was never recovered. After presenting its replacement to Lord Kinnaird in 1911, the third trophy was commissioned at a cost of 50 Guineas. Then, in 1958, Harry Burge, an 83-year-old man, confessed to having stolen the original trophy to melt down for a stack of counterfeit half-crowns. Wear and tear to the third cup, incidentally, meant that a fourth was crafted in 1992.

Built in 1873, Scotland's national stadium, Hampden Park, was named after English Parliamentarian John Hampden who died at the Battle of Chalgrove Field during the civil war in 1643. He had given his name to a terrace, which then lent its name to the ground. A clubhouse was added a year later at a cost of £21, while, a couple of years after that, the first grandstand was built for just £306.

The issue of paying players had always been discussed but it wasn't until 1882 that an FA committee was set up to investigate the often covert practice. Many Scots had travelled south to play with teams such as Blackburn because, although they wouldn't be paid as such, they would receive good job offers and other perks. Accrington were immediately expelled from the League and Preston from the FA Cup. This created such a furore that the FA were eventually forced to back down and payments to players gradually crept in, though the sides in the south were considerably slower on the uptake. The average weekly wage gradually increased from £1 in 1880 to around £4 at the turn of the century.

By the 1960s, though, Welshman John Charles (who was in Italy at the time having been the first British player to transfer abroad [for £65,000]) scoffed at the £100 a week earned by Johnny Haynes, claiming that the Italians wouldn't play for such a pittance. Maybe so, but this was considered an outrageous amount of money in Britain. Now, of course, the average wage is something like 130 times that amount…

The English FA finally permitted payments to players in 1885. As a result, agents appeared out of nowhere and travelled to Scotland to try and lure the best players north of the border to the top English sides, teams like Preston North End. In search of a better living, and knowing that they would be paid for the privilege of playing the game they loved, many hundreds of Scots made the journey south. With the wage cap in place though it was difficult for players to make a good living, and most had to continue working in another capacity, albeit part-time.

Glasgow Celtic's first ground at Celtic Park opened in 1888. The team's immediate success forced the landowners to increase the rent in response to rising crowd numbers though, and the side were pushed out of their ground. You can appreciate the good sense behind the move two hundred yards down the road to a new Celtic Park when you find out the rent had been increased by 900%, from £50 to £450 a year.

The first sod of turf was laid at the new ground in 1890, and it was promptly stolen! The site eventually went on to host not just football but athletics and cycling as well. Floodlights erected in 1893 were removed after the ball kept hitting them and smashing the bulbs, a costly exercise over the course of a season.

Tottenham were almost stripped of their amateur status when, in 1893, they supplied a player with a new pair of boots after his old ones had been stolen. The FA suspended the club for a couple of weeks because it deemed the ten-shilling cost of replacements as a payment to the player! He was then ordered to repay the money or face being suspended indefinitely.

Walsall's players went on strike before their game against Newcastle in 1894. They protested that they were not being paid enough and would therefore not take the field until an agreement over pay was reached. Having been persuaded to play by the management, the 'strikers' were promptly sacked afterwards.

Goalkeeper Jack Hillman was transferred from Dundee to Burnley towards the end of the 19th century for the princely sum of £130. The reason for the transfer was that Hillman supposedly wasn't trying hard enough for the Scottish side. He was suspended by the FA in 1900 for allegedly bribing Nottingham Forest players to lose to his side, and then banned for the 1906-07 season for accepting illegal payments while at new club Manchester City. In fact 16 team-mates were axed at the same time, all for financial irregularities. Their first game that season was against the Arsenal, and the City side, thrown together from the reserves and youth teams, were hopeless. The fact that the temperature reached 90 degrees Fahrenheit didn't help either and they finished the match with only five men, the rest having been sidelined with heatstroke!

In 1905 Sunderland's Alfie Common transferred to local rivals Middlesbrough for £1000, then the largest fee agreed in world football. Though this amount of money caused observers at the time to shake heir heads in wonder, it is a tiny amount when compared with today's transfer fees, although allowing for currency changes and inflation the figures are actually comparable. The investment proved to be shrewd however, as Middlesbrough avoided relegation, a good share of the credit for the escape going to Common.

Middlesbrough chairman Colonel Gibson Poole was due to stand in the 1910 General Election, and he knew that a good win against local rivals Sunderland would surely increase his chance of overturning Liberal candidate Penry Williams's majority. Boro's club secretary Andy Walker thought he could increase their chances of scoring the win if they paid for it, and he offered the Black Cats £30 to throw the game. Captain Charlie Thomson refused and reported Walker to the FA, and the association immediately began an investigation. They found all sorts of dodgy financial goings-on and both Colonel Poole and Walker were suspended indefinitely. Middlesbrough ended up winning the game anyway but the good colonel was trounced in the election all the same.

Morton players were promised a lamb by a local butcher for every goal scored in the 1910-11 season. Tommy Gracie netted just the once and named his winnings Toby, but there is no explanation for the hapless creature's death in the changing room bath after the match.

In 1913 West Brom captain Jessie Pennington scuppered a plan to bribe players to throw a match. He lured the culprit into making an offer of £5 a man, and then turned the evidence over to the police. The offender received a five-month prison sentence for his trouble.

Two years after this, Manchester United and Liverpool were accused of conspiring to rig the result of a game. Nine players ended up being suspended because they had won large amounts of money on the game, when an 1892 law strictly banned the practice.

Elland Road in Leeds was home to Holbeck Rugby club, but by 1904 the ground had been sold and football was now the main sport. After the First World War it seemed that rugby would return because Leeds had been expelled from the League for refusing to publish its accounts, specifically the illegal payments it had made to players. Then, in 1919, Leeds United was formed and Elland Road has hosted the side ever since. In 1985 the stadium was sold to the city's council to help pay off its rising debts. When David O'Leary took over as manager in 1998, he was promised a hefty budget if he delivered success. The side made the semi-finals of the UEFA Cup the following season, though their campaign was soured in Turkey when two fans were stabbed to death. The 2000-01 season saw O'Leary and the side make the semi-final of the Champions' League, but then their fortunes declined. It soon became clear that the management had overspent their budget (£100 million), and then some, and the club's financial situation deteriorated with debts mounting to over £80 million.

Their fall from the dizzy heights of European football was complete when their fans invaded the pitch before the end of their vital 2007 League clash with Ipswich. They had been leading 1-0, a result which, had it stood, would have given them some chance of avoiding relegation to the third tier of domestic football. As it happened, Ipswich equalised late on and the home fans piled onto the pitch. The referee ushered the players off and many thought the game would be abandoned. The other option was to let the result stand. The referee had other ideas though and brought the players back out half an hour later to complete the last minute. Leeds couldn't find an extremely late winner and were then left with a nine-goal deficit to overturn to avoid the drop in their last game.

Dundee's Dens Park ground was reopened in 1921, the layout having been designed by noted architect Archibald Leitch. One of the old stands remained, however, though not for long. Somewhat conveniently, it burned down almost immediately, allowing the ground to be completed to Leitch's specification with the insurance money. The fireman who tackled the blaze was not surprised, as it was the third such fire in the stand that season. He was surprised to learn that he'd been given the sack for his efforts in stemming the blaze though...

The Preston women's factory team, Dick-Kerr's - which would later become General Electric - were a star-studded outfit that toured all over the world in the early 1920s. The FA had all but banned them from playing matches at home (even though they once sold 50,000 seats at Everton's Goodison Park), so they took their show on the road. Playing against American opposition on their 1922 tour, they got off to a bad start and only managed two draws and two losses from the first four matches. The fifth, against New Bedford Men in Massachusetts, was billed as the 'Fair Leather Booters' vs. The USA. It was a close game in front of a big crowd of over 5000, all hoping to see the teams fight hard for the £1000 prize money, a considerable sum at the time. The Preston ladies didn't disappoint and scored their fifth, the winner, in the last minute, the waif-like Jenny Harris volleying home from close range.

The FA sold the rights to film the 1923 Cup Final for £1000. To make sure they got their own shots of the match, many rival film companies smuggled in cameras disguised as rubbish bins and the like.

Manchester United's Frank Barson was promised a pub if he managed to engineer the side's return to the top flight within five years of their 1922 relegation. He was rewarded with the landlord's position in 1925, but the pub in Ardwick was so busy that he resigned after a quarter of an hour and left the establishment to a lucky barman instead!

A disagreement over payments to amateur players led to the four home unions withdrawing from FIFA in 1928. The governing body stipulated that amateur players should receive compensation for playing, if, by doing so, it meant they missed out on their work-related salaries. These so-called broken time payments were dismissed by the FA, and the home unions not only left FIFA but also refused to compete at the Olympics. As a result, no home country appeared at the World Cup until 1950. The Pro-am split was only fully resolved in 1974.

And in the same year (1928) Bolton's David Jack became the first footballer to be transferred for a five-figure sum when he went to Arsenal for £10,000.

Clubs from the lower leagues have always found survival hard. Gate receipts are barely enough to cover wages, travel expenses and a thousand other monetary outlays necessary for them to exist. And Halifax Town were in especially deep trouble at the end of the 1920s. The club was reported to the FA for its dire financial situation, mainly because the players were not getting paid. Fans chipped in with donations to keep them afloat for the 1930-31 season but it was clear that the club would fold the next year unless they somehow survived to the latter stages of the FA Cup, an extremely unlikely proposition. The first round pitted them against Newark and they had to fight until the last minute to hold out for a draw. They won the replay and then managed a further two matches before being eliminated against Bournemouth. Amazingly, survival for another few months was assured on the back of this short run. And gate money earned by reaching the fifth round the following season just about ensured their security. During that season, however, they suffered a humiliating 13-0 defeat at the hands of Stockport County. It was sometime in the second half that Danny Ferguson asked Hugh Flack what the score was. Somehow keeping a straight face, Flack replied:

"I don't know, but I think we're losing"

Paraguay's Arsenio Erico was recognised as one of the finest players in the world in the early 1930s, so it was a surprise when he transferred from Club Nacional to Independiente in Argentina for just £1, with a proviso being that the club donated the same sum to the International

Red Cross! One of Paraguay's national stadiums now bears his name, a fine tribute to the man Alfredo di Stefano called:

"The greatest ever"

Leeds United toured Canada just before the outbreak of the Second World War. To commemorate a fine goal by Bill Wainscot after a slick passing move, the opposition in one match offered him an oil well!

Paying the referee didn't become common practice until about 1938, when their match fee was set at three guineas, double that of the linesmen. Arnaldo Coelho received £500 for officiating the 1982 World Cup Final between Italy and West Germany, while the top Premiership referees today get around £70,000 a year plus up to £1000 per match.

Tommy Lawton was considered one of the finest centre forwards England has ever produced. He broke the transfer fee record when he moved from Chelsea to Notts County in 1947 for £20,000. That same year he was invited to play for Great Britain against the Rest of Europe in a bid to raise money for the beleaguered FIFA organisation. The match was a huge success, with Britain demolishing the Europeans 6-1 and putting £30,000 into FIFA's coffers.

A gracious fan sent Arsenal goalkeeper Jack Kelsey £5 in 1953 after making the best save he'd ever seen! Imagine that happening nowadays. David James would be the lowest paid player on the planet.

Together with Stanley Matthews, Tom Finney guided English football into its golden era of the 1950s. He played big parts in their record wins over Portugal and Italy, and was soon being courted by foreign clubs. He turned down an offer from Italians Palermo that included £10,000 for signing on, followed by a car, villa and huge salary, preferring instead to stay with Preston North End.

Everton's Goodison Park became the first ground in the country to have under-soil heating installed in 1958. The cost was a substantial £7000.

The Welsh winger Cliff Jones was instrumental in taking his national side to the quarter-final of the 1958 World Cup. He was so good that

Tottenham offered him first team football at the end of the tournament and signed him for a then record fee of £36,000. The investment proved shrewd, for Jones helped the side to the League and Cup double in 1961, the FA Cup again the following year, the Cup Winners' Cup the year after that, and the FA Cup again in 1967.

Yorkshire housewife Viv Nicholson won £150,000 on the pools in 1961. Her immediate reaction, as quoted in the national press at the time, was to:

"Spend, spend, spend!"

And that is precisely what she did, blowing the lot and losing her husband on the way. In 1977 she penned the story of her life, which told how she was back in a tiny house having experienced life's full circle.

Player Speak 3

"Alex Ferguson is the best manager I've ever had at this level, well he's the only manager I've actually had at this level. But he's the best manager I've ever had"
DAVID BECKHAM

"Leeds is a great club and it's been my home for years, even though I live in Middlesbrough"
JONATHAN WOODGATE

"I can see the carrot at the end of the tunnel"
STUART PEARCE

"I took a whack on my left ankle but something told me it was my right"
LEE HENDRIE

"Keith Gillespie just lacks a little bit of inconsistency"
GRAEME LE SAUX

"Germany are a very difficult team to play. They had eleven internationals out there today"
STEVE LOMAS

"I always used to put my right boot on first and then obviously my right sock"
BARRY VENISON

"If it happened again tomorrow I'd stand here today and do exactly the same thing"
JOHN TERRY

"The Brazilians were South America and the Ukranians will be more European"
PHIL NEVILLE

"All that remains is for a few dots and commas to be crossed"
MITCHELL THOMAS

"The opening ceremony was good, although I missed it"
GRAEME LE SAUX

"One accusation you can't throw at me is that I've always done my best"
ALAN SHEARER

"I'd rather play in front of a full house than an empty crowd"
JOHNNY GILES

"Sometimes in football you have to score goals"
THIERRY HENRY

"I was surprised but I always say nothing surprises me in football"
LES FERDINAND

"It's a great honour [to be awarded an OBE] and it's an honour to be with Her Majesty. Obviously I'm very honoured to be given this honour"
DAVID BECKHAM (INCIDENTALLY, AN ANAGRAM OF 'DAVID AND VICTORIA BECKHAM' SPELLS 'BRAVO, VICTIM AND DICKHEAD....)

Money Talks (continued)

Manchester United's Denis Law became the first UK based player to be transferred for more than £100,000 when he went to Torino in 1961.

Chairman of the Professional Players' Association, Jimmy Hill lobbied for dissolving the maximum wage as he felt it restricted players who wanted to have a hand in negotiating transfers and salaries. Before 1961 a top professional could expect to earn no more than £1000 a year, but with the dissolution of the wage structure Fulham's Johnny Haynes was immediately offered £5000. By a strange quirk of fate, Hill, now a manger, had to find the money to pay his star players, and initially he struggled.

One of the founder members of the Football League, Accrington Stanley had a long and distinguished history. Sadly, by 1962, that was coming to an end. Their match against Crewe in the snow that year was a disaster and they went down 4-0. Immediately afterwards there was a meeting to discuss the club's future. It emerged that Stanley were about £60,000 in debt and as such could not continue. The directors, who had been paying the players' wages for some time, needed to find £400 to ensure heat and light at the training ground. The cash was not forthcoming, despite a last minute 'Save Our Stanley' campaign, and the club folded.

Betting on the outcome of matches had always been big business for punters, but the 1892 ban meant players couldn't have a few quid on the results. The ban was lifted in 1957, however. By December 1962 it was suggested that three Sheffield Wednesday players had put money on their team losing to Ipswich in a league match. Three years passed before investigator Michael Gabbert, who was working for the Sunday People, discovered that Jimmy Gauld had used players Peter Swan, Dave Layne and Tony Kay to make money on the 2-0 defeat, and that he'd probably been involved in match-fixing for quite some time, netting himself around £10,000. Kay had gone on that season to win a Championship medal after transferring to Everton for £55,000. Two Bristol Rovers players were banned for life at the same time for their part in trying to rig results.

Stoke City players were paid the princely sum of one shilling per hour to pour the concrete foundations for the Victoria Ground's new stand in the early 1960s.

The winter of 1962-63 was particularly harsh and a large number of games were abandoned as a result. This led to some confusion over what should be done about money gambled on the games by way of the pools. The simple solution was to assemble a panel of experts who would predict the outcome in all of the games. If any were cancelled, their fictional result would stand and punters could then collect if they had the right amount of points. Lord Brabazon chaired the first panel, which consisted of former internationals Tom Finney, Tommy Lawton, Ted Drake and George Young.

Most of the rival pools companies then gradually fell by the wayside until only one remained. With the massive increase in sponsorship in the 1970s, it was only a matter of time before the FA Cup followed the League Cup by having a logo attached to it. Littlewoods Pools became its first sponsor in 1994 having shelled out £14 million to secure the deal.

England's World Cup winners were each given a £1000 win bonus, a considerable sum in the mid-'60s. Sadly for them they then had to endure a lengthy court case before it was decided that they shouldn't have to pay tax on the amount.

Argentina's Racing club offered its players £2000 and a car if they managed to beat Celtic in the 1967 World Club Championship. As discussed a little later, the game was a fractious affair, which Racing went on to win 1-0. Celtic, on the other hand, were fined £250 a man for their on-field behaviour.

The Turkish side that was due to face West Germany in 1970 was offered a win bonus of a different kind. Local belly dancing star Sether Seinz put her 'services' up for grabs to anyone scoring a goal. Several of the defenders were said to be gutted and vowed to boycott the game if the offer wasn't revised.

Cyril Grimes became the first really big money winner on the pools when he collected £512,683 for his 30 pence stake in 1972. Since then there have been several million-pound winners of course.

When Johann Cruijff moved from Ajax to Barcelona in 1973 he became the first million-dollar man. He was also one of the first players to employ an agent, fully realising that he could make a great deal of money away from the game with sponsorships and a share of the gate receipts. He committed a huge gaffe in the eyes of the Dutch, however, when he refused to go to the 1978 World Cup - a tournament where they reached the final - because he had promised his wonife he wouldn't take part.

Pelé retired from football in 1974, but was forced to reconsider his position a year later having blown most of his fortune. He signed for New York Cosmos for $4.5 million in 1975 and helped the side to victory in the Soccer Bowl in 1977. Having earned enough money in the United States to retire for a second time, he then hung up his boots for good.

The British transfer fee record was broken again in 1979 when Trevor Francis moved from Birmingham City to Nottingham Forest for a cool million, in so doing becoming the first seven-figure footballer. He had gained the nickname 'Superboy' having scored 15 goals in his first 15 starts for the club as a fresh-faced 16-year-old, but felt Brian Clough's outfit could offer him the chance of European glory. He was right.

Francis took a leaf out of his then manager's book when he went into coaching too. Unimpressed when Alex Kolinko laughed when Bradford scored against Crystal Palace, Francis marched onto the pitch and clipped his player round the back of the head. He was fined by the FA immediately afterwards. Old Big 'Ead would have been so proud.

Whittle Wanderers' James Condon had his leg broken by Khalsa's

Gurdever Basi in a lower league game in 1980. The tackle was so bad, and the break so serious, that Condon had to take nearly a year off work to recover. During that time he spoke with a lawyer who advised him to sue Basi for damages and loss of earnings. He issued a writ citing negligence and deliberate and wrongful assault as the cause of his injury and the case went to court in 1984. Basi, who had apparently slid in with studs raised from about four yards away while the ball was some distance beyond Condon, was found guilty, and Condon was awarded £4,900. Footballers are bound by a duty of care on the field and the judge ruled that Basi had not taken reasonable care with his actions.

Liberian players had a win bonus of yet another different kind offered to them during the 1980 African Nations Cup. If they won they would be allowed to live, but if they lost they would be executed. Somewhat predictably, they drew, proving the great Bill Shankly wrong with his comment about football not being a matter of life and death. On this occasion the players were spared, however.

The Crown Prince of Kuwait offered the national side cars, homes, gold and cash if they qualified for the World Cup Finals in Spain in 1982. With incentives like that to play for the side performed above themselves and made it through to the tournament proper. Zaire's president, incidentally, had offered similar bonuses to their players for making it though the 1974 Finals. He then withdrew his offer when the team was dumped out of the competition without scoring a goal.

Dunfermline captain Jim Brown was stretchered off after a horrendous two-footed lunge by St Johnstone's John Pelosi in a match in 1981. Pelosi's studs caught Brown just below the knee, severing his ligaments. Despite a couple of operations, Brown never recovered his former fitness and was forced to retire. A volatile player who had already received a red card and a suspension for dangerous play, Pelosi was sent off and banned for another six months by the Scottish FA. Brown was advised to sue both the player and his employer and raised a civil action over the lack of reasonable care taken by Pelosi. The St Johnstone side countered that injuries were part of the game and could always be expected to happen by accident. St Johnstone eventually backed down and made a payment to Brown believed to be in the region of £20,000.

The International Monetary Fund, an organisation more used to receiving requests for assistance from beleaguered treasuries, was approached by non-League outfit Netherton United in 1982. The IMF offered an apology but said it could not help the club out of its dire financial situation. Staff at IMF headquarters did have a whip-round however and came up with £25, a sum that was immediately sent to the Nottinghamshire side.

In a similar story to the one that unfolded in Italy in 2006, Hungarian teams were punished for their roles in match fixing in 1983. In all, 75 people were convicted of conspiracy from the 260 players and 14 officials involved. Backroom staff at Belgium's Standard Liege were implicated in a similar scandal the following year.

In 1985 Trevor Senior scored a hat-trick for Reading against Cardiff. Instead of collecting the match ball, as was customary, he was told he could only keep it if he paid £40!

Swindon Town were the first club in England to be denied promotion on monetary grounds. In 1990 they were accused of making irregular payments to players and remained in the second tier as a result, thus denying themselves huge television revenue. The other major domestic scandal of recent times involved players Bruce Grobbelaar, Wimbledon goalkeeper Hans Segers and club-mate John Fashanu. All three were implicated in attempting to fix the results of certain games, with Grobbelaar actually admitting some deliberate goalkeeping errors while being stung by a national newspaper. He claimed he knew the reporters' intentions and was just playing along, however. Solicitor Mel Goldberg successfully defended the trio, who supposedly had links with a Malaysian businessman, saying that evidence for match fixing couldn't be corroborated.

There was a bidding war between terrestrial and satellite television for the rights to show the bulk of the new Premier League games in 1992. Sky eventually beat off the opposition, though they had to pay over £300 million for the privilege.

French champions Marseille were allegedly involved in a match fixing scheme in 1993. They strenuously denied any wrong-doing but the club's reputation remained tarnished for some years afterwards.

Having already been sent off six times, Vinny Jones was fined £20,000 for bringing the game into disrepute in 1993 after releasing a video called 'Soccer's Hard Men', which taught players how to commit the perfect professional foul. He also received a six-month ban suspended for three years.

Jimmy Greaves was less than impressed with the former hod-carrier, saying, on hearing about Jones's selection for the Welsh in 1994:

"We've had drugs, bribery and the Arsenal scoring two at home, but just when you thought there were no surprises left, Vinny Jones turns out to be an international player"

Tottenham Hotspur were thrown out of their best competition, the FA Cup, and then docked 12 points for making illegal payments to players in 1994. Chairman Alan Sugar fought the case on behalf of the club and managed to get both rulings overturned.

Alan Shearer's move from Blackburn to Newcastle in 1996 for £15 million broke the world record for a transfer fee. Only a year later Brazilian Ronaldo moved from Internazionale to Real Madrid for £20 million. By the time the 1998 World Cup Final came around, the French and Brazilian players between them had been involved in transfers totalling nearly a half a billion pounds!

The 1998 First Division play-off final at Wembley was a tense affair. Both Sunderland and Charlton knew that promotion to the Premier League would guarantee them a minimum of £7 million from TV revenues and increased gates the following season. The background to these games still feels a little strange though. The top two teams are automatically promoted and then the next four contest two 'semi-finals'. So the third team to get promoted are the champions of this mini tournament, who must feel like League winners if they emerge victorious in front of 80,000 at Wembley. (Let's face it, this is a money-making scheme, no more.)

A Clive Mendonca goal was the difference at halftime, Charlton leading 1-0. Niall Quinn and Kevin Phillips then put Sunderland ahead, before Mendonca equalised. Quinn then restored Sunderland's lead with his second. Charlton's Richard Rufus restored parity with his first goal in 145 Charlton starts. Mendonca's hat-trick came up in extra time and cancelled out Summerbee's earlier strike, and the match finished at 4-4. Even the penalty shootout proved how close the two teams were matched and it went to 6-6. But then Shaun Newton scored for Alan Curbishley's Charlton, while Michael Gray's left-footed shot was stopped by Sasa Ilic after three hours of deadlock. Sunderland fans were left shell-shocked, though their side would eventually make it into the top flight the following year.

The owner of Doncaster Rovers, Ken Richardson, was questioned by police in 1999 after he was allegedly involved in a plot to claim insurance money if the ground was destroyed by fire. He is said to have organised for the main stand to disappear, which it duly did.

German company Leo Hirsch paid £1.5 billion for the rights to broadcast the 2002 and 2006 World Cups, more than ten times the fee paid to show the 1998 tournament in France.

Frenchman Zinedine Zidane transferred from Juventus to Real Madrid in 2001 for the staggering sum of $60 million!

After eleven years at Arsenal, David Seaman was given a testimonial in 2001. More than thirty thousand fans packed into Highbury to watch them play Barcelona, earning the veteran 'keeper more than half a million tax-free pounds (almost as much as he used to earn in a week!).

Manchester United received £1 million as part of sell-on clause from Preston for Jon Macken in 2002, while West Bromwich Albion reportedly accepted nearly £2 million when Aston Villa sold Ugo Ehiogu to Middlesbrough in an £8 million deal in 2000. West Ham are said to have been paid £3 million after Michael Carrick's transfer from Tottenham to Manchester United in 2006. The biggest sell-on fee received by a non-league side is the £700,000 Kidderminster collected after Lee Hughes' £5 million transfer to Coventry in 2001.

The BBC's Panorama program claimed to have unearthed a series of managerial bungs in 2006. The practice first came to the wider public attention when Arsenal manager George Graham was accused of taking payments to grease player transfers back in the 1990s. The program went undercover and implicated several Premiership managers, all of whom used devious ways to hide the payments from the regulatory bodies.

Ukrainian striker Andriy Shevchenko equalled the most expensive signing in British football history in the summer of 2006 when he joined Chelsea from AC Milan for £30 million. Rio Ferdinand joined Manchester United from Leeds for the same fee in 2002.

Towards the end of the 2006-07 Premiership season the weekly wages commanded by the top players was scarcely believable, and no matter how vehemently you're prepared to argue over whether they're worth it, you must remember that some mug is willing to pay them what their agents ask for. Take Manchester United's Cristiano Ronaldo for example. He was one of the most hated men in England immediately after the 2006 World Cup, and many thought he'd be forced out of Old Trafford, but at the end of March 2007 he signed a contract reportedly worth £110,000 per week. Yes, per week, something like six times the average annual wage of the working person in this country. Remember, too, that they only train for about 20 hours to earn that. Ronaldo was immediately linked with several other clubs, though not all of them could afford the £50 million price tag. It was also said that his £6 million a year could be trebled with advertising and sponsorship deals, and that, at only 22, he probably had ten years of top flight football in him. Allowing for inflation and the ridiculous increases in the amount of cash in football, Ronaldo, should he avoid serious injury, could pocket over £250 million before retirement!

Chelsea's midfield maestro Frank Lampard also renegotiated his contract at the end of March 2007. Ronaldo probably had the right to feel a bit short-changed as Lampard managed to procure £10,000 a week more, though it's unlikely he sent him a bottle of L'Oreal with a note saying:

"Because you're worth it"

Chelsea may be owned by a man with some of the deepest pockets in football - indeed he's invested over £500 million in the club - but even Abramovich must be concerned that the business reported losses of £80 million in 2006. Someone should stop paying those players. The average weekly wage in the Premiership in 2007, incidentally, was £13,000 per week, one tenth of what John Terry was asking for when he wanted a nine-year contract drawn up in April 2007. He also wanted a clause in the contract giving him an option to manage the club after his playing days. Don't ask for much, do they? Remember too that when Ashley Cole was offered in the region of £80,000 a week to stay at Arsenal, he replied:

"Their wage offer is taking the piss"

These figures tend to make a mockery of the single-figure fines dished out to players, and their clubs for that matter, who receive yellow cards in a match. Even if a team has a rather dubious disciplinary record and collects six yellows in a match, the club is only fined £25,000.

It should be mentioned that the contracts discussed above are not binding for the player or club. Ronaldo is contractually obliged to stay at Old Trafford until 2012 according to the wording, but everyone knows this is meaningless. If Real Madrid said they'd pay £150 million for him, Ronaldo would be off immediately, no question, and the initial contract becomes worthless. This was not always the case though. In the early 1960s it was common for disputes to arise between the players and their clubs over their futures. Newcastle's George Eastham changed all that when he asked to be transferred to Arsenal. He was refused permission even though his contract with the Magpies had expired. He was temporarily forced out of the game until intervention by the Professional Footballers' Association meant that his case could be heard by the courts. The system ruled in Eastham's favour, and it's now the players who have the dominant role in controlling their careers, not their clubs.

West Ham continued the trend of welcoming foreign investors to top flight English football. In November 2006 Icelandic businessman Eggert Magnusson shelled out £108 million for a controlling stake in the club. Sadly two of the Argentine stars brought in after the 2006 World Cup, Tevez and Mascherano, were actually ruled as ineligible to play even though they'd already started a number of games. The club was fined £5.5 million instead of having ten points deducted at the end of the 2007 season.

Magnusson wasn't out of the woods yet either. A mysterious letter containing an unidentified white powder arrived at the club addressed to him just weeks after he'd taken over. The police feared an Anthrax outbreak and called in chemical weapons experts. The letter actually contained bath salts sent by a religious fan...

The new Wembley Stadium opened in March 2007, over two years late and, at £798 million, £400 million over budget. The first match to be held there was a charity event in which Mark Bright scored the first goal. The official curtain-raiser was an Under-21 international between England and Italy which turned out to be a thriller, ending 3-3. Some might be wondering why the stadium took so long to build and cost so much, especially when compared with the 75,000 capacity Berlin Olympiastadion, which hosted the 2006 World Cup Final (£165 million), Portugal's new 65,000-seater Luz stadium ((£67 million) and the Sapporo Dome that helped host the 2002 World Cup in Japan & Korea (£80 million). The Chinese Olympic stadium in Beijing seats 91,000 and cost just £203 million. By way of an aside, the first Wembley, named the Empire Stadium, was built in just 300 days and at a cost of £750,000. It was completed in time for the 1923 Final of White Horse fame.

The Czech Republic team were fined about £24,000 for having a party after their 2-1 defeat to Germany in the Euro 2008 qualifiers. The fact that it was defender Tomas Ujifalusi's birthday seemed lost on the management.

Eighty Sunderland fans were left abandoned in Cardiff after the crew of their flight home refused to take off. Chairman Niall Quinn climbed onboard as one of the last passengers and the remaining fare-payers burst into a chorus of the popular chant:

"Niall Quinn's disco pants"

This was too much for the flight crew who deemed it unsafe to leave. Though Quinn felt it was all in good humour, the fans then had to trudge back into the airport to await the next flight, which, as it turned out, didn't leave until the morning.

Quinn, presumably feeling slightly responsible for the situation, forked out £8,000 of his own money so that everyone could get a taxi for the 300-mile journey home!

Former prime minister of Thailand, Thaksin Shinawatra, the man who made an unsuccessful bid to buy Liverpool in 2004, approached Manchester City with a £90 million offer in 2007. Upset at the club's lack of direction, Oasis song-smith Noel Gallagher, a lifelong fan, had already voiced his opinion on the same subject in 1998:

"I've had enough. I'm going to buy that place, then walk in and say: 'You, fuck off. You, fuck off. You, make me a cup of tea'"

And once he'd told the band what to do, he'd have started with the club's staff...

Liverpool's CEO Rick Parry earned just shy of £400,000 in 2006-07, though a half-million-pound bonus, approved just before the club decided to accept a takeover bid, certainly helped with the weekly shop at Waitrose. The club was eventually bought for £470 million by American investors Tom Hicks and George Gillett, who promised £40 million for new players in early 2007. The club also looks likely to move across the road to a £215 million Stanley Park stadium within five years. Newcastle chairman Freddie Shepherd (he of 'Newcastle girls are all dogs' fame) announced a £300 million facelift for St James' Park at the same time, taking capacity up towards 60,000. And Portsmouth announced plans for a new £600 million, 36,000 seat stadium to replace Fratton Park. If the proposal is accepted by the local authorities, the side could be playing at this futuristic venue by 2011.

American billionaire Paul Allen is reportedly interested in buying Southampton. The Microsoft executive already owns the Portland Trailblazers and the NFL's Seattle Seahawks and is worth in the region of £10 billion.

The Premier League secured a television deal worth £2.7 billion early in 2007. Half of that went to the teams for the rights to screen them exclusively live, a quarter was then divided up according to League position, and the final quarter related to the number of televised appearances per club. The Tottenham - Blackburn match at the end of the 2006-07 season was the 1000th live game broadcast by Sky TV, the company having already pumped well over £3 billion into the Premier League.

These are the riches that await the winners of the Championship play-off match. This is supposedly a far bigger game, in money terms alone, than the Champions' League or FA Cup Finals as it guarantees the winners £60 million. Even so, the promoted teams traditionally struggle in the top flight. The teams going the other way receive a fair amount of help too. The Premiership's bottom side still earn £30 million for their League position and then they are awarded £11 million in parachute payments to help them survive in the lower division. Spare a thought for the teams who don't make it through the play-offs though. They receive a paltry £1 million.

In these money-oriented times it's particularly sad that some teams from the lower leagues don't actually want to be on television as their gate receipts fall by more than they get from the viewing rights.

Player Speak 4

"They've taken the horns by the scruff of the neck"
TONY CASCARINO

"I want to win the Nobel Peace Prize, and I'm going to fight as hard as I can to make it happen"
RONALDO

"Maths is totally done differently to what I was teached when I was at school"
DAVID BECKHAM

"I'd love the person who taught Jose Mourinho English to taught me"
STEVE CLARIDGE

"Even though two and two might look like four, it could be three or five"
KEVIN KEEGAN

"Mark Hughes crossed every I and dotted every T"
ROBBIE SAVAGE

"His right leg collided with himself there"
MARK BRIGHT

"The manager couldn't even talk to us at the interval. He said we were bad"
JOHN TERRY

"I've had fourteen bookings this season, eight of which were my fault and seven which were disputable"
PAUL GASCOIGNE, THANKING HIS LUCKY STARS THAT HE DIDN'T GO TO THE BECKHAM SCHOOL OF FURTHER MATHS...

"The Belgians will play like their fellow Scandinavians, Denmark and Sweden"
ANDY TOWNSEND

"I didn't say them things that I said"
GLENN HODDLE

"The world is my lobster"
KEITH O'NEILL

"I was a young lad when I was growing up"
DAVID O'LEARY

"It's like a toaster, the referee's shirt pocket. Every time there's a tackle, up pops a yellow card. I'm talking metaphysically now of course"
KEVIN KEEGAN

"Ian Pearce has limped off with what looks like a shoulder injury"
TONY COTTEE

1234567891011

International Oddballs

We've already had a good look at the quirky side of the domestic game. Of course, if you've studied Geography under Townsend or Keegan, you'll know that the world isn't quite as big as the UK, but there are still some odd matches that deserve our attention.

Though England's first official full international fixture is recorded as being against Scotland at Hamilton Crescent in Glasgow in November 1872, the Scottish FA had not yet been formed, and wouldn't come into existence until early the next year. Strictly speaking the match should have been billed as England vs. Queen's Park - Scotland's oldest club side. The match ended in a rather dull 0-0 draw. The first unofficial international had been held at the Kennington Oval in London between the same sides in 1870, with the home side winning 1-0. The word 'nil', incidentally, is an abbreviated form of the Latin *nihil* meaning nothing. It wasn't until 1885 that a match involving two other countries was played, that between Canada and the USA. The first international match to be played outside Great Britain was won 5-0 by Austria against Hungary in Vienna in 1902. The Fédération Internationale de Football Association (FIFA), the world governing body for the sport, was formed in Paris in 1904.

Fixture congestion is not a new problem, though Ferguson, Wenger, Mourinho and company will all tell you they suffer the most from it now. England found themselves having to play two home union internationals on the same day three times in the 1890s. They somehow managed to win all six games. In 1916 Celtic beat Raith Rovers 6-0 and then, later on the same day, beat Motherwell 3-1 to reduce their League burden. That's pretty impressive, you might think, but in 1987 Rangers played a home match against Hamilton Academicals and an away fixture at Dundee simultaneously, no doubt thankful for their large squad!

England won the gold medal at the London Olympics in 1908, and they cemented their reputation four years later when they beat Denmark in the 1912 final in Stockholm. At a time when there was no official World Cup, this proved what most already knew, that the English were the strongest side in the world. Things were to change pretty quickly after that, with both the Austrians and Hungarians threatening the dominance of the home unions.

Football was often the only common ground between British and German soldiers during the First World War. During lulls in the fighting, conversations between the two sides invariably turned to the 'Beautiful Game'. December 1914 was a torrid time for soldiers in the trenches of northern France but both sides managed to put aside their differences for a couple of hours on Christmas Day. Instead of charging at each other with rifles and bayonets, they brought out a football and competed, for once, on a level, if slightly muddy, playing field. Of course the next day they had to get back to the more serious business of killing one another.

Some ten months later, the 18th London Regiment played a slightly different form of attacking football when they went 'over the top' towards the German lines at Loos in September 1915. The unit dribbled a football as they stormed enemy lines, much as the 8th Battalion did at the Somme the following year. Captain W.P. Nevill, who had provided the ball for the latter assault, was killed in action. Fifteen of his company were decorated on a day when the allies made considerable gains. Indeed Bradford Park Avenue's defender Lieutenant Donald Bell, despite being killed during the battle, was posthumously awarded the Victoria Cross for his bravery, the only League player to have the honour bestowed upon him.

The 1920 Olympic gold medal match in Antwerp was between hosts Belgium and Czechoslovakia. It was all going smoothly until English referee John Lewis made a decision that angered the home side. They marched off in protest and, for some inexplicable reason, were awarded the gold medal by default.

Though the event was left off the program in Los Angeles in 1932, there being some dispute about whether to pay the players, it was back for the 1936 Berlin Olympics held in the shadow of the Nazi rise to power. A number of teams withdrew from the competition in protest, and the Italy - USA match descended into violent farce when one of the Italians refused to leave the field having been sent off by the German referee.

The Franco regime encountered much resistance in Spain in the 1920s and '30s. Barcelona fans were particularly vocal in their opposition and Franco shut the club down after a chorus of whistles greeted the royal march played at halftime during one match. They were back up and running with plenty of time to make Pope John Paul II an honorary member in 1982 however!

When Argentina met Uruguay in the final of the 1930 World Cup at the Estadio Centenario in Montevideo, the teams couldn't agree on which ball to use (both countries had provided one). After the toss of a coin the Argentinean ball was used for the first half, which they ended up leading 2-1. The Uruguayan ball proved even luckier for the home side in the second half though, and they went on to win 4-2.

The tournament four years later in Italy was dogged by controversy. Mussolini himself invited the Swedish referee to officiate at the semi-final between the hosts and the Austrian Wunderteam, and the move paid off. The Austrians were on the end of a number of dubious decisions and Italy made it through to face the Czechs in the final. There, the same referee ensured the same result. They played England shortly afterwards in the Battle of Highbury, a match billed as the biggest in the history of the sport. The world champions lost 3-2.

Italy's star man at the time was undoubtedly their captain Giuseppe Meazza, the only man in the squad given preferential treatment, such as being allowed to smoke, by the management. In fact he was also allowed the occasional drink, something he liked to do the night before a match. He was once so drunk that he slept in until half an hour before kick-off and was thus banned from doing so again. Typically he then went out and scored a hat-trick!

The great Austrian striker Franz Binder, known as 'Bimbo', became the first European player to score more than 1000 goals. In a career spanning twenty years Binder netted 1006 times in just 756 games, a phenomenal strike rate.

"The management allowed Italy's captain
to smoke and to drink."

Matthias Sindelar, perhaps the finest player of his generation, was a team-mate of Binder's, but that changed when the Nazis annexed Austria in 1938. Sindelar refused to play for the combined Germany team and aroused so much interest from the Nazis that the Gestapo had a secret file on him, claiming that he was sympathetic to the Jewish cause. He was found dead with a prostitute, Camilla Castagnola, at the age of just 35. His death, which was investigated by the Nazis and 'discovered' to be by accidental gas poisoning, was far more likely to have been at the hands of the Gestapo, or a jilted ex-girlfriend, or even by the pimp, Amerika Maxl. More than 15,000 Viennese turned out for his funeral.

The Indian side withdrew from the 1950 World Cup in Brazil, the first tournament for which they had qualified, because they weren't allowed to compete in bare feet! Abdul Salim, Celtic's star man in the 1930s, also refused to play in boots, wrapping bandages around his feet for protection instead.

Welshman John Charles played for Leeds in the 1950s but he, somewhat surprisingly, transferred to Italian giants Juventus in 1957. He was an instant hit despite deliberately missing an open goal when he knew he'd accidentally fouled the opposing centre-half in his first Turin derby. Over the next five years he scored 93 goals in just 150 starts in a country renowned for its defensive prowess, and he helped his side to three League successes and two Italian cups. Around the time of his death in 2004, Il Buon Gigante - The Gentle Giant, was voted Serie A's greatest foreign player, and when you consider who he was up against (Maradona, Marco van Basten and Adriano to name just three), the achievement is all the more remarkable. Another fact that helped him earn his nickname was that he was never cautioned in his career.

Though England had lost at home before (Scotland's Wembley Wizards demolished them 5-1 in 1928 and Ireland won 2-0 in 1949), they were not beaten at Wembley by any team outside the home unions until Hungary's visit in 1953. Though the 100,000 crowd expected England to win comfortably, they were tactically out-thought and physically completely out-played. Even though greats Stan Mortensen, Stanley Matthews and Alf Ramsay all scored, Hungary bagged six, Nandor Hidegkuti scoring a hat-trick. Their revolutionary 4-2-4 formation confused the English to the extent that they had to defend nearly forty shots, with the 'Galloping Major', Ferenc Puskas, completely dominating the game. It had all turned out rather differently from expectation, one of the England team saying this on seeing Puskas before kick-off:

"Look at that little fat chap over there. We're going to murder this lot"

The return match was billed as the chance for England to avenge this defeat but they were even more comprehensively thumped, 7-1. Tom Finney summed up the thoughts of a nation with:

"It was like carthorses playing racehorses. We haven't been the so-called best side in the word for some time"

Puskas once had the audacity to put on his army uniform, barge into the Ministry of Defence and demand that his friend - who was suffering from tuberculosis - be seen by the local military hospital. The Minister, who was in a meeting with ten top generals at the time, recognised Puskas and granted his request immediately! His overall record of 83 goals in 84 games for Hungary remains the most outstanding strike-rate in international football.

The Maracanã stadium in Brazil holds the record for the highest attendance for a football match. 199,854 fans watched the deciding game of the 1950 World Cup Finals between hosts Brazil and Uruguay. It is believed that some 10,000 more found ways in without paying.

Brazil went 1-0 but ended up losing 2-1. The name Maracanã is more of a nickname and is taken from a local species of parrot found in northern Brazil. The stadium was officially named Estádio Jornalista Mário Filho after a journalist who backed the stadium both financially and vocally. Pelé made his international debut against Argentina in front of 140,000 there in 1957, and it was also where he scored his 1,000th career goal when Santos beat Vasco de Gama 2-1. Pelé has scored more goals for Brazil at the Maracanã than any other player (30 in 22 starts). (Recently the stadium has been undergoing major renovations as the concrete surrounds were being corroded by fans' urine!) Another Brazilian holds the record for the most goals, just eclipsing Pelé's record in fact. Arthur Friedenreich netted 1329 times during his 26-year career in the early part of the century. Only one of those goals survives on film.

Frenchman Just Fontaine scored 13 goals in just six appearances at the World Cup in Sweden in 1958. This tally remains a record for a single tournament, though Brazil's Ronaldo, with 15 from 1998, 2002 and 2006, has more Finals goals overall. Fontaine went on to score 30 goals in only 21 full internationals for France.

Bangor City of the Konica League in Wales are a little known commodity in terms of world football, but they had a couple of games to remember in 1962. The non-leaguers had somehow won the Welsh Cup the year before and had thus qualified for the Cup-Winners' Cup. When they were drawn against Serie A opposition in the form of Italian giants Napoli, however, the game was expected to be somewhat one-sided. It was. Bangor won the first leg at Farrar Road 2-0! Incredibly the Welsh then travelled to Italy and only lost 3-1, a score that nowadays under the away goals rule would have seen them through to the next round. Sadly for them though, a decider was needed, which the Italians shaded 2-1 at Highbury.

The great Alfredo di Stefano, of Real Madrid fame, was capped by three different countries, Argentina, Colombia and Spain. Only two other men share that distinction. Ladislav Kubala played for Hungary, Czechoslovakia and Spain, while Jim Kennaway started for the USA, Canada and Scotland.

Di Stefano, of course, was part of the Madrid side that went unbeaten in the Santiago Bernabeu from 1957 until 1965, an astonishing 122 matches, of which 114 were won and only eight were drawn! In 1963 he had been kidnapped on a tour of Venezuela, but the kidnappers soon realised that if anything happened to the great man they would be hunted down like dogs and killed. They released him almost immediately.

Until 1965 important European matches were settled by the toss of a coin if the scores remained level after the replay. Clearly this was an unsatisfactory way of resolving big games and the away goals counting double rule was introduced. Dynamo Zagreb had been put out of the 1964 Cup Winners' Cup by the toss of a coin but they were the first to benefit from the new system. They beat Dunfermline Athletic having scored four away from home, and then they went on to win the competition.

North Korea were the surprise package at the 1966 World Cup in England. The team, affectionately christened the 'Diddy Men' on account of their small stature by impressed English fans, was not expected to pose a threat to Russia, Chile or group favourites Italy, and many argued that they shouldn't even be at the tournament when teams like Czechoslovakia hadn't made it. They didn't do themselves any favours by going down to Russia 3-0 in their opener, but they found new friends after a spirited 1-1 draw with Chile. Still, the mighty Italians would send them home, wouldn't they? Not a bit of it. Pak Du-ik scored the only goal of the game at Ayresome Park and it was Italy who were out instead. (The Italians decided to sneak home late at night to a mystery airfield to hide their embarrassment, but they were still terrorised by angry fans throwing tomatoes!) The quarter-final against Portugal was expected to be another walkover for the Europeans but North Korea scored three in the first quarter of the match, and Goodison Park acknowledged their sublime passing and movement. Only one man could spoil the party, and that was the Blank Panther, Eusébio. He scored two brilliant individual goals, two penalties, and then set up team-mate Augusta for the winner. The Koreans were widely praised thereafter for their contribution to the tournament. Just ask the Italians…

This next story could have made it into this book under virtually any of the chapter headings but as an oddball game it, and the build-up to it, stand alone. Two rival soccer Leagues were operating in the United States towards the end of the 1960s. The National Professional Soccer League found it hard to get TV funding and had to resort to paying the referees to blow for non-existent fouls every few minutes so that the sponsors could fit in breaks for adverts, while the United Soccer Association invited established clubs from around the world to compete under different names in an American championship. Strangely, the time and effort spent promoting both sides of the game to a largely unreceptive audience was slowly paying off as teams from around the world attracted bigger crowds across the country. It was through these knockout matches that Aberdeen (or Washington Whips as they were billed) came to meet Wolves (Los Angeles Wolves) in the final at the Memorial Coliseum in 1967. The build-up had not been easy. Two League matches (Detroit Cougars vs. Houston Stars and New York Skyliners vs. Cleveland Stokers [yes, Stoke City!]) had been abandoned after a series of brawls between players and fans.

Thankfully the final was a good-natured affair. It was 1-1 after an hour, but then the goals started flying in; four in four minutes! Aberdeen's Jim Smith was sent off towards the end but after ninety minutes the game was level at 4-4, David Burnside having netted a hat-trick. Derek Dougan put Wolves ahead once more but Frank Munro scored his second last-minute equaliser and the game went to sudden death. Incredibly, after all that had gone before, it was decided by an own goal, the ball ricocheting off Aberdeen's Ally Shewin in the 126th minute!

England arrived in South America to prepare for the 1970 World Cup in Mexico as world champions. But Sir Alf Ramsey and team were not made to feel welcome in their first ports of call, Colombia and Ecuador. While out shopping in Bogota, jewellery assistant Clara Padilla accused captain Bobby Moore of stealing an emerald and diamond bracelet worth about £600. The England defender strenuously denied any involvement and he was allowed to continue the tour with the team. Having arrived back in the capital a few days later the mood had changed however, and Moore was detained by police while the squad began final preparations in Mexico. It then emerged that several other high-profile guests staying in nearby hotels had also been accused of stealing from the same store, and while most had paid up to avoid scandal, Moore had decided to clear his name. Having been released he joined the team in Mexico, a hero before the competition had even kicked off.

Manager Speak 4 - More Drivel

"I'm afraid they've left their legs at home"
RON ATKINSON

"If I walked on water my accusers would say it's because I can't swim"
BERTI VOGTS

"There's nobody fitter at his age except maybe Raquel Welch"
RON ATKINSON

"He wanted us to sign Salford Van Hire because he thought he was a Dutch international"
FRED AYRE

"I think the referee should be allowed to blow up now, as a mercy killing, if you like"
RON ATKINSON

"I know what is around the corner. I just don't know where the corner is"
KEVIN KEEGAN

"It's a conflict of parallels"
SIR ALEX FERGUSON

"I'm not disappointed, just disappointed"
KEVIN KEEGAN

"I'm a firm believer that if the other side score first you'll have to score twice to win"
HOWARD WILKINSON

"We're going to start the game at 0-0 and go out and try to get some goals"
BRYAN ROBSON

"We probably got on better with the likes of Holland, Belgium, Norway and Sweden, some of whom aren't even European"
JACK CHARLTON

"Argentina are the second best team in the world and there's no higher praise than that"
KEVIN KEEGAN

"They've got Kanu, a guy with a heart as big as he is"
KEVIN KEEGAN (THIS IS ANOTHER OF THOSE DAVID COLEMAN/ASA HARTFORD-STYLE GAFFES BECAUSE KANU HAD EARLIER BEEN HOSPITALISED AFTER A HEART SCARE.)

"Neil Lennon wasn't sent off for scoring a goal and that's what annoys me"
MARTIN O'NEILL

The second leg of the second round of the 1971 UEFA Cup-Winners' Cup between Glasgow Rangers and Sporting Lisbon will be remembered for a number of odd happenings. Rangers had won the first leg at Ibrox 3-2, the only downside being that they had conceded two vital away goals. The return leg saw the Scots go behind twice but Colin Stein clawed both goals back. Then, with a quarter of the match to go, and after a serious injury to Ron McKinnon, Sporting scored again. Rangers managed to hold out for the remainder of the match and it went to extra time, both teams having scored three home and two away goals. The next half an hour saw both teams score one and, as they were still level, referee van Ravens signalled for penalties. Rangers contrived to miss all theirs, while Sporting scored three. Game over? Well, not quite. Shortly after the match it was pointed out to van Ravens that Rangers had scored three away goals during the 120 minutes, and, as they counted double, the Scots should be through instead. The Dutchman held up his hands and admitted he'd got it terribly wrong. UEFA sacked him immediately and Rangers did indeed make it to the next round. In fact, they went on to win that year's trophy. After all that, there's got to be a good pub quiz question in there about a team missing all their penalties and still winning the tie…

Zaire made it to the World Cup in Germany in 1974 on pure footballing skill. Sadly for them they fell down during the finals proper because they didn't seem to know the rules of the game. Whenever they faced a free-kick for example - most notably against Brazil and Scotland - they assumed the ball was back in play once the referee had blown his whistle, and they repeatedly charged up to it and hoofed it clear, particularly Mwepu Llunga, who almost 'scored' at the other end with one. Sadly the referees had little sympathy for them and repeatedly booked the offending players. Peru have also been involved in some strange World Cup happenings: In 1978 their goalkeeper, Ramon Quiroga, had come up for a corner against Poland, but the ball was cleared to one of the Polish midfielders. The 'keeper of course had to backtrack quickly but ended up rugby tackling the ball carrier in the wrong half, thereby getting a yellow card instead of conceding the score!

North Korean coach Pak Du-ik, the man who'd scored the winner to eliminate Italy from the 1966 World Cup, watched his team fight hard for a 3-3 draw with Hong Kong in the colony in 1975. After extra time had finished it was time for the dreaded penalty shootout. The teams couldn't be separated after the initial six, both sides scoring five. The goalkeepers then contrived to save a few, while the strikers managed to miss a few, and soon it was time for the 'keepers themselves to step up to try and break the stalemate. They couldn't, and the cycle had to begin again. Hong Kong eventually missed their fourteenth penalty but North Korea's Kim Jung-min stepped up to bury his and win the match 11-10 after 28 spot kicks! (Someone in the crowd suggested it might have been quicker to play another match.) The Koreans progressed to the Asia Cup Final where they beat China a couple of days later. The same score-line, incidentally, was reached in British domestic football when Aldershot met Fulham in 1987, the Shots eventually proving too accurate!

Controversy surrounded hosts Argentina's final second round game in the 1978 World Cup. Brazil had just beaten Poland 3-1, which meant Argentina would need to thrash Peru to progress on goal difference. The Peruvian goalkeeper Ramón Quiroga had been born in Argentina and had, up until that point in the tournament, only let in six goals in five matches. Argentina hadn't exactly been smashing goals in for fun either, scoring just six so far. Some utterly inept defending then saw the Argentineans bury the Peruvians under an avalanche of six goals, so they went through, and then went on to win the tournament. The Brazilians, quite understandably, cried foul but the result was allowed to stand. One reporter even went as far as to say:

"If Brazil had won 50-0 against Poland, Argentina would probably have beaten Peru 54-0"

Sylvester Stallone was in goal, while Michael Caine, John Wark, Bobby Moore, Max von Sydow, Ossie Ardiles, Pelé and the remainder of Ipswich Town's 1st XI played outfield. It could only be a film, and it was. John Huston's *Escape to Victory,* though not well-received by the critics, was an entertaining movie about allied prisoners of war taking on their German captors in a football match. Pelé, injured during the course of events, retakes the field and buries a bicycle kick to ensure a draw. The players then escape during the pitch invasion that follows.

A game between the North Palm Beach Golden Bears and the Palm Beach Piranhas in 1984 set a new world record as the longest ever. It lasted just over 68 hours. The players, having organised the event for charity, were only allowed a five minute rest every hour, and as they tired and were hauled off with exhaustion, the match officials were eventually forced to abandon the tie because there were only six fit men on each side.

The era of crowd participation arrived with the advent of the Mexican Wave at their World Cup in 1986. If the action on the pitch was particularly boring, the crowds spontaneously decided to liven things up a little by starting the wave. It has been noticed that these waves generally travel in an anti-clockwise direction in the northern hemisphere, the opposite to what usually occurs in the southern hemisphere. Despite several scientific studies into the phenomenon, there has never been a satisfactory explanation for this.

It had long been the case in England that matches abandoned before full time should either be replayed in their entirety or have the score-line stand if enough of the match had been completed. In 1989 a match between Osasuna and Real Madrid was called off after forty-three minutes. The remaining forty-seven were played at the end of the season, with Madrid's Sanchez scoring a rather belated equaliser some ninety days later. And while we're in Spain, the 1995 Cup Final between Deportivo and Valencia almost lasted until the end but eleven minutes had to be played two days later.

A rabbit once stopped play in a Spanish League game, as did a seagull in a Celta Vigo - Real Madrid clash. One of the players was nipped as he tried to escort it from the field, though the bird should be excused as it probably wasn't too happy at having a tracksuit top thrown at it. Of course most will remember the Arsenal squirrel, which made an appearance in their 2005 tie with Villareal in the Champions' League. The joke going round at the time was that the animal had more European experience than local arch-rivals Spurs as it had actually come onto the pitch for a few minutes. A chicken, pig, family of ducks, fox and any number of dogs have halted play at some point in Europe alone, of which one of the latter defecated on the grass, prompting the manager to shout:

"Who's just shit on the pitch?"

Four players put their hands up and one answered:

"But I'm okay in the air, boss"

And the Feyenoord 'keeper killed an airborne pigeon with a punt recently…

When Franz Beckenbauer managed the West German side to World Cup victory at Italia '90 he became the first, and so far only, man to captain and manage a winning team. Of course he'd captained the side that won the 1974 World Cup at home.

In a UEFA Cup tie between club sides from Bulgaria and Belgium, the Eastern Europeans were confident of winning the game given that they were 3-1 up with 90 minutes on the clock. The Belgians weren't going to go quietly, however, and they scored three goals in injury time to take the unlikeliest of victories.

AC Milan's 'keeper Sebastiano Rossi was preparing to defend a Parma corner when he was struck by an object thrown from the crowd. He went down as if a sniper's bullet had found its mark and was writhing on the turf until amused team-mates showed him the missile. It was a toilet roll, and he immediately staggered to his feet to play on, a rather sheepish look on his face. Could it be coincidence that the object cleaned him up?

And staying in Italy for a moment... In a Fiorentina - Milan match the crowd invaded the pitch at the end and forced all the players to remove their kit!

A swarm of bees in the goalmouth halted proceedings during a game in Italy in the 1980s. The fans tried to take matters into their own hands but only ended up angering the bees with scarves and belts. Thankfully, before anyone got hurt, the local beekeeper arrived. A similar situation arose in a World Cup qualifying match between Zambia and Congo in 2006. A floodlight pylon collapsed during the game and dislodged a beehive. The angry swarm then had spectators running for cover.

Sergio, Alviedo's fullback, was battling for the ball when he trod on the linesman's foot. Of course the referee's assistant took a leaf out of the players' book and crumpled to the turf in apparent agony. And Liverpool's Patrick Berger once took out a linesman with a sliding tackle. He flagged for the throw-in instead of the foul, however!

Switzerland's Stefan Chapuisat did everything but score in a match in 1996. His shot beat the 'keeper but not the unconscious defender lying in the goalmouth and the ball went out for a corner!

Jan Skorkovsky, a skilful Czechoslovakian player, juggled a football - without it ever touching the ground - while he ran the Prague Marathon in 1990!

A variation on the football game is practiced in Indonesia. Players attach fireworks to their bodies and demonstrate their courage/stupidity (you decide) by smashing bricks over their heads before kick-off. The game itself is played with a ball that has been doused in petrol and set alight. Thankfully the teams manage to avoid getting burned as their feet are only in contact with the ball for fractions of a second at a time, but it is not known what happens if the ball lands in the crowd, or if the star man levels his house after returning home with the match ball having bagged a hat-trick! You sense that these players are desperate for that elusive Darwin Award, the trophies dished out (posthumously) at an annual ceremony honouring those who remove themselves from the gene-pool by unnatural selection…

In the middle of a Leeds - Southampton match at Elland Road the pitch-surround sprinklers came on by accident. The same thing happened in a club match in Brazil some ten years earlier giving the players a thorough soaking.

Norwich City were the only British side to beat the mighty German side Bayern Munich in the Olympic Stadium. A Jeremy Goss goal gave them victory in the third round of the 1993-94 UEFA Cup. Of course Bayern now play in the Allianz Stadium, a thoroughly modern edifice built for the 2006 World Cup and one of the most innovative designs.

The 1994 Shell Cup match between Barbados and Grenada will be remembered for one of the oddest incidents in football. Barbados needed to win by two goals to qualify for the next round, and they were winning 2-0 at the break. You'd think they'd just knock the ball about and play out the time but, against the run of play, Grenada pulled a goal back. In the dying seconds the Barbados players, unable to score the one they needed, hatched a plan to get themselves through and scored a deliberate own goal. This took the game to extra time, where, somewhat confusingly, any goal scored would count double. This left them with half an hour to find the single winner, which they then managed.

A similar situation arose in an ASEAN Cup tie between Indonesia and Thailand in 1998. The Indonesian players realised that they would have to play Vietnam in the next round of the competition, which they were not prepared to do, preferring instead to play Singapore. So they calmly knocked the ball about for a while before Mursyid Effendi scored a deliberate own goal, this despite desperate Thai strikers trying to prevent the shot. Both teams were heavily fined, and both lost their next matches, while Effendi was banned for life.

Not wanting to see his team lose, a fan in a South American game ran on and stole the ball from the penalty spot. He then booted it into the stands to give his goalkeeper time to compose himself while the opposing striker would have to sweat it out. Sadly the plan backfired and the striker sent the 'keeper the wrong way and scored.

The 1994 World Cup brought the football circus to America in an effort to improve the standing of the sport there. Sadly the competition started and ended with missed penalties. Pub quiz experts will no doubt know this but Diana Ross kicked off the competition at the opening ceremony. No club in the world showed any interest in signing her as she managed to miss a penalty from about half the usual distance. It was a truly dreadful strike, but one that Italy's Roberto Baggio will have every sympathy with. At the end of a rather turgid final against Brazil, the pony-tailed striker stepped up to keep the Italians in it. Of course he blasted the ball Chris Waddle-style into the stratosphere to gift Cafu and team-mates the trophy. Baggio was never picked for Italy again, but there were rumours about him becoming England's penalty-taking coach.

South Korean maestro Sam Ik managed to juggle a ball non-stop for over eighteen hours using virtually every part of his body in 1995.

While England were playing Colombia at Wembley in 1995, South American 'keeper René Higuita watched the ball sail towards the roof of his net after a speculative shot by Jamie Redknapp. Then, instead of catching it, he threw his upper body forward, and kicked his legs up behind him to clear the ball, a save that became known as the scorpion on account of his feet striking the ball in a similar motion to a scorpion's attack. This prompted commentator Ian Darke to announce, rather incredulously:

"My goodness. Have you ever seen anything like that?"

Sadly Higuita didn't have everything his own way between the sticks. In the 1990 World Cup he tried to beat Cameroon's ageless Roger Milla while twenty yards outside his own area. Of course Milla dispossessed him and rolled the ball in, eliminating Colombia from the tournament. He was lucky he didn't get shot.

The 'keeper's exploits don't end there though. Three years later he was imprisoned for accepting a $60,000 reward after securing the release of a kidnap victim. In Colombia it is against the law to profit from such a crime, and Higuita, clearly ignorant of this law during his act of mercy, was incarcerated for seven months.

Internazionale's Paul Ince felled an opponent with a look and a quick word of abuse while playing in Italy. The referee thought he'd punched the player, judging by his exaggerated reaction however, and sent Ince off instead.

In a Portugal - Angola friendly the African nation appeared not to understand the meaning of the word 'friendly'. A series of two-footed horror challenges, mixed with the occasional tackle from behind and scything ankle-breaker, meant that the referee had no option but to send four players off. Then when one of their strikers was hit on the thigh by the ball, he collapsed to the ground in apparent agony. He was stretchered off and the game had to be abandoned because there weren't enough Angolans left on the field to warrant continuing.

Velez Sarsfield goalkeeper Gaston Sessa was repeatedly targeted by a man in the crowd with a laser pointer in a match in 1997. Sadly the light put him off when a free-kick came in and he fumbled the ball for the opposing striker to net an easy winning goal. Later in the same match Sarsfield had a chance to equalise from the penalty spot but the obnoxious fan put the striker off during his run up and he missed.

Until its closure in 1997, Wales' Cardiff Arms Park - more commonly associated with rugby - was the oldest surviving football ground in the world. Wales lost (9-1) to England there in 1896, and the national side continued to use the venue for the next century. Of course it has since been knocked down to make way for the Millennium Stadium, but the new ground is still on the same site and one of the stands remains, although it has been modernised.

For those who believe in fate, the result of the 1999 Manchester United - Bayern Munich European Cup Final must have been written in the stars. On what would have been Sir Matt Busby's 90th birthday, the Nou Camp in Barcelona hosted one of the most extraordinary matches. Bayern were quickly into their stride and a low Mario Basler free-kick gave them a 1-0 lead after just six minutes. Then they started to play with the confident swagger of champions elect. But two moments of good fortune for United will haunt the Germans forever. Scholl lobbed Peter Schmeichel only for the ball to bounce back off the inside of the post. Then Janker hit a fierce drive into the bar. But despite the woodwork helping out, United could not break through the stout German defence. As Basler was substituted at the death, he saluted the crowd victoriously and watched as UEFA officials removed United's colours from the trophy. Then, as if galvanised by the prospect of defeat, United forced a corner, for which Schmeichel came up. This seemed to confuse the Germans and sub Teddy Sheringham turned in a scuffed Ryan Giggs shot. With the prospect of extra time looming, there was still time for some last-minute drama. Solskjaer forced a corner and then collected Teddy Sheringham's resulting nod down to fire home the winner. Assured of victory virtually until injury time, the Bayern players had been mugged in the last seconds and most collapsed to the turf in disbelief. For the Reds the result capped a glorious season, with the League title and FA Cup already in the bag giving them an historic treble.

This wasn't the first time an English club had had the opportunity to take the same three trophies incidentally. In 1970 Leeds United were on course in that they headed the First Division, were in the semi-final of the European Cup and had forced a replay in the FA Cup Final. Surely they'd take something from this remarkable season. Well, no, they wouldn't. In one of the great team implosions, they lost to Celtic in Europe, to Chelsea in the FA Cup and Everton in the League run in. Gutted.

Everton themselves also had a shot at three trophies in 1985 but they lost the chance to add to the Cup Winners' Cup and League title when Manchester United beat them in the FA Cup Final. Fellow Merseysiders Liverpool, in fact, had won the League, League Cup and European Cup the year before for their treble.

Manchester United had a shot at three trophies in 2007, the Champions' League, Premiership and FA Cup, while Chelsea, having already won the League Cup, briefly had a shot at all four. United were bundled out of the Champions' League by AC Milan, while Chelsea were pipped at the post by United in the domestic League.

British scouts watching the top European sides train in the last decade were surprised to see the players repeatedly perform a 'dying swan' act. It emerged that they were being taught how to fall over after a challenge so that the referee was more likely to award them the free-kick. Sadly, with the influx of foreign players in the Premiership continuing, the practice has caught on here. It is now not uncommon to see an English player diving theatrically to try and con the officials into giving them a penalty, and the yellow cards that should be given to the offenders are frequently not forthcoming.

It was rumoured in the 1970s that Malcolm Allison also coached his players to dive while he was in charge at Manchester City. Celebrated forward Francis Lee, known as Lee Won Pen for a short time for his knack of being awarded spot kicks, was particularly associated with the practice even though he strenuously denied it.

Play had to be halted during a children's match in Japan recently after an F1 tornado ripped across the pitch and caused minor damage.

Julius Agahowa celebrated his winning goal for Nigeria against Algeria in the 2002 African Cup of Nations with an outrageous routine. He completed seven consecutive somersaults from the Algerian penalty box back to the halfway line.

"Agahowa completed seven consecutive somersaults."

Dutch fans had something to cheer, or, rather, jeer when first round rejects from their version of Pop Idol were allowed to perform Tina Turner's 'The Best' at half time in a Vitesse Arnhem game in 2005. The crowd, understandably, were pleading with the hopefuls to stop after the first couple of lines but they continued to the ear-shattering and excruciating climatic chorus. Ouch!

Liverpool were 3-0 down to AC Milan at halftime in the 2005 Champions' League final. A Steven Gerrard-inspired comeback enabled them to claw back the deficit in an incredible second half, and then, with no more goals in extra time, it went to a penalty shootout. Liverpool held their nerves better and Jerzy Dudek, emulating the goal-line antics of predecessor Bruce Grobbelaar, saved from Shevchenko to win the most dramatic final. As mentioned earlier, AC Milan avenged this defeat in the 2007 final.

Commentator Speak 5

"Don't tell anyone coming in the result of this fantastic match, but let's have another look now at Italy's winning goal"
DAVID COLEMAN

"The Baggio brothers, of course, are not related"
GEORGE HAMILTON

"He knows all about the Italian opposition now that he plays in Turkey"
JOHN MOTSON

"You need at least eight or nine men in a ten-man wall"
MARK LAWRENSON

"Billy Gilbert hit a kamikaze back pass which Justin Fashanu pounced on like a black Frank Bruno"
IAN DARKE

"Was the ball entirely over the line? It didn't cross the line when it landed, unless it was over the line when it hit the bar"
BARRY DAVIES

"Goodnight, and don't forget to put your cocks back"
JIMMY HILL

"One or two of their players aren't getting any younger"
CLIVE TYLDESLEY

"It's Brazil 2 Scotland 1, so Scotland are back where they were at the start of the match"
BARRY DAVIES

"Some teams are named after letters of the alphabet. Brentford are the Bs, Leyton Orient are the Os, and everyone knows Manchester United are the Cs"
DES LYNAM

"Well what do you think of Manchester United's three Rs? Rooney, Ronaldo and van Nistelrooy"
ROB MCCAFFREY

"That would have been his second yellow card, if he'd already got his first one"
TREVOR BROOKING

"This game is balanced in Arsenal's favour"
JOHN MOTSON

"McCarthy gave Harte a special cuddle after he pulled him off"
BARRY DAVIES

Fighting Talk

"Serious sport has nothing to do with fair play. It's war minus the shooting"
GEORGE ORWELL

This is meant to be a light-hearted stroll through football's quirky past and as the nightmarish events of Heysel have already been touched upon, we'll leave the tragic side alone after this paragraph. Throughout the 1970s and 1980s both the game and its reputation here in Britain suffered at the hands of a minority of mindless hooligans. These people, if we can call them that, only sought to destroy the beautiful game, indeed many gangs still arrange to meet each other for bouts of extreme violence after matches today. The only difference is that mobile phones are used to coordinate the attacks whereas in the past the meetings were prearranged. Surprisingly, many of those participating are addicted to the rush of confrontation, and may include people who otherwise hold socially acceptable positions and careers. There is also a hard core who follow England to away games and invariably cause problems abroad. There hasn't been a major competition in recent times where England fans haven't been arrested. Sadly the other home nations are also responsible for letting out of control fans into Europe. In the Rangers - Osasuna match in Pamplona in March 2007, riots erupted inside and outside the Spanish stadium. Football violence looks here to stay unless the authorities find a way of coming down hard on the instigators, thereby putting off the followers. Instead of concentrating on the murky underworld, the shameful side of football, though, I'd like to look at the interesting and funny - though often tragic - spats and brawls, the handbags if you will.

I've also included a few occasions where players have been sent off for violent behaviour, but, again, emphasise that a simple list of players given their marching orders would fill several volumes. So I've tried to stream the candidates for inclusion using a series of criteria instead. How important was the game in which they were playing? How and why was the offence committed? Were there any broken bones involved? What were the repercussions? If the incident involves a number of interesting points then it's likely to be included, though, of course, you may judge that for yourselves.

Domestic Violence

In 1908 Manchester United embarked on an ambitious month-long tour of Europe. Towards the end of the trip they were pitted against Ferencvaro in Budapest. The Reds dominated the game and were soon seven goals clear. The referee, who didn't speak a word of English, then seemed to lose the plot and tried to send off three United players for no apparent reason. He claimed afterwards that they had infringed Hungarian laws, whatever they were. In pleading with the official, two United players gripped him by the shoulders and sparked all-out war. The fans saw this as a blatant attack on the ref and started hurling stones and other missiles at the players. The police tried to calm the crowd but the damage was done and the players were taken off.

The Auld Firm derby between Glasgow's two giants, Rangers and Celtic, sees perhaps the most keenly contested local match in the world, even rivalling the Rome derby between Lazio and AS Roma. Such was the tension north of the border for the 1909 Cup Final that the two sets of fans went at one another in pitched battles. The first match was drawn, as was the replay, but the trouble was so bad the Scottish FA felt they couldn't risk hosting a third encounter and the trophy was not awarded that year. The word derby came to football from the horserace at Epsom. It was adopted because football fans saw the race as an epic clash, and local games between the likes of Manchester's two clubs, and Tottenham and Arsenal were revered in the same way.

In 1912 Belfast Celtic's Windsor Park was the scene of a riot between the Catholic following of Celtic Park and the Protestants supporting Linfield. Trouble flared at halftime with Linfield leading 1-0. The players and officials were in their changing rooms when gunshots rang out across the park. No one seems to know what triggered the confrontation but it raged for more than half an hour and involved thousands. Miraculously no one was killed, though the local hospital had to deal with a hundred casualties with injuries ranging from fractured skulls to gunshot wounds, facial lacerations to broken bones. The match was abandoned and the players eventually left their changing rooms having been locked in for the duration of the skirmish. A terrorist's bomb destroyed a large section of the same ground in 1972.

Referee William Williams died after being attacked by Wattstown's Hansford in his changing room after their match against Aberaman in South Wales in 1912. It beggars belief but the player was only sentenced to a month in prison - for manslaughter - while Williams's family were offered no compensation because the match had finished and he wasn't on the pitch.

Millwall's ground, The Den, has been closed on more occasions than any other League ground in the country, the chief reason being football violence. Matches in 1920, 1934, 1947, 1950 and 1978 all left the stands in disarray and the club was forced to repair the damage. Goalkeepers were protected from missiles by using netting like chicken wire instead of conventional nets. The last game before they moved to the New Den in Docklands in 1993 was marked by crowd trouble, a pitch invasion, the theft of balls and the posts, and the letting down of the opposition's coach tyres. Nice place to go then…

The offside rules had to be changed in 1925 because, among others, Newcastle's fullback Bill McCracken worked out a way to perfect the offside trap. As a result, most of the star strikers in the country were nullified and the game became increasingly boring to watch. On one occasion there was even a pitch invasion as disgruntled fans tried to stop McCracken springing the trap. Though he escaped injury, the FA agreed with the fans and changed the rule to restrict the number of defenders from three to two who had to be goal-side as the through ball was played towards the front men.

The 1926 General Strike saw many matches arranged between local police and the strikers themselves. In Plymouth, tramcar workers became entangled with the law in a pitched battle on the streets one moment and the next they were facing each other at Home Park in a football match. The strikers (!) won 2-1 in front of 10,000, most of whom then went on the rampage through the town afterwards, breaking windows and scuffling with the police.

Rangers' centre-half Willie Woodburn was a volatile player who frequently found himself called before the disciplinary panels of his day. He was banned for a total of nine weeks one season for persistently tackling dangerously, and was then shocked to be given a life ban after punching Stirling's Alec Patterson in 1954. The Scottish FA wouldn't go back on their decision for three years, by which time Woodburn was past his best and no longer able to play at the highest level.

The 1965 FA Cup Final pitted Liverpool against Leeds, a match which the Merseysiders won 2-1. The following year the blue half of the city was represented, and they faced Sheffield Wednesday. As the two sides were introduced, Princess Margaret reportedly asked Everton captain Brian Labone a question:

HRH: *"Tell me, Mr Labone, where exactly is Everton?"*
BL: *"In Liverpool, Your Highness"*
HRH: *"Oh, we had your First Eleven here last year"*

Big Jack Charlton was a tough, no nonsense player and manager. He helped Leeds to the League and FA Cups in 1968 and 1972 respectively, as well as being voted footballer of the year in 1967, the season after England's historic World Cup win, in which he played an integral role. It is said that he carried round with him a little black book containing the names of all the players whom he'd have liked to have launched over the touchline. Denis Law once claimed the book contained only two names, and that he was one of them. Charlton, of course, went on to have great success with the Irish national side, taking them to the quarter-finals of the 1990 World Cup.

Liverpool's Jimmy Case was involved in a scrap with future team-mate Graham Souness at Anfield in the 1970s. They'd both been tussling for the ball but decided it was far more interesting to go at each other instead. There is a famous photo with Souness standing over the flat-out Case still waving his fists at him.

"...still waving his fists at him"

While managing Turkish side Galatasaray in 1996 Souness courted more controversy by planting the club's flag in the middle of arch rivals Fenerbahce's pitch. Not such a good idea.

Bill Shankly, the legendary Liverpool manager, always hated the trip down to the south coast to meet Southampton. After a number of bruising encounters had left several of his players injured, he referred to the Saints as:

"Alehouse brawlers"

This nickname was taken up by opponents and remained in use for some years afterwards.

Stoke's John Ritchie was sent off just 40 seconds after coming on in their match against Kaiserslauten in 1972, and that meant he didn't even touch the ball, a feat emulated by Kilmarnock substitute Bobby Houston in 1979. Vinny Jones, of course has multiple entries in this section. He was booked after just five seconds while playing for the Blades against Manchester City in 1991 and was eventually sent off. He managed to better the record the following year, reducing the time to three seconds in Chelsea's 1992 fixture with Sheffield Wednesday at Stamford Bridge.

He was clearly worked up just before kick-off and was prowling round the centre circle like a caged tiger. As soon as the referee blew his whistle Jones steamed in, took his own player out and then nailed the Wednesday striker. Then, as if he had done nothing wrong, he berated the official with:

"Referee, what was that for?"

As if he didn't know. Of course Jones also picked up his fair share of red cards in his career, though not quite as many as Roy McDonagh, who managed a staggering 21, 13 of which were in the English League, a record!

Nottingham Forest looked certain to score an FA Cup upset at St James' Park against Newcastle in 1974. They were 2-1 up and hunting for their third when Duncan McKenzie was fouled in the area by David Craig. Gordon Kew awarded the visitors the spot kick and George Lyall converted. Newcastle's Pat Howard was still arguing about the foul while the ball was being returned to the centre spot so Kew sent him off. Things looked bleak for the Magpies, that is until the crowd decided to intervene. Around 400 charged onto the pitch and began attacking the Forest players. In all 23 people needed hospital treatment and police were forced to delay the restart by nearly ten minutes. When the game finally got underway, the Forest players were clearly unhappy about the situation and performed well within themselves. Newcastle took full advantage and scored three late goals.

Their delight at going through was short-lived. An FA enquiry into the pitch invasion ruled that the game should be replayed at a neutral ground. The sides fought out a goalless draw before Newcastle's Malcolm MacDonald won the replay, both matches being played at Everton's Goodison Park. They eventually lost to Liverpool in the final however.

The 1974 Charity Shield (the first at Wembley) between Liverpool (1) and Leeds (1) was notable because the game boasted the first red cards shown to British players at the famous old stadium. Kevin Keegan and Billy Bremner were sent off for fighting, a brawl they apparently continued afterwards. Both men were so disgusted with the decision to dismiss them that they removed their shirts in protest and were both hit with five-match bans. Leeds manager Brian Clough was very clear about who he thought was to blame, and the outburst further soured the relationship he had with his own club:

"Bremner seemed intent on making Keegan's afternoon an absolute misery. He kicked him just about everywhere, up the arse, in the balls, until it became only a matter of time before a confrontation exploded"

*

The 1975 Derby - Leeds clash will be remembered for the clash it spawned. Francis Lee and Norman Hunter were known as two of the most volatile players around and it didn't take much of a spark to ignite the touch paper. Norman 'bites yer leg' Hunter threw a nice roundhouse right which almost put Lee down but he recovered in time to see the ref send them both packing. As they marched off, and they knew further punishment was all but meaningless, they decided to finish what they'd started and began going at it again. Even the dressing room door seemed to be no match for the warring pair as they continued the punch-up into the tunnel and beyond!

Two Stranraer players were sent off for fighting during a League match in 1975, the odd thing about the story being that they were scrapping with each other. A similar situation arose in the 1979 third round FA Cup tie between Charlton and Maidstone at the Valley. Charlton strikers Mike Flanagan and Derek Hales had a brief misunderstanding over the timing of a through ball with a few minutes to go and all of a sudden the gloves were off. Referee Brian Martin stood by the law, even though the trouble was between team-mates, and sent them both off for violent conduct. Nine-man Charlton held on for a 1-1 draw. The replay attracted a five figure crowd and they were treated to three goals before the floodlights failed! Charlton held on to win (2-1) when the match resumed.

There were more problems north of the border in 1994 when Hearts and Raith Rovers met in a pre-season 'friendly'. Hearts' Graham Hogg and Craig Levine had a disagreement over their defensive qualities and decided to sort out their differences at middleweight under the

Marquis of Queensbury rules, the only difference being that the gloves were certainly off. Both men landed with a couple of good shots before Levine put Hogg down and he had to be carted off on a stretcher. Added to the fact that he lost the fight, he broke his nose, was red carded and suspended. Levine fared somewhat better. He was made captain!

It is rumoured that Neil 'The Razor' Ruddock broke Robbie Fowler's nose, the one of touchline snorting fame, in 1995 because the striker stole his expensive shoes on a return flight from Eastern Europe. In reality, Fowler had warmed the bench for the match against Vladikavkaz and was not in a great mood on the flight home. He fell asleep but woke up to find his shoelaces had been clipped. When he went to his bag to replace them he found his bag handles and spare shoes had suffered similar treatment. Narrowing down the culprit to Steve Harkness, John Barnes or Ruddock, he then eliminated the first two, probably incorrectly as it happens. Fowler then borrowed some scissors from the flight crew (those were the days) and chopped up Ruddock's brand new £300 shoes, which didn't sit too well with the big defender. The Razor demanded a new pair, and Fowler told him to:

"Fuck right off"

So Ruddock smacked him. Fowler retaliated on the coach but was restrained by David James, who somehow managed to keep hold of him.

The Liverpudlian was involved in another scrap, this time with a certainty to make the Premiership's all-time worst XI, Tottenham's Mauricio Tarricco, in 2003. Tarricco was baiting the striker about his mythical drug habit by repeatedly calling him 'Smackhead'. So Fowler turned round and asked the Argentinean how the Falklands War had gone, shutting him up immediately.

Graeme Souness arrived at Liverpool in 1978 and immediately began helping himself to trophies. He was known as a midfield enforcer, a hard-man, and manager Tommy Docherty backed this up, much to the player's disagreement, by saying:

"They serve a drink in Glasgow called the Souness. Have one

*

Pensioner Sam Phillips, a lifelong Ledbury Town supporter, was banned from all home matches after he assaulted the referee in 1981!

Sheffield Wednesday fan Robert Montgomery tried, unsuccessfully as it turns out, to sue the club over a match they played in 1983. He saw their performance as so terrible it was not actually football at all, and vowed to get his money back under the Trades Description Act!

In 1985 Luton Town made a couple of changes that were to have a ripple effect in English football. First they installed an artificial pitch so that they could play in all kinds of weather, and then they introduced a member's only scheme for fans. Both ideas were doomed from the start and the pitch lasted only three years. The membership scheme then somehow proved irksome to visiting Millwall fans later that season and they, somewhat predictably, started a riot. Along with the tragic events from earlier that year (Heysel), this led to the government's increasing, though not always popular, involvement in the sport. Prime Minister Margaret Thatcher even went as far as to say that premises should be licensed to admit members only and believed that without such a scheme the future of the game in England was tenuous at best.

Two Argentinean players made the headlines for all the right reasons in the late 1970s and early '80s. They were succeeded by a certain Alberto Tarantini, however, who made his mark in a different way in 1987. Having played just 23 games for Birmingham City, the World Cup winner marched over to the opposition fans and started swinging. He was kicked out of the country shortly afterwards, never to return.

Leicester City met Burton Albion in the third round of the 1985 FA Cup at Derby's Baseball Ground. Both clubs were sponsored by breweries and there had clearly been a fair amount of the amber nectar flowing that afternoon. The fans of both were very boisterous and soon cans began raining down on the pitch. The match was finely poised at one each when Burton 'keeper Paul Evans was struck on the back of the head by a missile. A doctor advised him not to continue after the halftime break but he ignored the advice and shipped another five goals. A formal complaint about the Leicester fans was lodged after the game and the FA deemed that the match should be replayed behind closed doors at Coventry. Leicester won 1-0.

There was never any doubt as to where Bill Shankly's allegiance lay when asked about teams in the northwest:

"This city has two great teams: Liverpool and Liverpool reserves"

Bob Paisley, a servant to the club in some capacity for an incredible 56 years, was equally forthright about the red half of Merseyside, much to the annoyance of their rivals down the road at Goodison Park:

"We've had some bad times at Anfield. One year we came second"

Brian Clough was, according to a number of players, essentially a dictator. He's credited with initiating a number of confrontations, such as this one with Nigel Jemson in the Nottingham Forest dressing room:

BC: *"Have you ever been punched in the stomach, young man?"*
NJ: *"No"*
BC: *"Now you have"*

Clough also came to blows with two fans during a pitch invasion at their end of their 1989 League Cup quarter-final against Queen's Park Rangers, a match they won 2-1. He was fined £5,000 for bringing the game into disrepute, and banned from the touchline for the rest of the season. Another instance involves Everton players, who, having been beaten, thanks to a controversial goal, wrecked their dressing room. Clough knew the two would clash again in the League three days later and asked the cleaners not to bother tidying up. When Everton arrived at the weekend, the changing room was in the state in which they had left it.

St Mirren's William Abercromby managed to get himself sent off three times in the same match. He was shown a second yellow, and thus a red card, after an illegal challenge, but he argued the decision so vehemently that he was shown a further two red cards. Despite being fined and banned, he led the club to victory in the 1987 Scottish Cup having only just come off the transfer list!

Opposing players used to call Wimbledon 'keeper Dave Beasant 'Lurch' on account of his supposed resemblance to the vast but slow butler in the Addams Family. It has to be said that Beasant looked nothing like the character but the nickname stuck anyway. He didn't do himself any favours while playing for Southampton against Liverpool in 1996. He charged towards the corner flag to stop the ball going out and then cleared it straight to John Barnes who knocked it in.

Tommy Docherty is arguably more commonly remembered for his turn of phrase than his turn of pace. This line from 1988 was echoed up and down the country by all enemies of Manchester City:

"There are three types of Oxo cubes: Light brown is used for chicken stock, dark brown for beef, and light blue for laughing stock"

A certain former Southampton manager made this observation about Alan Shearer in 1989:

"He couldn't trap a bag of cement"

Shearer had the last laugh though. He went to Blackburn in 1992 and won the Premiership title in 1995, before moving to Newcastle for a then world-record fee of £15 million. There he eclipsed the great Jackie Milburn's goal-scoring record for the club. With England he was a prolific marksman, scoring 30 goals and helping them to the semi-final of Euro '96. He will surely be remembered as one of the finest home grown players of his generation. Perhaps Mr Nicholl will accept that he probably put his foot in that cement when making his observation.

Shearer did manage to tarnish his reputation though by craftily elbowing opponents while backing into them throughout his career.

And it was his vicious boot to Leicester's Neil Lennon's face during the 1997-98 season that almost prevented him from going to the World Cup in France. Instead of receiving an instant ban, Shearer reportedly threatened to walk out of the squad if he was punished. He wasn't of course.

It's rare to get an all-out brawl on the pitch between opposing players, and even rarer for the players involved to be team-mates, but thankfully for this chapter, it does happen occasionally. Liverpool's Steve McManaman failed to clear a corner against Everton in 1993 and Mark Ward collected the ball before driving it past Bruce Grobbelaar. McManaman knew he was partly to blame and apologised, but Grobbelaar was having none of it and chased him up the pitch throwing a mixture of hand slaps and abuse at his midfielder.

Long-time Reds manager, Alex Ferguson can usually be counted on to deliver a good line or two about opposing players, though perhaps not while aiming sharp objects (or pizzas) at effigies of arch rival Arsène Wenger:

"Dennis Wise could start a fight in an empty house"

This statement appeared to be borne out when Wise was convicted over a scrap with a taxi driver in 1995 and ended up enjoying a brief stay at Her Majesty's Pleasure. As player/manager at Millwall he put himself on with five minutes remaining against Sheffield United in 2003. He was off almost immediately after a nasty two-footed lunge at Chris Armstrong. Red cards always accompanied the red mist with Wise.

Volatile Dutchman Pierre van Hooijdonk angered a few Nottingham Forest players and fans by saying the team wasn't good enough for him. Manager Dave Bassett summed up their thoughts with:

"If he offered me an olive branch I'd stick it up his arse"

Bassett, incidentally, doesn't appear to know how to end a sentence when he's been asked a question and he continually looks for longer ways to reply to them, as he so ably demonstrates every time we have to sit through his mindless punditry on the television, which, as you can imagine, is almost as annoying as trying to get to the end of this paragraph, though you might have launched this book across the room or expired from lack of oxygen by now…

Eric Cantona was singled out for a fine bit of abuse by the Daily Star, after his kung-fu kick into the crowd at Crystal Palace in 1995 landed him in all sorts of bother with the authorities:

"The sh*t hits the fan"

The Frenchman had just been sent off for an appalling tackle on Richard Shaw, but as he was walking off the pitch he was being subjected to a fair amount of stick from the stands. The red mist suddenly descended and Cantona leaped over the advertising hoardings to boot one startled fan, Matthew Simmonds. Not a good example for all the younger viewers to follow. Peter Schmeichel came to try and help restore order but only ended up wearing a cup of tea intended for the Frenchman instead! As the recriminations gathered pace, Cantona was banned for nine months, fined £20,000, stripped of his country's captaincy and was ordered to do 120 hours' community service (he enjoyed the latter - teaching under privileged kids - so much that he claimed there was no punishment in it at all). The incident also dented United's chances of taking any silverware that season. They lost the League title race to Blackburn, and Everton knocked them out at the final hurdle in the FA Cup. Simmonds, incidentally, was charged with incitement of racial hatred and banned from all grounds. He immediately tried to attack the prosecuting solicitor and ended up behind bars.

The National Portrait Gallery was approached two years later to exhibit a painting of the Frenchman, but critic Gavin Stamp was quick to say why this wouldn't happen:

"He's a footballer, he's a thug, and he's French"

A similar incident occurred in Central America five years later during a club game between Olympia and Mantagua in Honduras. One fan got more than he bargained for after repeatedly abusing the players. One of them decided he'd had enough, took a leaf out of Eric's book and attacked the man for a good few minutes. What security personnel there were thought it best to let the scrap reach its natural conclusion before stepping in, though by then team-mates had come to the rescue of the fan.

You couldn't have a chapter on football violence without some reference to Roy Keane. Before he joined Manchester United he was with Nottingham Forest under legendary manager Brian Clough. Old Big Head himself reportedly only had one major bust-up with his star midfielder but recalls:

"I only ever hit him the once but it can't have been very hard because he got up"

Then, in a match between Manchester United and Leeds at Elland Road in 1997, Keane suffered a serious knee ligament injury in a tussle with Alfe-Inge Haaland. Though he hadn't seen how badly Keane went down, Haaland suggested that the midfielder might have dived and told the prone Irishman exactly that. Keane spent the next four years seething with anger, and revenge seemed the only way to repay the insult. Haaland had moved to Manchester City during that time and the local derby provided Keane with the opportunity for which he'd spent years waiting. Instead of going for the ball, he raised his studs and brutally chopped Haaland down in front of referee David Elleray, who supposedly bore a grudge against Keane. There can be no argument about this sending off though, which was made even clearer to Elleray when Keane spat at the injured man. It was a shocking tackle designed to maim and finish Haaland's career, as Keane claimed in his autobiography:

"I fucking hit him hard"

Then Keane, in the process of marching off, remembered the little word Haaland had in his ear. So he strolled over the prone Norwegian and said:

"Take that, you cunt!"

Keane was fined a record £150,000 and banned for five matches, though some would think even this was far too lenient for such a dreadful tackle. He managed to get himself into more trouble the same year by claiming that:

"The home fans probably have the prawn sandwiches and don't realise what's going on out on the pitch"

Of course this was simply a dig at the number of corporate hospitality guests allowed in to watch the home matches, often at the expense of the true fan.

I was lucky enough to be at Old Trafford for the last game of the 1997 season, that against West Ham. The Premiership trophy was presented before the match and then the Reds set about hammering the opposition. Sitting with my roast beef, Yorkshire pudding and all the trimmings in the directors' box, I couldn't help but notice that hundreds of guests refused even to face the pitch. I ended up sitting outside on the balcony on my own.

In an Orient - Stevenage match the ball was kicked into the crowd. When the Orient midfielder went to collect it, a fan threw it back with some force right into his face.

"A fan threw the ball back with some force..."

As he stepped up to have a quiet word with the fan, the entire section of the crowd rushed forward and dared him to try it. The player wisely backed down and the match continued.

Bolton players became embroiled in a brawl with the visiting Manchester United side in 1997. It was such a weak affair that John McGinley was moved to observe:

"It was like being on a girls' night out"

The Plymouth - Chesterfield match in 1997 was memorable for the number of red cards dished out. An Argyle player was sent off for a two-footed lunge which sparked a mass brawl. Four more players, including Kevin Davies, were sent off following Bruce Grobbelaar's late intervention. And in December of the same season, five players were red-carded during the Bristol Rovers - Wigan Athletic match.

Birmingham's Steve Claridge delivered a nice line about the skills of Barry Fry in 1997:

"Someone said you could write his knowledge of management on a postage stamp, but I think you would need to fold it in half"

While managing Barnet, Fry came up with a novel way of not being sacked. Owner Stan Flashman reportedly gave the coach his marching orders on at least a dozen occasions, but Fry simply turned up for work the next day as if the conversation had never happened. When he finally gave in to the barrage of criticism, he fired a parting shot at Flashman:

"He's a complete and utter shit"

But let's go back to Steve Claridge for a moment. While at Cambridge United he had a touchline altercation with manager John Beck. Within a week the striker had been sold, while Cambridge slipped down the division and were relegated.

Manager Speak 5 - Whatever Next?

"At this stage of the season, I just tell the players to get points under their bags"
GEORGE GRAHAM

*"He's carrying his left leg, which,
to be honest, is his only leg"*
STEVE COPPELL

*"The important thing is that he shook
hands with us over the phone"*
ALAN BALL

"I've had an interest in racing all my life, longer really"
KEVIN KEEGAN

"We must have had 99% of the match. It was the other 3% that cost us"
RUUD GULLIT

"Michael Owen is a good goalscorer but not a natural born one, at least not yet. That takes time"
GLENN HODDLE

"The problem at Wimbledon seems to be that the club has suffered a loss of complacency"
JOE KINNEAR

"Think of a number between 10 and 11"
RON ATKINSON

"Hunt has proved on a few occasions that he's a clever type, but his challenge on Nick Montgomery earlier in the game wasn't clever either"
NEIL WARNOCK

"Football is like a big market place. People go to the market every day to buy their vegetables"
BOBBY ROBSON

"Although we're playing Russian Roulette, we're also obviously playing Catch 22 at the moment, and it's a difficult scenario to get my head round"
PAUL STURROCK

"If Glenn Hoddle said one word to his team at halftime, it would have been concentration and focus"
RON ATKINSON

"On reflection of this game it was probably an awkward time for us to score the third"
GLENN HODDLE

"Luis Figo is totally different to David Beckham and vice versa"
KEVIN KEEGAN

"You've got to miss them to score sometimes"
DAVE BASSETT

Blackburn Rovers were playing a Champions' League tie against Spartak Moscow in 1996 when David Batty and Graeme Le Saux collided while chasing a through ball. Instead of continuing their runs, the players decided to get the handbags out and start swinging, and eventually had to be separated by team-mates.

It's unusual, but not unheard of, for players to come to blows behind closed doors at training. West Ham's Eyal Berkovic had a main course of John Hartson's boot in front of the TV cameras in 1998 though, the action costing the volatile striker £20,000 and a three-match suspension. It wasn't the first time that Hartson had put his foot in it (got into trouble with the authorities, that is, not presented Berkovic with a leather sandwich), but his poor team-mate can't have expected to get his jaw broken. The incident prompted a caller to a TV phone-in show to ask Hartson's then girlfriend:

"What's it like living with a lunatic?"

Dennis Wise again failed to live up to his name when he scaled the dizzy heights of the bottom bunk to attack team-mate Callum Davidson while the Leicester City man was sleeping during their pre-season tour of Finland in 1998. The punch connected, the jaw was broken, the wise man was sacked. He lost his appeal for unfair dismissal and is now at Leeds having answered an advert with 'no brain cells required' somewhere in the wording. Or perhaps it was 'financial knowledge unnecessary'... Rumour has it that the club is going to adopt the Status Quo anthem 'Down Down' on account of how many times opposition fans seem to sing it at Elland Road.

Okay, so most of us have had a few too many at the office Christmas party before. But when Manchester City's Jamie Tandy was offered a celebratory cigar by Joey Barton in 2004, he can't have expected the thug to stub out the Montechristo in his face. Put that in your eye and smoke it. Of course the other version of the story had Tandy earning the assault by setting light to Barton's shirt, while he was still in it…

More recently, Kieron Dyer and Lee Bowyer came to blows while playing for Newcastle against Aston Villa at St James' Park in 2005. The home side were three goals down and Bowyer was becoming increasingly upset about Dyer refusing to pass him the ball. The problem gradually escalated until the two were trading punches. The referee then rightly sent them both off for violent conduct, thus giving them plenty of time to contemplate their stupidity. Bowyer received a £30,000 fine from the FA, while Newcastle docked him six weeks' wages and gave him a seven-match ban. Dyer got away comparatively lightly, receiving only a three-match ban.

Bowyer was also involved in an incident in the town centre that led to an Asian man, Sarfraz Najeib, being hospitalised, though the midfielder was cleared of any wrong-doing by the courts in 2001. Rodney Marsh quietened the chorus of voices hinting at racial motivation for the alleged assault:

"I don't think he's racist at all. He would stamp on anyone's head"

Now it's time to move into dark territory with the player branded 'The most hated man in football', Australian hard-nut Kevin Muscat. Ian Wright reportedly left a ball to strike partner Dougie Freedman when he got the call from behind in 1999. Wright then turned round to see Muscat grinning like a Cheshire…well, you know, and the defender cleared the ball instead. He wasn't just a bit cheeky though. Oh no. He was well known for charging in to tackle opponents from behind, especially when the ball and referee's gaze were nowhere near the action. He seriously injured both Craig Bellamy (okay, so we're not too bothered about that) and Frenchman Christophe Dugarry, the latter with a terrible lunge in 2001 that was described as "an act of brutality" by French manager Roger Lemerre given that the match was supposed to be a friendly. Remember, this is the man made captain of Millwall by Dennis Wise. If that doesn't worry you, then perhaps this does:

In 1998 Charlton's Matt Holmes was hospitalised after an encounter with the defender almost left him with only one leg. Seriously. Some TV channels were asked not to show the incident until after the 9 pm watershed. Surgeons were contemplating amputating the limb, but after four operations they managed to save it. A lawsuit filed at the High Court in 2004 resulted in Holmes winning almost £750,000 in damages.

You'd have thought that this would have calmed the 'player' down a little. Not a chance. Muscat moved back to Australia and was immediately banned for violent conduct. Then, in 2006, he decked Adelaide United coach John Kosmina while the latter was simply returning the ball. Muscat, incidentally, spent some time with Rangers, but he was never selected to play in the Auld Firm match. Can you guess why? I think they should have played him. If he lasted the match, I'd have chucked him in the stands with the Celtic fans for a while. That would have taught the 'man' a lesson he wouldn't forget in a hurry.

Arsenal's Patrick Vieira was known for taking the occasional theatrical tumble when the tackler's leg was somewhere within three feet of him, but he was also lost a good deal of respect by proving he could spit a bit too. In their 1999 encounter with West Ham, Razor Ruddock had been getting right up his nose with a series of abusive rants and hard tackles and Vieira suddenly decided he'd had enough. He lost his cool and committed his second yellow card offence, which resulted in the obvious red. He steamed back into the fray only to be met by Ruddock, who was now giving him his marching orders too. So he mustered a mouthful of phlegm and deposited it squarely on Ruddock's chest, which didn't go down too well.

Aston Villa's Savo Milosevic, dubbed Miss-a-lot-evic, for obvious reasons, endured a stormy time in the Midlands. Manager Brian Little became frustrated with the striker and was apparently on the verge of letting him go, when Little himself got the boot. Milosevic cemented his bad boy image by piling into the crowd and spitting at them. One disgruntled fan was moved to write to the Evening Mail in 1997 to complain that Milosevic:

"is the most one-footed player since Long John Silver"

*

Robbie Fowler celebrated a goal against Everton in the 1999 Merseyside derby by crouching next to the goal-line and pretending to snort it like cocaine. This was a supposed dig at Everton's smack-heads, or so claimed the media, presumably not realising that 'smack' is a slang term for heroin. The player said afterwards:

"I suppose I shouldn't have been so obvious in taunting the Everton fans, but I can't believe how much stick I got for it"

Fowler decided to try and renew his season ticket at the bottom of the Mersey when he scored another against Everton, only this time it was for Manchester City a couple of seasons later. He ran along the touchline smacking his head, for obvious reasons, not the wisest course of action in the northeast.

He offended some in the south too by repeatedly wagging his backside at Chelsea's Graeme Le Saux in 1999. He was insinuating that Le Saux was gay, this despite the Londoner having a wife and family, so the Chelsea player clipped him round the ear. They made a public apology afterwards but everyone knew there was no meaning behind the words. Le Saux received a one-match ban and Fowler a two-game suspension. The Scouser was in trouble again after being caught drinking heavily in 2003. He was reportedly:

"So wrecked that he snorted the salt for his tequila"

"...he snorted the salt"

Seasoned drinkers, however, will know that this is all part of the 'Suicide Slammer' routine, where the salt in snorted, the tequila set alight and drunk, and the lemon is then carefully squeezed into one eye... Oh, well, I suppose I'd better insert a disclaimer of sorts here. Please don't try this at home as it's not very clever and should be restricted to professional footballers and idiots only. No need for a Venn diagram there then...

The Sheffield United - West Brom match in 2002 will be remembered for all the wrong reasons. There were a number of terrible two-footed challenges and referee Eddie Wolstenholme had no option but to dismiss three Blades players. The first to go was 'keeper Simon Tracey who handled the ball outside the area after just ten minutes. Santos and Suffo were then brought on as substitutes but they both set the rather dubious record of being immediately sent off. Santos was red carded for yet another dangerous tackle, while Suffo head-butted an opponent in the melee after the incident (they never played for United again). At this point United were 3-0 down and defeat looked certain. But then an injury to Rob Ullathorne changed all that. He limped off, and, as Neil Warnock had already used all his subs, United didn't have enough players on the pitch to continue and the match was abandoned. This was the first time in British football that a match had to be called off for a lack of legal players, though the FA eventually decided that the result should stand.

One of football's most famous incidents occurred in the dressing room at Old Trafford in February 2003. Manchester United had just lost to Arsenal in the FA Cup and manager Alex Ferguson wasn't too pleased. In a fit of rage he kicked a boot across the room, which just so happened to fly into David Beckham's face, cutting him above the left eyebrow. Of course the fans already had something lined up when Beckham, stitches and all, appeared on the pitch for United's next match:

"Do you think I'm Becksy?"

(This wasn't the first time, and it was never going to be the last either, that Ferguson had blown his top with his players. Apparently Peter Barnes heard Ferguson thundering round the dressing room shouting his name in the 1980s. Barnes, thinking quickly, dived headlong into the communal bath and held his breath until the fuming manager had disappeared.)

Even Dame Barbara Cartland got stuck into the Beckhams when she heard they might become neighbours:

"I dread it; they have lots of money but no class"

George Best was equally derogatory about David's ability as a footballer:

"He can't kick with his left foot, can't head the ball and can't tackle"

And here are Bryan Robson's thoughts about John Fashanu:

"Not blessed with talented feet. He'll knock people out of the way to get the ball"

John's brother Justin was also singled out for a rather unfair helping of abuse when, in 1989, he revealed his homosexuality. He found immediately that although he was a footballer of some talent, the top clubs refused to negotiate with him. The story has a tragic ending too, for Justin killed himself in 1998.

Chester captain Mark Jackson was given a second yellow card, and thus his marching orders, after aiming a boot at Rochdale manager Mick Docherty while the latter was calmly sitting on the bench. Jackson should have been retrieving the ball but he thought he'd have a quick dig at the opposing coach first. Not very sensible considering the referee was only five yards away at the time.

In 2003, the Arsenal - Manchester United rivalry that had been simmering, and occasionally boiling, finally came to a head in a League match. Ruud Van Nistelrooy had leaped all over Patrick Vieira's back and had knocked the big Frenchman to the ground. Vieira reacted angrily and lashed out with a boot, which Van Nistelrooy claimed had been aimed at his groin. Vieira was sent off but felt he had to let the Dutchman know exactly what he thought of him, and not even the intervention of legendary hard-man Roy Keane could put him off. Van Nistelrooy had the chance to rub salt into the Arsenal wounds by scoring a last minute penalty to win the game, but, you guessed it, he missed, sparking yet another round with the handbags drawn. Ray Parlour gave him a nice little dig in the ribs to thank him for hitting the bar, before Martin Keown clouted him on the back of the head, somehow contorting his face to appear even more repulsive than normal and then launching into a blistering four-letter-word tirade.

The managers then decided to get in on the act after an encounter in October 2004. The match had been pretty bad tempered, a foregone conclusion given the recent history between the two, and afterwards Wenger was reportedly quite ready for a punch-up with Ferguson in the Old Trafford tunnel. Sadly the tension was alleviated when the two ended up trading pizza instead. Thankfully neither man decided to top himself...

They did have a few choice words for each other though:

AW: *"It's wrong that the fixtures are delayed so their players can rest and then win everything"*
AF: *"He's a complete novice who should keep his opinions about football in Japan"*

Many believe that the bad blood between the two clubs stemmed from the 1990 encounter, when a Nigel Winterburn tackle on Brian McLair precipitated an all-in brawl. The United player objected to the strength of the challenge and repeatedly booted Winterburn while he was still on the ground. Of course the other players soon joined in though McLair was the only man to see red.

The 2004 Barcelona - Celtic UEFA Cup tie was also a bad tempered affair. Celtic defender Bobo Balde was inspired, despite a couple of nasty challenges that for some reason went unpunished, and Thiago Motta was unable to make any penetrating runs from Barcelona's midfield. As the players left the pitch at halftime a brawl erupted in the tunnel. Motta was red carded immediately, and was thus assumed to be the trouble-maker, but it was unclear who was on the receiving end of his handbag.

"...of course the other players soon joined in"

Though it's likely it was Balde or 'keeper Rab Douglas, who claimed he acted as peacemaker, there are some that say Motta was trying to wing team-mate Ronaldinho! Douglas was the one who was sent off though. Back on the pitch, things were calm for a minute or two of the second half before Saviola launched another attack - of the physical kind - on Thompson, an assault that earned him a red card too. Celtic eventually won 1-0 and Barca were out of the competition.

Becky Hendrie wasn't too pleased to find out that husband Lee, then an Aston Villa player, had a teenage mistress in 2004. She decided the best place to vent her fury was on the side of his new Porsche Cayenne Turbo, scratching:

"Prick - Wanker"

Not a bad double-barrelled surname as it happens.

Craig Bellamy arrived in Newcastle in 2001 with a message for Tyneside legend Alan Shearer:

"You're too old and too slow. You couldn't even kiss my arse"

Shearer was none too impressed with the volatile front-man and replied:

"If you ever step foot in Newcastle again, I'll knock your block off"

Indeed Bellamy's time in the northeast was marred by confrontation. He admitted that he'd threatened to fake an injury ahead of an Arsenal match, and then accused manager Graham Souness of lying about his condition. Two days after the match he was fined two weeks' wages, and on transfer deadline day in 2005 Bellamy was shipped off in a loan move to Celtic. He was then offered a chance by Birmingham City, but reportedly sent a text to Souness and chairman Freddy Shepherd saying:

"I am Craig Bellamy. I don't play for shit football clubs. You are a rubbish boss"

In September 2006 Magpies assistant manager Terry McDermott called him:

"A little upstart, he was hated at Newcastle"

On this evidence the Welshman could certainly teach Shane Warne a thing or two about texting though.

Commentator Speak 6

"And I suppose Spurs are nearer to be being out of the FA Cup now than at any other time since the first half of the season, when they weren't ever in it anyway"
JOHN MOTSON

"Arsenal are quick to credit Bergkamp with laying on 75% of their nine goals"
TONY GUBBA

"They've maintained their fine unbeaten record between the legs"
BARRY DAVIES

"They weren't even breathing at times thanks to their fitness and strength"
GAVIN PEACOCK

"He's got a knock on his shin just above the knee"
FRANK STAPLETON

"Roy Keane going to Celtic would be a case of out of the goldfish bowl and into the fire"
RADIO COMMENTATOR

"That was the perfect penalty, only he missed it"
ROB MCCAFFREY

"He had defenders swarming around him like a wet blanket"
GERRY ARMSTRONG

"When England go to Turkey there could be fatalities or, even worse, injuries"
PHIL NEAL

"Scholes has four players in front of him - five if you count Gary Neville"
DARRAGH MOLONEY

"For those of you watching in black and white, Spurs are in the all yellow strip"
JOHN MOTSON

"You cannot fail to be unimpressed by the work Pearce has done"
MARK LAWRENSON

"Van Persie's adjusting his undershorts with Van Nistelrooy in his sights"
PETER DRURY

"Germany, not for the first time this century, invading Czech territory"
RON ATKINSON

"Football today is like a game of chess. It's all about money"
NEWCASTLE FAN

Arsène Wenger has shifted his attention to Chelsea boss Jose Mourinho since the self-proclaimed 'special one' arrived in London. He accused Chelsea of tapping up (making an illegal approach for) Ashley Cole in January 2005, and was further angered by Mourinho's refusal to shake his hand after a match at Christmas the same year.

Mourinho is fast becoming an expert on winding up opponents. He and Bryan Robson almost came to blows after he was accused of keeping the West Brom manager waiting after halftime in 2005, and then he refused to shake his hand. This resulted in a few choice words passing between the two, Mourinho's Portuguese clashing strongly with Robson's, dare I call it, English.

And who can forget the 2005 Carling Cup Final against Liverpool. Mourinho angered the Liverpool fans by holding his finger to his lips and shushing them when Chelsea scored. It was a bizarre own goal as it turns out, in that captain Steven Gerrard scored a classic header at the wrong end. The gesture angered many neutrals - though some did manage to see the funny side - and indeed it must have upset the officials because Mourinho was banned from the dugout and sent to the stands instead. Chelsea went on to win 2-1. The Merseysiders had a revenge of sorts in the Champions' League semi-final at Anfield when thousands of fans held up 'Shut up Mourinho' boards. Liverpool, of course, went on to win the trophy that year.

Chelsea's William Gallas was given a headache after a cheeky butt from Everton's James Beattie connected in 2005. You can guess the headline:

"Beattie and Butthead"

Blackburn's fiery little striker Paul Dickov squared up to Portsmouth's six-footer Pedro Mendes recently after the two had collided during a 50-50 challenge:

"You're a fucking shithole! Fuck off!"

It's unclear what Mendes's knee thought of the striker's outburst…

Alan Sugar, the former Spurs chairman, has never been one to keep his opinions to himself. He delivered this famous line in 2005:

"Footballers are scum, total scum. If they weren't football players most of them would be in prison"

Manchester United's Gary Neville immediately tried to prove him right. That season he stormed over to the family enclosure at Goodison Park, contorted his face with rage (okay, I'll accept that no further contortions are possible given his current appearance, otherwise the entire crowd would have turned to stone), and yelled:

"You're a bunch of fucking wankers"

Well, there is a seven-letter word in there so his elocution lessons must be starting to bear fruit…

And Birmingham City supremo David Sullivan summed up the thoughts of many with:

"In the main, the average footballer is not a nice person"

Arsène Wenger and the then West Ham manager Alan Pardew had a touchline altercation in 2006 that led to the Frenchman being fined £10,000. In a break from tradition for the Gunners' boss he didn't claim not to have seen the incident. He was fined again for arguing with referee Steve Bennett in early 2007.

Sir Alex Ferguson traded abuse with referee Graham Poll during Manchester United's spring 2006 clash with old enemies Arsenal. Poll instructed Ronaldo to get to his feet after a collision with Alexander Hleb when Ferguson marched over and shouted:

Fuck off! He got the ball"

Poll was quick to dismiss the irate manger with:

"Hey, don't you 'fuck off' me again"

Manchester City's Joey Barton had a pop at both Steven Gerrard and Frank Lampard after they released their autobiographies in the wake of England's sorry exit from the 2006 World Cup. He, like any other fan, was disappointed in the midfield duo's performances and felt he was entitled to say what he thought:

"I played shit. Oh, here's my book"

The pair, who have recently been teamed up with Barton under new coach Steve McLaren, were not amused, Lampard replying:

"He said he was up every morning at 6 am running. The difference is we were doing that from age eleven. I realise being a pro you should not talk about other players though"

Don't then.

Manchester City's Ben Thatcher cemented his reputation as a dirty player when he knocked out Portsmouth's Pedro Mendes with a vicious elbow at the beginning of the 2006-07 season. Mendes required hospital treatment after suffering a seizure brought on by the assault. It wasn't the first time Thatcher had been warned about his eager use of the arm. Allan Nielsen, Nicky Summerbee, Ralph Welch and a number of others have complained about Thatcher's blatant thuggery.

Tottenham's Jermaine Defoe was lucky to stay on the pitch after being tackled clumsily from behind by West Ham's Javier Mascherano. The West Ham man was booked, as was Defoe for his immediate reaction, which was to bite the tackler on the arm. Now he might have been fooling about but this was hardly an example to set the children watching. Referee Steve Bennett showed him a yellow and not a red card.

Defoe was lucky again after another incident against Sheffield United in 2007. Spurs had gone 1-0 up but they'd then imploded and gifted the home side two goals. After being tripped for the umpteenth time that afternoon, Defoe finally lost it and began pushing and shoving the United players. It was described as a 'classic case of handbags' by the commentary team as there were no actual punches thrown.

On the same weekend Portsmouth's Pedro Mendes, one who truly manages to get himself in the wars, was singled out for some hard hitting tackles by Manchester City's Joey Barton. Mendes had just scored a spectacular thirty-yard half-volley so Barton decided to see him off with a nasty rake of the studs down his Achilles tendon. There must be something about Mendes that winds opponents up, possibly his haircut, which reminds older viewers of the great Charlie George.

Arsenal's Thierry Henry will be remembered as one of the world's nicer great players (in the pre-match build-up he'd given youngster Theo Walcott a hug for nearly half a minute), but he does have a nasty streak that we glimpse occasionally. In their 2007 clash with Wigan at the new Emirates Stadium, Wigan were a goal to the good and 'keeper Chris Kirkland probably reminded Henry of the fact each time the striker missed. When the ball finally ended up in Kirkland's net, due to an own goal from Hall, Henry picked the ball up and held it in front of the goalie's face while giving him a tirade of abuse. Kirkland, of course, replied with a simple:

"Fuck off, will you"

This angered the striker who seemed ready to continue the spat before he was led away by team-mates. Wigan manager Paul Jewell was incensed and marched angrily up and down inside his technical area, whatever that's supposed to be… Henry was booked for ungentlemanly conduct. Arsenal then rubbed salt into Wigan's wounds and elicited further outbreaks of bad-will with a late winner from Thomas Rosicky. Jens Lehmann, for example, was immediately booked for time-wasting and was lucky not to be sent off for dissent when he started arguing with the referee. Jewell steamed onto the pitch at fulltime to remonstrate with Phil Dowd, angered chiefly by a cast-iron penalty for a foul on Heskey that was not given. Heskey himself will wish he hadn't wheeled away in celebration during the match itself. He thought he'd scored but Lehmann somehow turned his shot onto the post. If Heskey had been alert, and not running towards the corner flag arms aloft, he would have easily knocked in the rebound and Wigan would probably have won.

While Harry Redknapp was in the middle of a TV interview one of his players thought it would be fun to aim a ball at the gaffer's head. Harry wasn't to happy, as you can appreciate, when the ball smacked him on the ear:

"Why the fuck have you hit that over here? You've got some fucking brains, haven't you? Oh, you were aiming for the goal, were you? Well that's why you're in the fucking reserves"

Here's another happy Harry comment after a recent loss:

"I'm going to grab a bottle of wine on the way home to knock myself out"

Personally speaking, I would have drunk it first…

Dennis Wise was sent off yet again in March 2007, only this time - and not for the first time - it was from the dugout to the stands. Referee Nigel Miller took offence to his tirade over a penalty appeal in Leeds' fixture against Southend and banished him. Wise remarked afterwards:

"I've had problems with him before. I hope the assessor puts him

down a couple of divisions"

He was probably thinking along the same lines, but would have liked to delete the last four words...

Jose Mourinho escaped punishment from the FA after calling referee Mike Riley a 'Filho da puta' or 'Son of a whore' during their FA Cup quarter-final tie against Tottenham in March 2007. Riley did not mention the halftime incident in his report and instructed the FA not to pursue the matter further.

Frank Lampard was on the receiving end of a healthy dose of abuse from a couple of Spurs fans, one of whom threw a punch at the midfielder after the Blues' 2-1 victory over their north London rivals in the quarter-final replay. Security guards and police eventually disentangled Lampard and Drogba from the melee, after which five arrests were made. The two fans were given £300 fines before being banned from White Hart Lane for life. Tottenham's coaching duo of Chris Hughton and Clive Allen avoided the crowd trouble but ended up trading insults with Mourinho's assistant Baltemar Brito instead.

West Ham's former Blackburn player Lucas Neil received a chorus of abuse from the Ewood Park faithful when he returned there in 2007. He thought the outburst thoroughly unpleasant saying:

"I was totally committed to the club for over five years. I never complained, never missed training, never missed games and always gave everything. I was disappointed with the disgusting reception"

Barnsley and Birmingham had just fought out a tense match at the end of their 2007 season when the players decided that not quite enough fighting had been done. Barnsley's Bobby Hassell and Birmigham's Neil Danns were immediately ordered off, even though Mike Russell had already blown the final whistle, before the management and both benches thought they'd contribute to the brawl.

Holmbury St Mary were battling it out at the top of the Guildford

& Woking Alliance League in their 2006-07 season when they visited Addlestone. The home side started brightly and were soon two goals to the good. Then, after launching a violent attack (headbutt and attempted punch) on George Archer, Addlestone's striker was sent off. Holmbury 'keeper Richard Stone then joined him on the sidelines after wrestling him to the ground and giving him a thorough verbal pasting (for which he received an eight-week ban). Addlestone's 'keeper was the next to go for a deliberate handball outside the area and Holmbury sensed a chance to peg back the lead. The prolific Brad Dougal and captain Mark Turner both netted, the latter with a perfect lob over the advancing 'keeper, to tie the scores at 2-2. And they were two men to the good five minutes later when Addlestone had another man sent off for a second yellow card. With twenty-five minutes to go and with ten against eight, you'd have thought Holmbury would run out comfortable winners. A defensive mix up and a wonder strike late in the game sunk their chances though as Addlestone pulled off the unlikeliest of victories.

The Chelsea team coach was struck by a brick on the way to West Ham's Upton Park in 2007. Though the window cracked, no one was hurt. If it had been thrown by one of the West Ham strikers, it probably would have missed, one observer noted.

Fulham's Michael Brown found himself in hot water with the FA after appearing to head-butt Liverpool's Xabi Alonso during their end-of-season clash in May 2007. And Blackburn's Jason Roberts managed to get two yellow cards in less than thirty seconds in their crucial UEFA Cup-chasing match with Tottenham a couple of days later. He'd tripped one of the Spurs men and been shown the first yellow by referee Rob Stiles, but decided the official needed to hear his opinion:

"You're a wanker"

Of course Stiles then showed him the second yellow and he was off. And the language got predictably worse accordingly:

"Now you're being a fucking prick!"

*

I've always wanted to be able to include my all-time favourite team in a book. Everybody must have a Greatest XI, and most would also have their best national side listed somewhere. There must also be a top Premiership starting line-up. Well, as this is the fighting talk chapter, I'm going to shun all the fabulous players and go for the Red Card XI instead. Imagine the look on your team-mates' faces if they had to play against these Premiership bad boys. I've had to play a couple of them out of position, but when you're only going to kick lumps out of the opposition, then neither tactics nor the ball assume any relevance. The formation, for what it's worth, is 3-4-1-2:

Paul Dichov   Craig Bellamy

El-Hadji Diouf

Lee Bowyer   Vinny Jones   Roy Keane   Robbie Savage

Ben Thatcher   Kevin Muscat (c)   Martin Keown

Mark Bosnich (GK)

Substitutes: Duncan Ferguson, Gary Neville, Jens Lehmann
Manager: Graham Souness
Coach: Dennis Wise

Commentator Speak 7

"I've seen players sent off for far worse offences than that"
ALAN BRAZIL

"Seaman, just like a falling oak, manages to change direction"
JOHN MOTSON

"He's got his tactics wrong tactically"
MICK QUINN

"That was only about a yard away from being an inch-perfect pass"
MURDO MACLEOD

"For such a small man Maradona gets great elevation on his balls"
DAVID PLEAT

"Stoichkov is pointing at the bench with his eyes"
DAVID PLEAT

"He reminds me of a completely different version of Robbie Earle"
MARK LAWRENSON

"That header was cleared off the line by the crossbar"
SIMON BROTHERTON

"Ruud Gullit is imposing his multi-lingual skills on this match"
JOHN MOTSON

"He says that he'll walk away from the game when his legs go"
RADIO COMMENTATOR

"The Bulgarians are doing all they can here to waste every last inch of time"
COLIN MACNAMARA

"Football's gone a little bit more corporate nowadays, and that's taken the man out of the street"
Lee Dixon

"Michael Owen has got the legs of a salmon"
Sky TV commentator

"Quite literally, you wouldn't have put your shirt on him"
Clive Tyldesley

1234567891011

International Incidents

There are numerous stories of countries trading insults and blows on and off the football pitch, so I've had to be quite selective with the anecdotes below. Hopefully most will tickle the ribs, while others might provoke a grimace or wince.

William Ashurst and A. Bowyer almost came to blows during an England - Wales encounter in 1925. Rumour has it that this exchange passed between them:

"Now then, my man, we want none of that here. Now, why don't thee just fuck off?"

When England met reigning World Champions Italy at Highbury in 1934, the match was billed as the most important game in the world since the end of the Great War. The largely Arsenal contingent soon found themselves on the receiving end of some awful tackling, the Italians retaliating after claiming that their star man Monti's broken toe was the result of reckless English play. Captain Eddie Hapgood suffered a broken nose as a result and many of the home side were repeatedly clattered from behind. It seemed that the match would degenerate further but the English players managed to control their tempers and held on to win 3-2. The Italians went home empty handed, literally. They had been promised vast sums of money and cars, and would also be exempt from military service had they won.

England travelled to Germany to play their hosts in the Berlin

Olympic Stadium in 1938, mindful of the background to the match. This was a time where war between the two countries was seen by many as inevitable and political tension was high. Hitler ordered the German team to stand to attention during the English national anthem, but asked the English players to give the Nazi salute as 'Deutschland Uber Alles' (Germany Above All) played in return.

The players were divided in their opinions, Arsenal's Eddie Hapgood being the most vocal in his stance against the idea. In the end the players agreed to give the salute, though their photos in the press back home caused outrage. Thankfully England scored a physical as well as moral victory over their hosts in that they won the match 6-3. The next day Aston Villa met a German club side, but they gave their opponents a two-fingered salute instead of politely raising their arms!

The Austrian side of the 1930s was also called the Wunderteam on account of their supremely gifted players. When their country was annexed by Germany in 1938, the side showed their displeasure by winning the 1939 German Cup and, two years later, their League as well. The Nazis, understandably, were none too pleased at this as their aura of Aryan invincibility was shattered.

The German invasion of the Soviet Union in 1941 resulted in many teams disbanding. However, Dynamo Kiev players formed a new side, Start, when a number of team-mates met up having been put to work by the Nazis in a bakery in the city. The occupying forces heard about the side and decided to form a military team to take them on. Start beat the soldiers comfortably 5-3. This irritated the German high command as their side was well-disciplined and well-fed, while the Russians were a malnourished scratch side. The Germans decided to organise a second fixture, but this time the opposition would be sterner. Start then beat PGS 6-0, the humiliation only angering the Germans into organising yet another game, this time against MSG Wal of Hungary, a highly rated outfit. The Start team dished out yet another hammering and saw off their opponents 5-1. A rematch was also won emphatically.

By now news of the matches had spread across Eastern Europe, and the Start side was being seen as a bastion of resistance to the hated Nazis. It was time to crush the movement with a game against elite German side Flakelf. You can guess the outcome. Start won 2-1.

A rematch was arranged but with an interesting caveat. If the Germans lost, the Start side would be executed. So the brave men from Kiev had to decide whether to live or be humiliated on the football field. They chose honour, and thrashed the Flakelf team so badly that the referee, a German, had to finish the match early, while the troops in the crowd fired their weapons in anger. The Start side, of course, were arrested as they left the field. This is the point at which a number of versions of the story spring up. The official Russian enquiry concluded that the team was immediately executed, though a watered down version has it that one of the players managed to escape, while two were reassigned to the labour camps. The rest were then shot and thrown into an unmarked ravine at Babi Yar while still wearing their kit. Since the end of the Cold War, however, a more likely scenario has the players being sent back to the bakery for the duration of the war. The players were then vilified by fellow 'inmates' for socialising with the hated Nazis. Sadly four, including goalkeeper Trusevich, were shot when a prisoner killed the commandant's dog and every fifth man in the camp was executed in punishment. Whatever the truth may be, a statue martyring the players was erected at Dynamo Kiev's ground at the end of the conflict.

There was always going to be another story behind the 1954 World Cup Final in Switzerland. The two teams that made it through were Germany and Hungary, and not many had forgotten the trauma inflicted on the Hungarian people by the German army during the war. Added to that, Hungary had beaten Germany in a qualification round 8-3, so there was an extra incentive for the Germans too. The match began well for the Magyars, German 'keeper Turek handing them a couple of early goals. The Germans fought back well and were level by the break, however. As the Hungarians tired late on, the Germans only seemed to get stronger, and they scored a third somewhat inevitably. But the magnificent Ferenc Puskas (nicknamed the 'Galloping Major' on account of his ties with the Hungarian military) wasn't done and he thought he'd scored an equaliser in the dying seconds. Sadly for him, he was ruled offside and the Germans held on to win 3-2. For the so called 'Golden Team' - the 'Magnificent Magyars' - defeat was unacceptable and riots broke out in Budapest. Then the players and their families were targeted by gangs on the streets.

Half a century later it emerged that some of the German players had been given injections before the match, and that the syringes probably didn't contain the innocent vitamins officials were led to believe. Puskas has voiced his concerns throughout the intervening years and both television documentaries and eye witness accounts now appear to back him up. It seems likely that his team was beaten by a group of performance-enhanced athletes.

This wasn't the only tough match of that year's World Cup, however. The Brazil - Hungary quarter-final became known as the 'Battle of Berne' because the players repeatedly stopped play to start belting each other. Santos and Tozzo were sent off for Brazil, with Hungarian Boszik joining them, not quite literally, for an early bath. In fact there was an all-out brawl in the changing room immediately after the game.

Coventry City faced Argentinean side San Lorenzo in a friendly on the South American's 1956 tour of the UK. FA Cup Final referee Arthur Ellis officiated, but things turned sour just before halftime when he awarded the home side a penalty after a push in the area. The irate Argentinean midfielder Jose Sanfilippo started kicking Ellis while shouting obscenities at him. He then refused to leave the field when shown the red card and carried on abusing Ellis instead. Several players intervened, some trying to help the referee escape, others trying to help Sanfilippo give him a good shoeing. After a few minutes Ellis was forced to abandon the match because the player would still not leave the field. Sanfilippo was transferred to Boca Juniors shortly after returning home, but his new club also found him difficult to deal with and he was eventually sold after attacking the team coach - the man, not the mode of transport, though we wouldn't put it past him...

The Champion Clubs Cup in 1962 was between Santos (Pelé's club) and local rivals Penarol. The Chilean referee was forced to call a halt to proceedings twice as both benches were pelted with missiles from the stands. Having then gone to extra time, the game eventually finished 3-3 at one o'clock in the morning, some 210 minutes after kicking off!

The same tournament in 1970 pitted Penarol against Nacional and, in an ill-tempered match, a handful of players were sent off after a mass brawl.

"The game eventually finished at one o'clock in the morning."

Brazil's little genius Garrincha had to overcome polio as a child, but he still managed to set the 1958 and '62 World Cups alight with his wonderful football. The latter, in Chile, almost passed him by however after he was sent off and hit by a bottle during their semi-final against the host nation. Thankfully for him, President João Belchior Marques Goulart intervened and he was granted permission to play in the final.

In his later life he probably would have downed the contents of that bottle. Repeatedly hospitalised after bouts of heavy drinking, he died from alcoholism in 1983 aged just 46. After one binge, he'd recovered sufficiently by the morning to have a queue of nurses at the door waiting to sleep with him. Against doctor's orders, he was apparently satisfying them for most of the day!

This is how BBC commentator David Coleman introduced highlights of the Chile vs. Italy match from the 1962 World Cup, a match that would become known as the 'Battle of Santiago':

"Good evening. The game you are about to see is the most stupid, appalling, disgusting and disgraceful exhibition of football, possibly in the history of the game"

Having already watched the match live of course, Coleman knew what to expect. The match was an absolute disgrace, with players from both sides committing a number of dreadful tackles. There was one moment when six players were writhing on the turf at the same time and the referee, barely in control, was forced to send two Italians from the field. Things did not calm down in the second half and the police had to intervene on four separate occasions to restore order. The television audience was then even more shocked to see Chile's Leonel Hanchez break Humberto Maschio's nose with a blatant punch, an offence not seen by either of the linesmen or the referee. Chile went on the win the fight 2-0 but viewers hardly warmed to them after their roughhouse tactics. Perhaps they'd got away with it because they were the tournament hosts.

Nearly 100,000 turned up at Hampden Park to watch Scotland take on Austria in 1963. The first goal provoked an angry reaction from the away players as the linesman had clearly flagged for offside during the build-up. Referee Jim Finney had deemed Davie Wilson onside though and refused to blow his whistle. Wilson scored again a few minutes later and this time Nemec protested too much and was sent off. Denis Law then added a third before halftime. Immediately after the break the Austrians were down to nine men as Rafreider had to be taken off with a nasty leg injury. Denis Law scored again but then the Austrians pulled one back through Linhart. The Austrians were still smarting from Law's second, and barely seemed to notice their own score, when Hof was sent off for another dangerous tackle. Finney was left with little option but to abandon the game with ten minutes left because there was the very real possibility of further violence erupting. The Austrians by then of course were down to eight men and trailing 4-1...

Mexican striker Carlos Zomba scored four times for Atlanta against Los Apaches. He couldn't have imagined, however, that a Los Apaches fan would take the matter seriously enough to shoot him four times in the legs, thus bringing about an end to his career, though thankfully not his life.

The 1963 Ethiopia vs. Kenya fixture almost had to be abandoned due to trouble flaring up, first between the players and then between the fans. Seven years later, nine members of the Kenyan team were treated for injuries after being attacked by a section of the crowd. The game lasted just under an hour before it was abandoned for safety reasons.

England - Argentina always conjures up certain images. For the younger generation there were the Falklands War and 'Hand of God' incidents but relations had been sour between the two at least since the World Cup in 1966. The South Americans had clearly been told to rough the English up with some horrific tackles and foul-mouthed rants. Captain

Antonio Rattin was sent off for two reckless challenges, then spat at the referee and had to be escorted from the Wembley turf by policemen. Half the Argentine team had already been booked and FIFA officials threatened them with expulsion from the tournament if they didn't start playing. They never recovered and England won the scrap 1-0. Manager Alf Ramsay remarked, somewhat undiplomatically, afterwards:

"Our best play will come against a team who come to play football, not act like animals"

Such was Pelé's influence over international affairs that he managed to get Biafra and Nigeria to declare two days off from their war in 1967! It is not known if he was any help with the following conflict however.

The poor Central American countries of El Salvador and Honduras were pitted against one another in the qualifying stages of the 1970 World Cup which was to be held in Mexico. Though their borders were quite distinct, the nations overlapped considerably in that several hundred thousand Salvadorans lived and worked inside Honduras. This was not an ideal situation, and as the match approached the two governments decided to ramp up the tension. They each accused one another of illegal manufacturing practices, and began personal attacks on their ministers. The Honduran government then issued an order for 300,000 Salvadorans to return to their own country within a month. By now, however, the El Salvador team was already in the Honduran capital Tegucigalpa. The night before the match their hotel was surrounded by an angry mob and the noise prevented the players from sleeping. They then lost the first leg 1-0.

The second leg a week later was incident packed. The team hotels were again bombarded with makeshift missiles, and a bomb even made it through one window. Luckily for Marco Mendoza it didn't explode. A dirty dishcloth was run up the Honduran flagpole during the anthems before the game, and shortly afterwards violence erupted, requiring two Honduran supporters to receive hospital treatment. El Salvador won and forced a play-off in Mexico City, but not before Honduran troops had rounded up the remaining peasants, of whom two were killed, and forced them back over the border.

The final match was played in front of about 15,000 and it went off without major incident, Mauricio Rodriguez giving the Salvadorans a deserved 3-2 win. The same could not be said for the events unfolding back in the two capital cities. The governments broke of diplomatic relations and on July 14th 1969 the two countries went to war for four days. Thankfully economic sanctions imposed by the West brought a halt to hostilities before the crisis escalated further. Even so, it was estimated that there had been 6,000 deaths, and the two countries would remain in sporting isolation from each other for the next decade.

El Salvador then needed to play Haiti for a place at the Finals proper. They won the first leg but a Haitian witch-doctor cast a spell on them in the return and another play-off loomed. The match, played in Kingston, Jamaica, was another closely fought contest, with El Salvador scoring the first goal in extra time. The immediate appearance of the witch doctor angered El Salvador coach Gregorio Bundio so he took matters into his own hands and decked the shaman! El Salvador held on to win. Sadly for Bundio, however, even though he had guided his team through war, pestilence and witchcraft to reach the World Cup, he was then sacked for trying to get his players a better deal on pay. They lost all their matches at Mexico '70.

Boca Juniors' stadium was filled to capacity with fans waiting to see their team take on Peru's Sporting Cristal in a Libertadores Cup match in 1971. The game started peacefully enough but Boca's captain Ruben Zune soon saw to it that the game would be remembered for a spectacular punch-up. He was tackled, scythed to the ground more like, and he rolled over in agony. He then stood up and belted the tackler. This sparked the fight which involved nineteen players and both teams' entire benches. Referee Alejandro Otero had no hope of restoring order so he called in the police. Only the two goalkeepers and Boca centre-half Menendez had abstained from the fracas, while the rest were sent off, all nineteen of them! Zune needed stitches in a gaping head wound, Mellan had a fractured skull and another player had a broken nose. Though the nineteen were sentenced to a month in prison they managed to secure suspended sentences instead. Still, it would take six weeks before both sides were fully restored.

The word friendly conjures up an image in the head, but matches thus called can often be anything but. Benfica, as champions of Portugal, played Arsenal in one such game in 1971. They lost (6-2) to the North Londoners and all eleven players then proceeded to attack referee Norman Burtenshaw. UEFA were left with no option other than to report the side for its terrible behaviour.

Rioting Rangers fans almost prevented the European Cup Winners' Cup from being presented to the team after the 1972 Final against Dynamo Moscow. Instead it was left to manager Bill Waddell to beg the disciplinary committee in Barcelona for forgiveness. UEFA relented and the trophy was on its way to Scotland, just.

Kenyan national league side Abaluhya were two goals to the good after the first leg of their 1974 African Club Championship tie against Ethiopians Asmara. For security reasons (see above for previous incidents involving sides from the two countries) the game was moved to the Haile Selassie Ethiopian national stadium, but trouble was already brewing and police were forced to quash a disturbance in the first half. The violence overflowed onto the pitch in the last ten minutes, by which time Asmara had pulled a goal back. The score-line was of little consequence, however, when the heavy-handed police stepped in to stop the crowd throwing bottles with machinegun fire. At least two spectators were killed a number of players and fans were injured.

Leeds reached the final of the 1975 European Cup but they lost to Bayern Munich in the Parc des Princes in Paris. Their fans, known as some of the most volatile in the country, then went on the rampage and the club was banned from European competition for three years.

The Rome derby match, or the Derby della Capitale as it's known in English, is the biannual game between Roma and Lazio held in the Stadio Olimpico. The game is usually extremely tense and has been marked by a number of major crowd disturbances over the years. More recently, racist banners have begun to reappear after several decades of (mostly) peaceful confrontation. One commentator has suggested that:

"There are few games on the world stage that can match the bitterness, rivalry and sheer passion of the Rome derby"

Sadly the rivalry between the two often boils over into outright violence, with two events in particular leaving their mark on this fixture. Lazio fan Vincenzo Paparelli became the first football riot-related fatality in Italy when he was hit in the eye and killed by a flare thrown by a Roma fan in the Curva Sud stand in 1979. Lazio fans in the Curva Nord stands retaliated, chanting sfottò (highly offensive remarks) focusing on the socio-economic origins of the Roma fans, principally that they were dishonest because they stole the game from the Laziali (Lazio was founded nearly thirty years before their arch-rivals in 1900). The Roma fans then replied with the standard line about their opponents not really being from Rome.

Recently Lazio fans have been bringing the game down with racist chants, though the Roma fans responded in kind and were equally derided in the Italian media. In 2001 Lazio's Fabio Liverani came in for a huge amount of abuse, not just from the fans, but from his own players because it was discovered that he was a Roma fan as a child. Despite the obvious pressure to leave the club, Liverani responded through strength of character and is now worshipped by the Laziali.

In 2004 the underground movement known as the Roma Ultras forced the game to be abandoned four minutes into the second half after spreading false, as it turns out, rumours that a child had been killed by police before the match. A riot broke out immediately and fireworks were exchanged. During the trouble three hardcore fans walked onto the pitch to ask Roma captain Francesco Totti to lead his team off. Adriano Galliani, the League President, then spoke with the match officials and decided that the best course of action would be to postpone the game for safety reasons.

The violence continued after the abandonment with a running battle between police and rival fans. Though they used teargas and riot controls to try and stop fans torching first the stands and then the cars outside the ground, the trouble still left more than 150 policemen were injured. They only managed to make 13 arrests.

The match was replayed at the end of March and thankfully it passed peacefully. The 1-1 score-line ended Roma's championship aspirations and the title went to Milan instead.

Random Balls 7

"I think the big guns will come to the boil here"
JIMMY ARMFIELD

"He's not George Best, but, then again, no one is"
CLIVE TYLDESLEY

"Many of Don Revie's faults are good qualities carried to extremes"
KEVIN KEEGAN

"The new West Stand casts a giant shadow over the entire pitch, even on a sunny day"
CHRIS JONES

"Sarajevo isn't Hawaii"
BOBBY ROBSON

"Ardiles strokes the ball like it was part of his anatomy"
JIMMY MAGEE

"And there's Ray Clemence looking as cool as ever out there in the cold"
JIMMY HILL

"The news from Guadalajara, where the temperature is 98 degrees, is that Falcao is warming up"
BRIAN MOORE

"In comparison, there's no comparison"
RON GREENWOOD

"I don't want to be either partial or impartial"
FRANK MCLINTOCK

"If he opens his legs he'll be hard to handle"
GRAHAM TAYLOR

"We thrashed Romania 0-0 in the first half"
KEVIN KEEGAN

"We just haven't had the rub of the dice"
BOBBY ROBSON

"It's nice for us to have a fresh face to bounce things off"
LAWRIE SANCHEZ

"Footballers are no different from human beings sometimes"
GRAHAM TAYLOR

"Steve McCahill has just limped off with a badly cut forehead"
TOM FERRIE

"This was that game that finally put the Everton ship back on the road"
ALAN GREEN

"The game has gone rather scrappy as both sides realise they could win this match or lose it or draw it even"
KEVIN KEEGAN

West Ham were forced to play the second leg of their 1980 Cup-Winners' Cup tie against Spanish side Castilla behind closed doors after crowd trouble had spoiled the first leg in Spain. Fifty Londoners were expelled from the ground and one was later hit by a bus and killed. The Hammers were fined and ordered to play their next matches at neutral venues, a lenient sentence when you consider that three British clubs, including Manchester United, had been completely banned from European competition for similar offences. West Ham issued a statement on how they would deal with the issue, and promised 500 police for the return leg, provided they could play in an empty stadium at Upton Park. Their proposal was accepted and the match went ahead. West Ham scored three to Castilla's one, an exact reversal of the first leg. David Cross then completed his hat-trick in extra time and the Hammers went through.

This next outburst is not so much fighting talk as sheer relief at a job well done and a chance to gloat at the hapless losers. The Norwegian television commentator Borge Lillelien was getting quite excited as his side closed in on victory against England in 1981. After the final whistle sounded he began celebrating the 2-1 victory is his own inimitable style:

"We have beaten England; we are the best in the world! Lord Nelson, Lord Beaverbrook, Sir Winston Churchill, Sir Anthony Eden, Clement Attlee, Henry Cooper, Lady Diana, we have beaten them all. Maggie Thatcher? Can you hear me, Maggie Thatcher? Your boys took one hell of a beating!"

Mr Lillelien clearly never studied in England because there is no way any schoolchildren here could name that many influential figures from our history (he even spelt their names correctly in commentary…). I suppose you might get asked something that tricky for your PhD though…

Marinko Janevski was watching his native Yugoslavia play in 1982 when his wife turned the television off. He was so incensed that he strangled her before watching the rest of the game. He was given a lengthy jail sentence as a result.

Violence erupted at the end of the 1984 Spanish Cup Final, the Copa del Rey, which marked Maradona's last appearance for Bareclona before his £6.8 million transfer to Napoli. He was subjected to chants of,

"Indian, Indian, Indian!", which, though highly insulting, galvanised him into action, and he scored twice. Opponents Athletic Bilbao made sure he took home some painful memories by subjecting the Argentinean to at least five horrendous tackles though. They then spoiled his farewell by winning the trophy with a late goal. After the final whistle the challenges became somewhat more brutal. Maradona sparked the main brawl himself after a well-directed knee knocked out Bilbao's 'keeper. Then both sets of players went at it in a kung-fu-style contest for the next several minutes until police and the officials managed to restore order.

The man himself was to court his fair share of controversy in the next World Cup, that held in Mexico in 1986. The quarter-final pitted Argentina against England in the first match between the two since the end of the Falklands War in 1982. There was clearly an undercurrent of hostility between players and fans alike but Maradona ensured the match was remembered for another reason. He challenged Peter Shilton for a high ball after a failed clearance from Steve Hodge ballooned into the air above the penalty spot. Maradona climbed above the 'keeper, but, instead of heading the ball in, he punched it past the stranded Shilton with his left fist for a 'goal'. Despite vehement protests from the English players, referee Ali Bin Nasser allowed the goal to stand.

There can be no argument about the Argentinean's second goal. It was a moment of World Cup magic. Maradona beat five defenders with a mazy run from inside his own half and then shot low past Shilton. It was, perhaps, the greatest individual goal ever scored (Barcelona's teenager Lionel Messi almost replicated it touch for touch against Getafe in 2007), but it couldn't quiet the protests over his earlier actions. Argentina won the match 2-1 and in the press conference afterwards Maradona announced that his first had been scored by the Mano de Dios, or, as it read in the full English version:

"A little bit by the hand of God and a little bit by the head of Maradona"

This, of course, angered the English further and Maradona - whose full name, incidentally, translates as 'Little God' and is an anagram of 'Oh dear, I'm a gonad' - was pilloried by the English people. He did nothing to help his reputation when he appeared to use his right hand to control the ball against the Soviet Union at Italia '90, a tournament unlike Mexico '86 because Argentina didn't go on to win, Germany gaining revenge for their defeat in the previous final.

Maradona made one more appearance at the finals, those held in the USA in 1994. This time he managed to get himself thrown out after failing a drugs test. Since then the troubled star has battled drug and alcohol addiction and has frequently ended up either in hospital or on the wrong side of the law. He shot and wounded four reporters with an airgun in 1994, almost died from respiratory and circulatory failure in 2004, and had his stomach stapled in 2005. In March 2007 it was announced that Maradona was back in hospital, suffering, as his doctor put it, from the effects of leading an overactive lifestyle and having an addictive personality. He actually meant hepatitis caused by alcohol abuse. It looks like the Argentinean's demons continue to haunt him (his doctor announced they were taking a holiday in Switzerland in Spring 2007 because Maradona was smoking too many cigars in hospital…). Thankfully he seems to have turned the corner now and is managing his national side.

The Bulgarian Cup Final in 1985 pitted Levski Spartak against CSKA. Before the match even started the players were trading blows in the tunnel, and this sparked crowd trouble on a massive scale. As a punishment the government forced both teams to change their names, Spartak playing as Vitosha for four years and CSKA playing as Sredec.

Ray Wilkins became the first man to be sent off for England at a World Cup Finals tournament (Mexico '86) during their match against Morocco. He'd thrown the ball at the referee, who deemed it an act of dissent, and was promptly shown the red card. Of course Allan Mullery was the first Englishman to be sent off for his country while playing Yugoslavia in 1968.

A thunderflash was thrown at Roma goalkeeper Franco Tancredi during their match with AC Milan at the Giuseppe Meazza stadium in 1987. The explosive device almost killed the player according to one report. The stadium, incidentally, got its name from the much celebrated Italian striker of the 1930s. Though Meazza spoke out strongly against Fascism, and was the only player not honoured by Mussolini after the victorious 1938 World Cup campaign, this only made him more popular with the masses. It was for this reason that the San Siro in Milan was named after him.

Frank Rijkaard and German Rudi Völler had a minor spat at Italia '90 after the Dutchman, well, spat at the striker with the notoriously bad hair. The Dutch and German meetings are always highly charged affairs. Events that took place during the Second World War still haven't been forgotten and the teams often bring their pasts onto the pitch. Holland's Frank Rijkaard took offence to Rudi Völler's perm in their 1990 World Cup clash and decided it needed some gel. So he lobbed two mouthfuls of phlegm at the German, the second after the referee had already seen enough of Völler and sent him off. The incident led to Rijkaard also being sent off.

George Weah almost took Fabien Barthez's head off with a challenge in a French League game in the early 1990s. The tackle sparked an all-in brawl featuring such established names as Ginola, Desailly and Angloma, two of who helped France win the World Cup in 1998. Another European brawl saw French team Panazni's players repeatedly stamping on the opposition striker after he committed a sly off-the-ball tackle. Having taken several boots to the head, Tropicana's front man was then sent off!

Colombian star Andrés Escobar Saldarriaga was killed having returned home after the 1994 World Cup in the USA. He'd scored an own goal for the tournament hosts and his team had been eliminated from the competition. To some people football is never just a game. A linesman in an Argentinean club match also paid with his life after giving a contentious offside call. The entire team was sent to prison for their part in his death.

FIFA were forced to postpone a recent Olympic qualifier between Morocco and Gambia because of the violence that had plagued relations between Gambia and Senegal. The Gambian squad were due to fly through Rabat for the game but the authorities were worried that it could spark more rioting. There had already been trouble at the Nations Cup qualifier between Senegal and Gambia in Dakar when Gambian fans began hurling stones and bottles. Senegal won the battle 3-1, even though soldiers had to be called in to try and control the fighting, which eventually spilled onto the streets outside the ground.

The Gambian capital Banjul was then besieged by Senegalese fans and the border between the two had to be closed to prevent further outbreaks of violence. The Gambian FA said it was still too risky to allow its players to travel through Dakar to Morocco and FIFA would have to decide on a new date for the game. Other African nations found it hard to complete their qualifiers for similar reasons. Ghana refused to travel to Liberia because rebel forces were closing in on Monrovia, and Mauritania refused the trip to Senegal because of an attempted coup in Nouakchott.

Brazilians Romario and Junior decided to start belting each other in a club match in the 1990s. It began as a simple disagreement but ended up with both teams piling in to an all-in brawl. One of their national club sides became involved in something far worse just after they'd defeated their Mexican rivals in an ill-tempered contest in 2004. Having won, the Brazilian players began flapping their arms, a gesture that angered a number of Mexican players and fans. Soon the violence erupted onto the field while a riot broke out in the stands. The Brazilian players initially tried to defend themselves, but, when it became clear they were going to be injured, they bolted for the dressing room, found it locked and had to kick the door in to avoid the situation escalating beyond control.

French coach Aime Jacquet was described by the media as an 'Unskilled country bumpkin' in the build-up to the 1998 World Cup. He silenced the doubters by guiding the team to victory and then promptly resigned so that he would not have to face the press again. He vowed never to forgive the newspapers for their personal attacks.

The referee sparked a fracas at Anfield after awarding a penalty to Roma for handball during their UEFA Cup tie against Liverpool in 2001. He then changed his mind and gave them a corner instead. So incensed were the Roma players that they vehemently protested, earning themselves two yellow cards in the process, one for Guigou and another for Zago.

Sao Paulo youth were attacked by opposition players and fans because they over-celebrated a goal in a lower league match in 2000!

In a Pacifico - Almonia clash in Argentina a Pacifico player was sent off for a violent tackle. This promoted the benched players to stream onto the pitch to attack the injured Almonia striker who was already down and hardly needed the shoeing he subsequently received. Riot police came on to restore order but this only seemed to anger the players and they began fighting the officials. Thirteen Almonia players spent the night in the cells as a result, probably not the result their coach had asked for at the beginning of the match however. It's strange how most of these stories seem to emanate from South America but perhaps that has something to do with the notoriously volatile Latin temperament. Mexican side Monarcas were 3-2 up on rivals Olmedo when one of the defenders, Prado, was sent off for a late tackle, about a day late to be fair. Somewhat predictably, he reacted angrily to the referee's decision and belted the opposing goalkeeper. Then he launched into a vicious assault on his opposite number, before finally having a kick at their coach! Not surprisingly, this precipitated a full on brawl.

A mass brawl erupted after a fierce challenge during the Jamaica - Torosneja match in Kingston. The fans quickly became involved, but even they didn't resort to ripping the chairs out of the stands and using them as weapons as the Mexican side's players were doing. The Jamaicans fought back having left the ground to search for comparable weapons, many returning with sticks and rocks.

The 2001 Atlas vs. Santos clash in Mexico started off with a couple of dangerous tackles and finished up as a mass punch-up. Though there was some initial pushing and shoving after another two-footed lunge, the referee appeared to have restored order. He hadn't counted on the volatile 'keeper Fabio Costa charging fully sixty yards before leaping long-jump style into the opposing striker though. This studs up tackle, that caught his opponent in the midriff, sparked yet another South American melee. Both teams were heavily fined for their parts in it.

When Portuguese star Luis Figo returned to Barcelona's Nou Camp stadium with Real Madrid in 2002, the crowd were so incensed that they started pelting him with objects, including, incredibly, a stuffed pig's head!

Roy Keane was famously sent home from the 2002 World Cup in the Far East because of a disagreement with Irish manager Mick McCarthy. At a meeting between the two intended to clear the air, Keane launched into this rant:

"You were a crap player and are a crap manager. Somehow you are the manager of my country and you aren't even Irish. You English cunt"

*

In 2003, Botswana's captain Modiri Marumo became the first goalkeeper to be sent off during a penalty shootout. He was given his marching orders for punching his opposite number, Philip Nyasulu, after the latter wished him luck during a cup tie against Malawi. Malawi went on to win the match 4-1 and in so doing they reached the semi-final.

Many think that disgraceful Bolton Wanderer El-Hadji Diouf should be banned from the game after a series of spitting incidents. While playing against Portsmouth in 2004 he snapped and launched a liquid tirade at de Zeuw. The Pompey man showed remarkable restraint by not lamping him, something that even referee Jeff Winter said he'd be tempted to do if Diouf spat at him. (Back in 1972 a similar incident had taken place in a Canadian League match, only this time the referee was on the receiving end. Two Italian players had taken aim and then let fly from close range. One salvo missed and the player was only banned for eighteen months, while the other hit, earning the player a four-year ban.) Diouf is not afraid to stick the boot in either, as Everton's Phil Neville found out in 2007. The defender was lucky not to have his leg broken by a terrible studs-up challenge. Is it just me or does anyone else think players like Diouf should be forced to repay their wages and then bundled off to annoy someone somewhere else, preferably some big bloke who is allowed to retaliate? The American street slang nickname Doofus (idiot) has been earned recently, and not a moment too soon. He probably thinks being offered a cortisone injection means he's getting a new car.

Wayne Rooney was sent off in England's vital World Cup match against Portugal in 2006. He had been subjected to a number of bad challenges himself but surely couldn't have thought he'd get away with stamping on Ricardo Carvalho's testicles in reply. And speaking of the nether regions, everyone but Paul Gascoigne 'fondly' remembers the photo of him grimacing as Vinny Jones really made sure he felt his 'tackle' in a Wimbledon - Newcastle fixture in 1988. It is rumoured that the two sent each other 'gifts' afterwards, a toilet brush and a red rose. Big-haired Colombian Carlos Valderrama also had his lower collar felt in a club game in the 1990s.

But let's go back to the Rooney incident briefly. The referee hadn't immediately gone to his pocket and perhaps thought the stamp was nothing more than Rooney stepping backwards and trying to find his balance. Then, up popped Cristiano Ronaldo to help the referee make his mind up. He gesticulated wildly at the official, who appeared to change his mind before producing the fateful red. Ronaldo walked off smiling, and then winked at team-mates, satisfied that he'd got the desired outcome. The Portuguese star was vilified by the English media who said he'd be kicked out of Old Trafford rather than face the wrath of Rooney on the training pitch. Time has proved the doubters wrong though. Rooney and Ronaldo appear to have patched up their relationship and have developed into two of the most feared players in the country.

Rooney of course has a few more memorable sendings-off to his name. In the Manchester United - Villareal Champions' League tie in 2005 he was booked by the rather overzealous Kim Milton Nielsen. As he was being shown the yellow card he applauded Nielsen at very close range. The referee, sadly, didn't see the funny side and immediately issued a second yellow card and Rooney was off.

Frenchman Zinedine Zidane will go down in history as one of the game's greatest players, but he will also be remembered for a couple of moments of absolute madness. In the 2006 World Cup Final against Italy in Berlin he engaged Italian defender Marco Materazzi in a number of verbal exchanges. After one, in which the Italian reportedly abused Zizou's family and heritage, and suggested he might be a terrorist, the Frenchman overreacted and savagely butted him in the chest. Referee Horacio Elizondo consulted with his linesman and then gave Zidane his marching orders. Italy, of course, went on to take the trophy. The Zidane incident has caused heated debate ever since because television replays of the exchange show that the linesman is not always looking at the players. Many people believe the red card was the first decision to be made, albeit covertly, by video referee. It is quite possible that the officials then received word in their ears from above…

Football violence has been on the rise again in Europe recently.

Dutch side Feyenoord were ejected from the UEFA Cup after their fans went on the rampage during a group match against Nancy in November 2006.

The Chinese Olympic team was involved in a mass brawl with QPR players during a friendly in early 2007. The game was halted after a punch up during which China's Zheng Tao had his jaw broken, lost a couple of teeth and was then knocked out. QPR chairman Gianni Paladini said that the brawl was quite unacceptable and that he considered sacking some of his players. Seven of their opponents were sent home in disgrace.

All domestic and international games in Italy were halted after a policeman was killed while helping to marshal a Serie A game between Catania and Palermo in Sicily in February 2007. Crowd trouble had meant the police were forced to intervene with tear gas, but the fighting continued after the game in the streets. More than a hundred people were treated for injuries, but hospital staff were unable to save the policemen who had been struck in the face by a homemade explosive. The tragedy followed the death of an official at a lower league Italian club the week before.

England captain John Terry apparently ripped his shirt out of Andorran skipper Oscar Sonejee's hands after a heated argument in the tunnel at the end of England's rather poor 3-0 victory over their hosts in Barcelona in March 2007. Manager Steve McLaren was also in a rather testy mood after the game. The fans had given him a rough time during the game and the media chipped in immediately afterwards, so the head coach ordered the bus driver to run over reporter Brian Woolnough. The journalist quipped that had McLaren been driving the bus himself, he probably would have missed!

Referee Mejuto Gonzalez failed to spot Lyon's Fred's blatant elbow on Cristian Chivu, a blow that left the Roma player bleeding heavily from his nose, in their 2007 Champions' League clash. Roma went on to win 2-0.

Manchester United's fans had been warned to watch out for the Roma Ultras during the club's trip to face AS Roma in the Champions' League tie at the Olympic Stadium in April 2007. Despite the warnings violence erupted after the first goal and the police moved in. Thirteen

United fans needed hospital treatment, mainly for baton wounds to the head and torso, while several others were stabbed outside the stadium. The incident reportedly lost the Italians the chance of hosting the 2012 European Championships.

"Fred's blatant elbow left the Roma player
bleeding heavily from the nose"

Crowd disturbances at AS Roma are not uncommon. In 2000 a Leeds fan was stabbed before a UEFA Cup tie, while five Liverpool fans suffered the same treatment in the following year's competition. Later that year, four more Liverpool fans were hurt as the bad feelings rolled over into the Champions' League clash between the two, and referee Anders Frisk was hit by a missile during their 2004 encounter with Dynamo Kiev. Three Middlesbrough fans were stabbed, with another handful injured, after a UEFA Cup match early in 2006. Apparently the preferred area to stab is the rear end, which, the Ultras tell us, is because it is a humiliating wound that prevents the victim from sitting comfortably during recovery.

Tottenham's UEFA Cup clash against Sevilla in the same week as the United - Roma match was also marred by crowd trouble. They lost 2-1, with the referee awarding the Spaniards a highly controversial penalty after Spurs' 'keeper Paul Robinson was alleged, rather harshly, to have tripped Claro Adriano Correia. These two incidents forced the FA to order all British clubs still involved in European competition to monitor their crowds with extra vigilance.

Manager Speak 6 - I think I know what they were trying to say

"Batistuta is very good at pulling off defenders"
KEVIN KEEGAN

"Anything from 1-0 to 2-0 would be a nice result"
BOBBY ROBSON

"The unthinkable is not something we're thinking about at the moment"
PETER KENYON

"It's understandable that people are keeping one eye on the pot and another up the chimney"
KEVIN KEEGAN

"The lads really ran their socks into the ground"
ALEX FERGUSON

"It's 60-40 against him being fit, so he's got half a chance"
GLENN HODDLE

"Doncaster will hit Villa with fire and broomstick"
JOHN GREGORY

"I just wonder what would have happened if the shirt had been on the other foot"
MIKE WALKER

"We threw our dice into the ring and turned up trumps"
BRUCE RIOCH

"Shearer could be 100 percent fit, but not at peak fitness"
GRAHAM TAYLOR

"Sometimes it's very hard to follow what would have happened, and sometimes it's hard to follow what has happened"
GRAHAM TAYLOR

"I was feeling as sick as the proverbial donkey"
MICK McCARTHY

"I can take the pressure of the clock ticking on the wall"
KEVIN KEEGAN

"I'd never allow myself to let myself call myself a coward"
GRAHAM TAYLOR

1234567891011

Injury Time

Now That's Got to Hurt

It was not uncommon for villagers to be seriously injured, and in some cases killed, during the annual riots that passed for a football match on Shrove Tuesday in the Middle Ages. Since the time of codification, and the advent of the FA to police the game, injuries have become rarer, but they do happen, and some are stomach-churning in the extreme. I've tried to limit the action here to the players and officials as it would be impossible to list all the incidences where fans have become involved, except in a couple of particularly interesting cases.

Who'd be a Goalkeeper?

Four Stoke City players, including Welsh international goalkeeper, Leigh Richmond Roose, were incapable of taking the field for the second half against Liverpool in 1902 because they all had food poisoning. The food in question happened to be the fish lunch, and it sank their chances of victory against the mighty Merseysiders. They eventually lost 7-0.

Dunfermline Athletic's goalkeeper, Slavin, had to be carried off because he was so drunk in 1911! And don't believe this kind of behaviour was uncommon. In the 1960s, Jimmy Greaves reportedly used to have a couple of beers at halftime, which, in all honesty, probably constituted a top up. And Holmbury's Dougal and Turner brothers are famous for taking the piss field - sorry, field pissed.

Legendary Czechoslovakian goalkeeper Frantisek Planicka helped his side to the 1938 World Cup Final with some inspired performances.

In the quarter-final against Brazil he broke his arm but carried on playing, ensuring their passage to the semis.

Manchester City's heroic goalkeeper Bert Trautmann broke his neck in the 1956 FA Cup Final but he played on, eventually claiming his winners' medal. Not realising the severity of the injury at the time, he finally went to the doctor three days later. Not surprisingly he was unable to play again until the injury had healed, which took some nine months. Trautmann started off his career with German club side Tura Bremen and was initially a striker. He has a number of League goals to his credit as a result.

The 1957 Cup Final was marred by the injury to Manchester United's goalkeeper Ray Wood. In the first minutes of the match he was deliberately, but legally, shoulder charged by Aston Villa's Peter McParland and suffered a depressed fracture of the cheekbone. Substitutes were not allowed and the poor 'keeper was patched up just so he could wander aimlessly up and down the wing for the rest of the afternoon. United's midfield maestro Jackie Blanchflower took over in goal but he couldn't stop McParland netting twice for Villa in their 2-1 victory.

While warming up for the second leg of the final of the World Club Cup against Argentina's Racing Club in Buenos Aries in 1967, Celtic's Ronnie Simpson was struck on the head by a brick and had to be replaced by reserve 'keeper John Fallon.

Now I could place this next section in any of the preceding chapters but as there were injuries to both goalies I'll keep it here. The first leg of the final had been won by Celtic in Glasgow, but Racing went on to win their home leg too. The decider would be held in Montevideo, Uruguay. Paraguayan official Rodolfo Oserio was prepared for trouble between the players and gave them a warning about it before the match, but only a quarter of the final had been played when he was forced to call both captains over again to warn them about some of the tackling. After a particularly bad foul on Jimmy Johnstone a few minutes later, Celtic players rushed to confront the perpetrator, Rulli. A fight was the only outcome and the police had to intervene when it became clear that Oserio could no longer control the players. Basile and Lennox were eventually shown red cards before both play and the fight continued up to halftime, with a further forty fouls being committed, several of which were on the goalkeepers. Just after halftime Johnstone retaliated after another bad challenge by punching Martin and he was rightly sent off. Then team-mate John Hughes was red carded for a dreadful challenge on the Racing 'keeper. Rulli finally got his comeuppance four minutes from time when he, too, was sent off. Celtic's Bertie Auld was then sent off in the midst of a brawl at the final whistle, which meant that for a brief instant it was seven against nine! And somewhere in the middle of the match a goal had been scored, though it went largely unnoticed, Cardenas making sure that Racing were crowned world champions in the 55th minute.

Scotland international Tommy Lawrence collided with the crossbar during the home tie against Wales in 1969. Sadly the injury he sustained was so severe that he was forced to retire from the game.

A contaminated bottle of beer put paid to Gordon Banks's chances of playing in England's crucial World Cup quarter-final against West Germany in 1970. Peter Bonetti deputised and things were looking good for England at 2-0, but then came a series of howlers and the tiring England side lost 3-2.

As a brief aside, during that campaign England, as holders, had met the pre-championship favourites, Brazil. The match was notable for a couple of reasons, not least of which was Bobby Moore's great tackling, which even Pelé was forced to accept as outstanding afterwards. There was also a miss to end all misses, that from West Brom's Jeff Astle, which would have given England a well-deserved 1-1 draw. And how could anyone forget the save from Gordon Banks that denied Pelé? The striker had risen beautifully to head a cross into the far left corner of the net, and he was wheeling away in celebration when Banks hurled himself fully five yards along the goal line low to his right. Somehow the 'keeper managed to get a hand under the ball just as it was about to cross the line, and he then flicked it up and over the bar. Pelé couldn't believe it, saying:

"I had to applaud him with all my heart. It was the greatest save I had ever seen"

And surely there's no higher praise than that. Banks himself was equally amazed that he managed to keep the ball out:

"Every time I watch it I know the ball is going in, and even I can't believe it when it doesn't"

A team of scientists recently inputted all the television data, the speed and trajectory of the ball, and Banks's position into a computer. It turns out that the 'keeper - according to all the laws of physics - should never have been able to make the save. Humans don't have the reaction time, so he must have anticipated the direction of the header before Pelé even touched it; once Banks has dived, he can't change direction, but somehow he manages to arch his back and adjust his upper body to reach the ball while both it and he were in flight.

Banks lost an eye in a car crash in the early 1970s but still finished up his playing career as the finest goalkeeper in the North American League.

Brentford's Chic Brodie was hospitalised after a dog ran onto the pitch during their game with Colchester in 1970. As he knelt to collect a back-pass from Gelson the hyperactive terrier leaped into him, smashing painfully into his leg. Brodie overbalanced and collapsed to the ground with a shattered kneecap, thus ending his professional career.

Brian Greenhoff had to replace Manchester United's Alex Stepney in goal after the latter dislocated his jaw shouting at his defenders during a game against Birmingham City in 1975. The midfielder then kept a clean sheet. He'll wish he had as much luck in the outfield though, as he once lashed the ball into his own net in a match against Arsenal when Armstrong failed to score.

And the Arsenal's Pat Jennings had to have a dart removed from his arm by the team doctor after he was struck by the missile while collecting a back-pass during a League match at Nottingham Forest. And understudy Bob Wilson (middle name - Primrose) almost knocked himself out when he dived into the post to save a miss-hit cross back in the '70s. Jennings also had a number of other objects come his way, including door handles, snooker balls and beer bottles. Sometimes he could even be hit by coins with the edges sanded down like razor blades, and once a Coca-Cola bottle hit him right on the crown of his head.

"...a number of objects came his way..."

The great West German goalkeeper Sepp Maier was partly responsible for his country's international success in the 1970s. They won the 1972 European Championships and the 1974 World Cup but also had good showings in the other tournaments that decade. Maier also won three consecutive (1974, 1975 & 1976) European Cups with Bayern Munich. Sadly his career was cut short after a near fatal car crash in 1979.

England's Ray Clemence was sidelined after only twenty-five minutes of their opener against Belgium in the 1980 European Championships after suffering from blindness caused by the excessive use of tear gas by the Italian police behind his goal. There had been trouble brewing in the crowd but their response after fighting broke out when the Belgians equalised meant Clemence had to be substituted.

Argentina's World Cup winning goalkeeper Nery Pumpido got his wedding ring caught on a nail in the crossbar and almost had to have the finger amputated.

Cypriot goalkeeper Andreas Charitou had a heart attack after being struck by a firework during a European Championship qualifier against Holland in 1987. Though the Dutch won the match 8-0, UEFA ordered it to be replayed on account of the incident. The fan was charged with attempted murder. In Mexico in the 1990s a disgruntled fan threw a homemade pipe bomb into the goalmouth injuring several players, including the stunned 'keeper. The fan was immediately targeted for abuse and assaulted by the Corona fans before being rescued by the police and escorted to prison.

First choice England 'keeper Chris Woods cut his fingers while trying to untie his tracksuit with a knife. This gave future star David Seaman his third England cap.

Liverpool legend Bruce Grobbelaar was hospitalised after being hit on the head by a rock thrown by an Egyptian fan during a World Cup qualifier with Zimbabwe in 1993.

One Brazilian stopper had his skull fractured by angry fans after cheering a goal his new club had just scored against his old club. The incident then escalated into a riot and the police had to escort him from the field.

Bulgarian defender Trifon Ivanov took a thunderbolt from Germany's Muller right in the gentlemen's area during their clash at USA '94. Even though Ivanov grasped the swollen contents of his shorts and writhed around before being carted off on a stretcher, the commentator helpfully explained to the younger viewers that he'd taken one in the stomach. Bollocks!

Don't believe that David Seaman had it all his own way throughout his career. He missed the first half of the 1996-97 season after bending down to pick up the TV remote and tearing knee ligaments. His future understudy, David James, also managed to let the remote control get the better of him, though he damaged a muscle in his back instead while attempting to change channel. And while trying to land a carp he tweaked his shoulder. You can bet he didn't go on about that for too long…

You wouldn't have thought it possible but Barry Town's Andy Dibble was hospitalised after suffering from chemical burns from diving on the pitch against Carmarthen Town in 1998. It is thought he had a reaction to the paint used for marking the touchlines.

Spurs' American goalkeeper Kasey Keller knocked his front teeth out with the head of a golf club while removing the bag from the boot of his car in 1998. Ouch!

Manchester United's legendary 'keeper Peter Schmeichel tore a hamstring trying to tackle Arsenal's Dennis Bergkamp at the end of a crucial match in 1998. The injury is all too common but Schmeichel was in Arsenal's penalty area attempting to score from a corner when Bergkamp collected the ball. Having retired the great Dane has been seen on celebrity shows such as 'Come Dancing', for which his son

Kasper, currently on loan at Falkirk from Manchester City, frequently gets ribbed. The away fans have been chanting (to the Arctic Monkeys):

"I bet your Dad looks good on the dance floor"

Aiden Davidson was decked by a hard-boiled egg thrown from the crowd during a play-off game for Grimsby against Fulham in 1998.

Mark Statham missed a game for non-leaguers Stalybridge in 1999 after getting his head trapped in a car door... That must be a wind up. Vinny Jones, of course, denied having anything to do with it.

Everton's Thomas Myhre broke his ankle in training in 1999 while with the Norwegian national squad. He was out for several months and then, just as he was ready to retake his place with the Everton side, he slipped over in the bath and broke the other ankle! The hapless 'keeper then managed to stay under the idiot radar for a few years until a Euro 2008 qualifier against Turkey went horribly wrong. He let the ball squirm under his body, Taibi-style, for one goal and then let another easy shot through his fingers to gift Turkey a 2-2 draw. Luckily for him they didn't get stuffed...

Spain's Santiago Canizares missed the 2002 World Cup in Japan and Korea after dropping a bottle of aftershave on his foot and severing tendons. Wimbledon's Dave Beasant knows how he feels. He dropped a bottle of salad cream on his foot which ruled him out for several weeks.

Liverpool's Michael Stensgaard somehow dislocated his shoulder while fighting with an ironing board, the injury curtailing his career. He should have thrown in the towel earlier.

Derby's Mart Poom struggled with an injury to his nether regions after a charity clash against a side assembled by legendary rockers Iron Maiden. And that's surely the last place you'd want your balls to end up.

High blood pressure occasionally caused Portsmouth goalkeeper Aaron Flauavan to faint. It happened twice just as he was about to take goal kicks and he was substituted immediately. He died in a car crash soon afterwards, the cause of the accident believed to be his blackouts.

Scotland's Jim Leighton dropped a contact lens during an important qualifying match and missed the rest of it as a result. He's more likely to be seen dropping bollocks now though. Then he almost decapitated himself by looking into the business section of a lawnmower while it was running. He has always been known as an unlucky 'keeper, and has lost any number of teeth plying his trade. He was also stretchered off with concussion during the Scottish Cup Final in 2000.

Richard Wright of Everton and England missed the start of the 2003-04 season after falling out of his loft and injuring his shoulder. He backed this up by then injuring himself before a match after landing on a sign instructing players not to practice there. The word 'idiot' doesn't quite seem adequate in this case.

At least Volkan Demirel (Fenerbache's 'keeper)'s injury took place while on the pitch, although the match had actually finished by the time he dropped his clanger. He threw his shirt into the crowd having beaten arch-rivals Galatasaray in 2004, then promptly fell over and dislocated his shoulder, forcing him to miss the next month of the season.

Five members of Newcastle United's squad were incapacitated by conjunctivitis before the 2004-05 Premiership season. It is rumoured that Republic of Ireland goalkeeper Shay Given brought the affliction to training.

Wycombe Wanderers' Australian goalkeeper Frank Talia fell over while mowing his lawn in 2004. He missed the start of the season when the mower cut off one of his toes. He and Jim Leighton should either form a double act or audition for The Clangers.

Vietnamese goalie Do Ngoc The was stabbed after keeping a clean sheet in a top flight home game for Danang. He was attacked outside a nightclub after his team had beaten favourites Song Lam Nghe.

Referee Markus Merk had to abandon the 2005 Milan Derby between AC and Internazionale because AC's Brazilian goalkeeper Dida needed treatment after being hit on the head by a flare thrown from the stands.

In 2006 Bayern Munich's reserve 'keeper Michael Rensing smashed a ball at first choice Oliver Kahn during the warm-up for their match against Arminia Bielefeld. It hit him full in the face and caused his eye to swell up. Unable to take the field for the match, Kahn, presumably exuding his legendary wrath, was forced to let Rensing start between the sticks.

Newcastle's Shay Given suffered a perforated bowel - believed to be the first injury of this type on a sports field - in 2006 after a collision with West Ham striker Marlon Harewood.

Blades' goalkeeper Paddy Kenny had his eyebrow bitten off in a drunken brawl in Halifax in 2006.

In a bad day for Chelsea 'keepers, first choice Peter Čech was hospitalised with a fractured skull after a collision with Stephen Hunt in their League fixture with Reading in 2006. Reserve goalie Carlo Cudicini was then knocked out in another clash with Sonko, leaving third choice 'keeper Henrique Hilário to complete the match. Doctors said at the time that Čech was lucky to survive the clash.

Worse Than Being Injured: Football Tragedies

During a heated football match in Rome in the mid-14th century an opposing player fell onto Canon William de Spalding's knife. Pope John XXII granted him special papal forgiveness as the incident was clearly an accident.

Sheffield's Jim Beaumont died after falling into a quarry in 1877. He was chasing the ball when he slipped down the incline and suffered fatal head injuries. In 1892 St Mirren's James Dunlop died from tetanus shortly after cutting his knee on a shard of broken glass during their match against Abercorn. And Ashton's Thomas Grice was accidentally tripped during a match in 1897. He fell on his belt buckle, which punctured his stomach, and he died shortly afterwards.

Leith's Billy Walker died from internal injuries sustained after a nasty tackle resulted in a kick to the stomach in 1907, while Welsh international Dai Jones suffered the same fate after developing septicaemia stemming from an open leg wound picked up during training a few years earlier. Jimmy Maine died after another poor tackle led to internal injuries in 1909, while the Arsenal's Robert Benson collapsed and died from a burst blood vessel a few years later.

In 1921 Dumbarton's Joshua Wilkinson died from peritonitis two days after a match against Rangers. Port Vale's Tommy Butler broke his arm during a game in 1923 but he wasn't offered the correct treatment and died from blood poisoning.

Jock Thomson, Celtic's goalie, fractured his skull after colliding with Sam English during an Auld Firm derby at Ibrox in 1931. Sadly the young 'keeper never regained consciousness after the incident and he died in hospital later. The goalmouth where the incident took place is rumoured to be haunted by Thomson.

Charlton 'keeper Alex Wright died demonstrating his technique near Torre Abbey Sands in Torquay in 1934. Diving into shallow water, his head hit a rock and he broke his neck. Gillingham's Sam Raleigh died from a fractured skull in 1934.

James Utterson died from a blow to the heart during a reserve game for Wolves in 1935. A similar incident claimed the life of Guatemalan Danny Ortiz after he was involved in an accidental collision with Mario Rodriguez during a Comunicaciones v Municipal game in 2004.

Alex Villaplane, the French national team captain at the 1930 World Cup, was executed by his own country in 1944 for his supposed collaboration with the Nazis.

We've looked at the impact and aftermath of the Munich air crash in 1957, but this is not the only disaster to claim the lives of several players. In 1949 the Torino side that contributed ten of the eleven players in the Italian national team was involved in the Superga crash on their way back from a testimonial in Portugal. No one survived. The replacement team still managed to reach the final of the Latin Cup, though they lost 3-1 to Sporting Lisbon.

The entire Chilean Green Cross side were lost in 1961. And a Bolivian representative side lost nineteen players and officials in 1969 in a crash similar to the one that claimed the Uruguayan Rugby team immortalised in the 1993 film Alive. Alianza of Peru, Surinam and Zambia have also had teams decimated by air crashes since 1987.

The Zambian side had just won a 1993 World Cup qualifier against Mauritius but they were not pleased to be flying to their next match in an antiquated Buffalo aircraft. Sadly their FA decided to save $25,000 by insisting they took the flight instead of using a commercial charter, and while just off the coast of Gabon it came down with the loss of the entire team.

Galatasaray's Ali Sami Yen Stadium was substantially renovated in the early 1960s. In the first game after its second completion, a safety barrier collapsed under the weight of fans trying to escape a small fire and seventy were injured. A similar incident occurred when a railing on the top tier collapsed at the Maracanã stadium in Brazil, pitching several fans thirty feet onto fans in the lower tier. There were some serious injuries, and three people were killed. And again in South America, a striker celebrated a goal with his fans only to watch helplessly as they charged forward into a retaining wall. The structure collapsed throwing fifteen people some ten feet into a pitch-surrounding trench. There were some minor injuries but thankfully no deaths.

Colombian side Santa Rose de Cabal's winger and stand-in 'keeper Libardo Zuniga died after an opposition forward deliberately kicked him in the testicles in 1977. Zuniga had been playing so well, it had angered the striker.

Jose Gallardo died from a brain haemorrhage a month after receiving a blow to the head in a collision during a Second Division game for Malaga against Vigo in 1987.

A bolt of lightning struck the waterlogged pitch during a match between Basangana and Benatshadi in Africa in 1998. The Benatshadi side had all been issued with boots that had metal studs and this factor contributed to the deaths of all their players as the charge was conducted into their bodies. The opposition escaped injury solely due to them wearing boots with synthetic studs.

Similar tragedies had struck the Highgate United - Enfield Amateur Cup match in 1967 when four players and three spectators were injured with one killed, while two players had been killed (Bertram Boardley and Kenneth Hill) during the Army Cup Final in 1948 between the Royal Armoured Corps and the Royal Artillery at Aldershot. Eight players and the referee were knocked down by the bolt, which, some say, had been attracted by the ref's whistle, and five of these were forced to stay in hospital overnight. A lightning strike was also responsible for injuring five players at the George stadium in South Africa during a Johannesburg Premier League match between Jomo Cosmos and Moroka Swallows in 1998, including international Cibi.

CSKA Moscow's goalkeeper, Serhiy Perkhun, died following an

accidental clash of heads during a Russian Premier League match in 2001.

Cameroon international Marc-Vivien Foé collapsed and died during the Confederations Cup semi-final against Colombia in 2003. The former Manchester City and West Ham midfielder supposedly had hypertrophic cardiomyopathy - an enlarged muscle inside the heart - which, though a cause of sudden cardiac death, had not been diagnosed.

In 2005 Benin 'keeper Yessouffo Samiou died after being attacked by a mob of angry fans following defeat by Nigeria in the opening game of the African Youth Championship.

Manager Speak 7

"Our current financial situation means that if we want to buy we have to spend"
KEVIN KEEGAN

*"That's not the type of header you want to see
your defender make with his hand"*
RON ATKINSON

"I don't blame individuals. I blame myself"
JOE ROYLE

"As one door closes, another one shuts"
HOWARD WILKINSON

"Yeading was a potential banana blip for Newcastle"
BOBBY ROBSON

"They can't change any of their players but they can change one of their players and he's the coach"
BOBBY ROBSON

"I can count on the fingers of one hand ten games where we've caused our own downfall"
JOE KINNEAR

"I've no regrets. None at all. My only regret is that we went out on penalties. That's my only regret but no, no regrets"
MICK MCCARTHY

"It would be foolish to believe that automatic promotion is automatic in any way whatsoever"
DAVE BASSETT

"If you count your chickens before they hatch they won't lay an egg"
BOBBY ROBSON

"That was an inch perfect pass to no one"
RAY WILKINS

"He's lightning slow"
RON ATKINSON

*"Nicolas Anelka left Arsenal for £23million, and they built a
training ground on him"*
KEVIN KEEGAN

*"There was nothing wrong with the performance, apart from we
threw away the game"*
GLENN HODDLE

*"We were in an awkward position against Yugoslavia in that in
order to win we needed to score more goals than them"*
JOSE ANTONIO CAMACHO

Ouch-Field Injuries: Who'd be a Player?

Some injuries are worse then others, but how many players can claim
this many medical mishaps? While at Stoke City, Denis Smith managed to
break his legs five times (not five legs as one report claimed) and his nose
four times. He also fractured his ankle, collarbone and a vertebra among
other assorted bones! Hull 'keeper Billy Bligh comes a close second with
13 career breaks, none of them too big sadly for him!

The Royal Engineers made it to the first ever FA Cup Final in 1872.
They would go on to become one of the most successful teams to
compete in the early years of the tournament. Sadly their first appearance
was marred by an injury to their fullback Lieutenant Creswell (broken
collarbone) and they lost the final 1-0.

Three floodlights failed at Kilmarnock during a match in 1878 and
the ground was plunged into darkness. Sadly for two of the players,
they were then involved in a blindside incident that finished both their
careers. It is said, though no one actually saw the challenge, that the men
collided at high speed.

Dragoon Guard Eddie Mason was a battle-hardened war veteran
who had fought with distinction in the bloodiest trenches of the Marne
and Ypres. In his first game after the Great War he was carried off with a
knee injury and missed the remainder of the season!

Ledger Ritson's leg was shattered in a tackle during a Leyton Orient game in 1948. The injury failed to heal properly despite the attentions of a number of experts and the limb was eventually amputated two years later.

After a playing career spanning more than twenty years, it was a broken leg that finally forced Joe Mercer to hang up his boots in 1954. His retirement as a player only pushed him straight into management though, where he would enjoy great success, particularly with Manchester City. Sheffield Wednesday's star striker Derek Dooley broke his leg during the same campaign, but his injury was so severe that he eventually had to have the limb amputated.

One of the most gifted players of his generation, Brazilian Didi couldn't secure a regular place at Real Madrid in the late '50s because the side contained the legendary Alfredo di Stefano, regarded by many, George Best and Matt Busby included, as being the best player of all time. Didi, however, was not going to be brushed aside and returned to Botofago before masterminding Brazil's 1958 World Cup win. In all he gained 72 caps, and was revered for his deadly striking ability. And it so nearly never happened. While still a teenager he damaged his knee and almost had the lower half of his leg amputated.

Elton John's uncle, Roy Dwight, scored and then broke his leg while playing for Nottingham Forest during their 2-1 win over Luton in the 1959 FA Cup Final.

Dave Mackay broke his leg not once but twice during Spurs' 1964 season. He eventually recovered and played on for a further eight years, often in considerable pain. Compatriot Allan Mullery missed that year's tour of Brazil with a serious back injury sustained, not while playing, as most would think, but while cleaning his teeth!

Aldershot were the visitors to Chester in early 1966 when bizarre injuries to both the home fullbacks occurred. Bryn Jones broke his left leg while trying to tackle the Shots' Derek Norman. The ball bypassed them both, however, and Tony Priscott scored for the visitors. Then, while Jones was lying injured, the second oddity of the day came about. A team-mate jumped on Priscott's back to help celebrate the goal, but Priscott thought he was being attacked in retaliation for the Jones incident and ended up in a fight with his own striker! The scores had moved on to 2-2 by the time Ray Jones broke his left leg in a mistimed tackle and he too was carted off to hospital. Chester then somehow managed to notch the winner.

The great Brazilian Jairzinho scored in every match of their glorious 1970 World Cup campaign, and he would go on to become a football legend. He was lucky to have had a career in the first place though, as he broke his leg twice while playing for Venezuelan outfit Caracas.

Charlie George, of Arsenal 1971 FA Cup fame, managed to cut off his toe with a lawnmower.

Scotland's fullback Danny McGrain was known as being slightly injury prone. He fractured his skull against Falkirk in 1972, was then diagnosed with diabetes in 1974, before struggling with a serious ankle injury a couple of years later. Despite all these problems he went on to captain the national side and played in two World Cups (1974, 1982).

Future England captain (Marvel) Bryan Robson broke his leg three times in the 1976 season. He can also consider himself unfortunate to be injured during England's World Cup campaigns of 1986 and 1990, both of which could have turned out differently had he been in the side for the crucial games against Argentina and Germany respectively.

The semi-finals of the World Cup in Spain in 1982 pitted Italy against Poland, and the free flowing French against the determined though rather gritty and unexciting West Germans. Italy overcame the eastern European challenge comfortably, and so to the second semi. The French were knocking the ball around with their usual flair when maestro Michel Platini played a beautiful through-ball to substitute Patrick Battiston. He calmly knocked the ball past the fast-approaching German 'keeper, pornstar-a-like Harald Schumacher, and prepared to roll it into the net. Schumacher had other ideas though. Leaping like a long-jumper from the take-off board at the Olympics he smashed his body into Battiston at full tilt. Schumacher was lucky that he wasn't seriously injured in the collision, but the innocent Battiston was not so fortunate. He had two teeth knocked out, his jaw broken in two places, was unconscious for nearly five minutes, and had to be rushed to hospital. Television replays showed the incident in all its terrible glory and Schumacher, though calmly walking back into his area, must have been expecting the red card. Then everyone watched in utter disbelief as Dutch referee Charles Corver awarded the Germans a goal-kick and motioned for play to continue. Of course the neutrals were now praying for a French win, though, somewhat typically, the Germans spoiled the party and went through to the final, where, thankfully, the Italians emerged victorious.

The image conjured up in your head when someone mentions defender Terry Butcher and his red England shirt is usually of the man with his head swathed in bandages and blood pouring down his white shirt. A clash of heads at the Rasunda stadium in Sweden in 1989 meant that Butcher had to be patched up quickly if he wanted to play on. Proudly drenching the three lions in claret Butcher soldiered on, defending mightily to ensure England didn't concede. The captain's performance ensured England qualified for the following year's World Cup Finals in Italy.

Leeds United midfielder David Batty managed to injure his Achilles tendon when one of his children ran him over with a tricycle!

Patrick Vieira's goal celebrations against Manchester United in 1997 - when he slid across the turf on his knees - damaged his legs so badly that he was out of the team for nearly a month. And Manchester City's Shaun Goater celebrated a Nicolas Anelka goal by kicking an advertising hoarding so hard that he damaged his foot and had to be substituted. In 1998 he actually broke his arm while celebrating.

Liverpool's defender Phil Babb was chasing back hard to try and prevent Chelsea from scoring in 1998 but Pierluigi Casiraghi ended up notching a fantastic goal for the Blues. Babb wasn't quite finished though. As he desperately tried to clear the ball, he ended up sliding in, straddling the goalpost at full tilt and cementing his own balls to the line, painfully.

Barnsley's Darren Bernard slipped in a puddle of dog excrement (no shit, I hear you cry) and tore his knee ligaments, an injury that left him out of the side for several months.

Arsenal's Patrick Vieira almost knocked himself out taking the field at Highbury. Jogging down the tunnel he smacked his head into the roof, and not even being laughed at by Ian Wright made him feel any better.

South African defender Mark Fish required 39 stitches in his back after first falling into a glass vase and then impaling himself on the remains of a coffee table as he reeled back through it.

Manchester United's fabulous goalkeeper, Peter Schmeichel, needed counselling after seeing the horrific injury to David Busst during their match with Coventry in 1996. The Light Blue man collided with Denis Irwin and Brian McLair while battling for the ball and turned his ankle over. Both the tibia and fibula shattered, and his foot was just about ripped from the bottom of his leg. Schmeichel vomited at the sight and several players had to be comforted while Busst's blood was cleared from the pitch. The injury was so severe that it required nearly thirty operations to repair the damage. Though he tried to make a comeback Busst's leg never fully recovered and he turned to coaching instead. (In Sheffield United's away fixture with Chelsea in March 2007, Blades' front man Rob Hulse suffered a similar injury after colliding with opposing 'keeper Peter Cech. He'd slid in bravely to try and turn in a Gillespie cross but only succeeded in breaking his lower leg in two places.)

Aston Villa striker Darius Vassell injured himself attempting a little DIY surgery on his own foot in 2003. He decided the best way to drain the blood from a blister under his toenail was to approach the haematoma with a power drill.

"He decided the best way to drain the blood was with a power drill."

Contrary to what you might be thinking, this is a perfectly good way of relieving the condition, though it's usually carried out by a medical professional, not a misguided footballer. Vassell, of course, made the problem worse. Then the wound became infected and he eventually had to have the nail removed completely.

In May 2000 Thierry Henry celebrated his winning goal against Chelsea by dancing at the corner flag. He then required treatment when the end of it caught him in the eye! Italian Marco Tardelli managed a similar injury during the World Cup Finals in Spain in 1982.

During a Swiss League match in 2004, midfielder Paulo Diogo scored for Servette against Schaffhausen. As he jumped into the crowd to celebrate, he caught his wedding ring on a fence and tore off the top half of his finger. He was then booked for the excessive celebration as the referee assumed his agonised thrashing was all part of the act!

Liverpool's Djibril Cisse suffered a horrific injury to his lower leg (not unlike that endured by David Busst some years earlier) while playing against Blackburn. Somehow he managed to recover, scoring a penalty in the 2005 Champions' League Final against AC Milan, but then he broke the leg again just before the World Cup in 2006, meaning he missed the tournament and the chance to play in the final itself. Thankfully he was able to mount another comeback, though he was released on loan to Olympique Marseille immediately afterwards.

Holmbury St Mary's star midfielder Dan Church suffered a horrific knee injury during a Second XI match against Shalford in 2006. The hospital was unable to diagnose the problem correctly but it seemed that Church had dislocated both the bones of his lower leg at the kneecap, as well as damaging the medial ligaments. Despite trying to make a comeback, the injury proved too severe and he retired from competitive football shortly afterwards. Some would say that was no bad thing...

Norwegian defender Svein Grondralen collided with a moose while out training. The player souffléd a serious injury and missed his next two international tarts.

Arsenal's Robin van Persie fractured his foot while celebrating a Thierry Henry goal in early 2007, the injury keeping him out for the end of season run in.

And don't go thinking the managers aren't in the firing line, literally, for some fans. During the second leg of the 2007 Copa del Rey match between bitter rivals Real Betis and Sevilla, a man in the crowd launched a missile (i.e. threw an object) at Sevilla coach Juande Ramos, striking him on the head and knocking him out. Indeed football in Spain has endured many recent crises, not the least of which was the racism that Arsenal's Thierry Henry claimed was rife in the country. Surely this behaviour, allied with the fact that the players and managers are now being bombarded with coins, mobile phones and other objects, must prompt the authorities into taking action. The referee for the Sevilla vs.

Real Betis match abandoned the cup tie and led the players from the field.

Preston's Simon Whaley missed the end of the 2007 season after suffering a freak injury during the squad's trip to Spain. While heading for the bathroom he stubbed his toe on the leg of a coffee table, a seemingly innocuous injury that led to far worse. The impact dislodged the table's marble top which then landed on his foot, fracturing a bone! Some coffee break…

"Simon Whaley suffered a freak injury"

Everton teenager James Vaughan was left with a severed artery in his ankle after a tackle with Bolton's Abdoulaye Meite. The accidentally collected injury was so severe that Vaughan was immediately taken to hospital. Thankfully he was released the next morning with no lasting damage.

Who'd be a Referee?

"When my eyesight started to go, I took up refereeing"
NEIL MIDGLEY

The 1878 FA Cup Final between the Royal Engineers and the Wanderers was refereed by a certain Mr Segar Bastard, a man whose name has become synonymous with the chief match official ever since. He probably wished he had been called Charlie Faultless as one Scots ref in the 1950s was christened.

The referee for a Sunderland match in 1954 managed to blow for the second half without realising he had no linesman in attendance. He was lucky though. Referees at Roker Park often had to be smuggled out of the ground disguised as policemen if they had angered the crowd. Full-scale pitch invasions were not uncommon and indeed a police horse was once stabbed there.

Before the last match of the 1970-71 English domestic season Leeds were looking good for the title. The visit of lowly West Brom to Elland Road promised two easy points and the Championship, but Leeds, somewhat against the script, were a goal down going into the second half. Then Mick Jones finished off a nice move and Leeds were back in the match, or so they thought for a brief moment. Referee Ray Tinkler disallowed it for offside, not the only contentious decision he was going to make that afternoon. With twenty minutes to go Jeff Astle raced past flagging team-mates to score the Baggies' second, but to the relief of all the hone fans, the linesman was flagging for offside against the exhausted Colin Suggett as he trudged back to the halfway line. Tinkler had other ideas though, claiming Suggett had nothing to do with the move and therefore could not be given offside. So he awarded the goal. All hell broke loose and some thirty home fans invaded the pitch and besieged the ref. Leeds players, who had been doing exactly the same seconds before, were then forced to protect Tinkler. Then the innocent linesmen, Colin Cartlich, was pelted with stones and cans, one scoring a direct hit on his head. Once order had been restored, Leeds clawed a goal back, but, having lost, they couldn't stop Arsenal taking the League title with victory at White Hart Lane a couple of weeks later.

Trevor Brooking accidentally collided with a referee in the 1970s. Bobby Moore picked up his whistle and blew it to halt the game, then checked on the official who was found to be out cold!

In a World Cup match between Italy and Peru in 1982, referee Walter Eschweiler dummied a ball that came towards him. Unfortunately the player failed to buy the dummy and clattered into him, knocking out two of his teeth.

It's quite common for South American referees to be attacked, either by players or fans. On one occasion the ref fought back, first, by laying out the striker who repeatedly abused him. And ref Choi Kuok-kun was in charge for a Macau vs. Hong Kong match in 2000 when he decided to get the first punch in. The Macau striker he'd just sent off refused to leave the field so Kuok-kun helped him on his way with a roundhouse right before a full-scale brawl erupted. The linesmen, too, are repeatedly targeted for abuse and often have to resort to using their flags as batons to keep troublemakers at bay. On one occasion the male ref was knocked to the ground by warring women players who then gave him a pretty good shoeing!

But let's nip back to South America for this next bout of madness. The referee for a League encounter issued a yellow card to the RACA goalkeeper in the hope that the prospect of another, and therefore a sending off, would calm the man down. The goalie responded by throwing a series of punches at the official who then had to take cover behind an army cordon. When order was restored he was of course sent off. Sometimes the officials are not so well protected though. The video footage of the terrified ref escaping over the perimeter fence before he's lynched by an angry mob makes for painful viewing. And there are numerous occasions where angry parents have taken their feelings out on the referee because the game didn't go well for their children. What is the world coming to?

While 'Razor' Ruddock was lying on the floor getting treatment for a knock, the referee casually strolled over to ask if he was okay. He received a painful testicle grab as his reply and the Liverpool man then made a speedy recovery!

A linesman for a Spanish league match was knocked out by a wayward clearance in 1991. In fact any number of officials have been struck and injured by the ball. And so have quite a few players, who should get a brief mention here. Newcastle's Olivier Bernard knows exactly how it feels to be pole-axed by the ball. He was knocked off his feet during a match against Leicester by a Laurent Robert pass in 2003. The initial impact made his knees wobble before they finally gave way and he slumped to the turf like a beaten boxer. Leeds United's Jimmy Floyd Hasselbank was also felled by a close-range free-kick.

Anders Frisk is not the most popular referee in England, so no doubt many readers will be pleased to hear that he's been attacked by fans on numerous occasions. Once, the fan actually charged thirty yards onto the pitch before knocking Frisk to the ground with a flying karate kick.

Nottingham Forest's Mark Crossley accidentally (apparently) punted the ball up-field into the back of the referee's head once. The blow knocked the official out cold, though none of the players, perhaps understandably, looked too concerned!

Barnsley referee Stephen Lodge ended up with a severely bruised ego during a Leicester City - Coventry match in 1999. He tried to give the ball back to the Leicester players with a deft back heel but ended up tripping over it and landing flat on his face instead. You can imagine the reaction from the stands....

Still, you'd rather look a bit of a plonker than have a two pound lump of ice crack you on the head. In Honduran side Cruz Azul's match with local club side America in Mexico City, the official had just awarded a penalty against Cruz when he was struck by the missile thrown from the crowd. Ouch. As a somewhat roundabout result of this, the players started warring with their opponents' coaches.

Commentator Speak 8 - Oh Dear

"We're not used to weather in June in this country"
JIMMY HILL

"The Dutch fans look like a huge jar of marmalade"
BARRY DAVIES

"Wimbledon are putting balls into the blender"
RODNEY MARSH

*"It's hands on hips and heads in hands
for the Charlton players"*
RADIO 5 COMMENTATOR

"It was one of those goals that's invariably a goal"
DENIS LAW

*"He is the type of player who will follow you to every end of the
box"*
KERRY DIXON

*"There's no in between, you're either good or bad and we were in
between"*
GARY LINEKER

"If in winning we only draw, that would be fine"
JACK CHARLTON

"Signori has all the tricks up his book"
RAY WILKINS

"It was one of the best goals that I've seen this millennium"
TONY GUBBA

*"The World Cup is every four years so it's going to be a perennial
problem"*
GARY LINEKER

"This is the end of season curtain raiser"
PETER WITHE

"There are two ways of getting the ball: one is from your own team-mates and that's the only way"
TERRY VENABLES

"Jim Leighton is looking as sharp as a tank"
BARRY DAVIES

1 2 3 4 5 6 7 8 9 10 11

The Final Whistle

And now we should look at a small collection of the seriously bizarre. Just when you thought you'd heard every oddity football had to throw up, you stumble blindly into this lot, God help them…

Just after the start of a match between Cambridge students and the townsmen of Chesterton in 1579, the townsmen began an all out assault on their opponents with sticks and clubs, and they eventually drove them into the river Cam.

Sunderland had only been in existence as a football club for two years when it was faced with dissolution through lack of funds. One of the board members saved the team from extinction by selling his prize canary for £1 in 1881!

After an injury to one of his players during their 1930 World Cup match against Argentina, American trainer Jock Coll ran on to the field to try and help. As he did so, however, he tripped, smashing a bottle of chloroform inside his medical bag. The chemical went to work on the hapless Coll and he passed out almost immediately. All efforts to revive him on the pitch failed and he had to be carried off!

Though this is the version commonly cited, the story has perhaps become exaggerated over the years. Another view is that Andy Auld sustained an injury to his mouth and one of the Argentinean players accidentally knocked Coll's smelling salts into his eyes! Either way, there was certainly an unusual incident. In the same year the referee at a Glasgow - Sheffield fixture sent himself off after realising that his shirt was the same colour as United's.

Manchester City goalkeeper Frank Swift was so exhausted at the end of the 1934 FA Cup Final that, as he bent down to pick up his gloves, he fainted and had to be revived by team-mates. A popular figure, he took up journalism when his playing days were over, but he was killed in the Munich crash in 1958.

When there isn't much in the way of cash in a club's coffers they might offer material gains to another side in exchange for players (Tony Cascarino moved to Gillingham from Crockenhill for a set of tracksuits in 1981). Surely one of the oddest incidences of this came when the Gills gave Aston Villa a player in 1937 for the princely sum of a typewriter, a goalkeeper's jersey, a couple of jars of weed killer, a member of coaching staff and three turnstiles (used)!

Austria's national Wiener Stadium was used as a barracks for German soldiers during the Second World War. As a result of this military activity it was listed as a priority target for allied bombers. In one raid alone it suffered nearly 300 hits.

Len Shackleton, otherwise known as 'The Clown Prince Of Soccer', transferred from Bradford to Newcastle in the late 1940s for a considerable fee. He justified the outlay on debut though by scoring six of the Magpies' 13 goals in a complete shutout for Newport County. He joked afterwards:

"And they were bloody lucky to get nil!"

He was equally complementary about his former side's fortunes in the 1970s:

"I know about players selling dummies but this club keeps buying them"

On one occasion though, the joke was on Shackleton. The FA failed to pick him for an international in the 1950s using the excuse:

"We play at Wembley, not the London Palladium"

★

The derby clash between Peñarol and Nacional in Uruguay in 1949 was notable for the actions of the referee. Peñarol scored twice in the first half while Nacional had two players sent off. Whatever was said at halftime in the Nacional dressing room then caused such a rumpus that the players did not come out for the second half. Some claimed the referee was incapable of keeping control, had awarded a dubious penalty and had then punched one of their players.

In 1951 Notts County's Jackie Sewell transferred to Sheffield Wednesday for around £35,000, thus, given the current financial climate, becoming the first player to be worth his weight in gold! The Australian side beaten 17-0 by a touring English XI the same year were relying on the services of one Norman Conquest in goal!

The suspension handed down to Trinidadian Selwyn Baptiste in 1955 was considered a touch draconian. He played in a match just a day after being given a two-year ban and was then prohibited from playing for the next thousand years! No prizes for guessing that he'd like to play his return match in the Millennium Stadium…

The magnificent Yugoslavian forward Dragoslav Sekularac helped his team to perform strongly in the 1956 Melbourne Olympics (where they took silver) as well as the 1958 and 1962 World Cups. He is perhaps best remembered for his temper though. At the height of his powers he decided to have a disagreement with the referee over a petty incident during a match for Red Star Belgrade and he laid the official out. Sekularac was then banned for a whole year!

The referee for a Danish cup game was about to blow for fulltime when his dentures fell out. While collecting them from the turf one side netted to make the score tooth-tooth. The official then ruled out playing extra time because of his error!

*"The ref was about to blow for fulltime
when his dentures fell out"*

In a time when money in football was just beginning to spiral out of control, it was noted that the Bolton side which won the 1958 FA Cup had been assembled for less than £150.

During a Watford - Grimsby clash in 1961, a two-foot hole suddenly appeared by the penalty spot at one end of the Vicarage Road pitch. Turf from the edge of the pitch then had to be used to fill the depression. Perhaps that's how £1 million investor Elton John got his nickname, 'The Brown Dirt Cowboy'; then again, there could be another explanation, after all he apparently wanted to rename the club Queen of the South…

Incidentally, directors at the club advertising for a new manager in 1971 were surprised to receive an application from a 12-year-old girl. By the end of the next season they were probably rueing the decision not to accept her as an error of judgement as the side was relegated!

A member of the Super Spurs side in the early 1960s, Scottish forward John White had little time to appreciate his success. He was struck by lightning and killed while playing golf near London in 1964.

One Swedish fan was so disappointed in his side's performance at the 1974 World Cup that he launched his television out of the window of his fourth floor flat at the end of one of their matches. He lost a bit more than he bargained for however, because the TV smashed through the roof of his car and wrote that off too!

Under Bobby Robson - as indeed they had been under Alf Ramsey in the late 1950s and early '60s - Ipswich Town went from relative nobodies to the upper echelons of the First Division. In 1978 he took them to the FA Cup Final against Arsenal, and a Roger Osborne goal with a quarter of an hour to go sealed victory for the Tractor Boys. Having scored, Osborne was so overcome with emotion that he almost fainted. Robson then noticed he was incapable of playing on and had to substitute him.

Bristol's Mike Bagley was so incensed with the referee's decision to book him that he snatched the official's notebook and ate it, an act that earned him a six-match ban!

Real Madrid were expected to beat Aberdeen comfortably in the 1983 Cup Winners' Cup Final but the Scots won 2-1. Fan George Dixon lived in Australia and couldn't follow the match so he rang family in Scotland and asked them to place the receiver next to the radio. He said listening to the victory was worth every penny of the £220 phone bill. The same side took the Scottish Cup a few days later, a remarkable and unique achievement.

Brazilian star Ramalho confined himself to bed for three days after swallowing a suppository intended to treat a dental infection!

Substantially renovated in the 1980s, the most famous stadium in Switzerland is called the Wankdorf.

Former Soviet President Mikhail Gorbachev was said to be an avid Wigan Athletic fan. It is rumoured that he even ordered an end to radio jamming on Saturday afternoons so that he could listen to their results!

Having won the 1984 European Cup against Roma - when their opponents were playing at home - the Liverpool players celebrated in style at a villa outside the city. In fact they got so drunk that they forgot to load the trophy onto the coach heading for the airport in the morning.

The former Scottish international goalkeeper Alan Rough walked out of his local supermarket with a stolen packet of beef in 1990. He was held by police for a few hours before being released without charge, but his career took an instant nosedive as a result. In his next match the fans were at the ready with this, to the tune of 'My Darling Clementine':

"Where's the mince beef, where's the mince beef, where's the mince beef, Alan Rough? It's in your pocket, in your pocket, in your pocket, Alan Rough!"

Aston Villa's vertically challenged fullback Alan Wright strained a knee stretching to reach the pedals in his new Ferrari. He then exchanged the sports car for a more pedestrian mode of transport, a Rover 416.

An Italian woman was injured when ornaments were knocked off her mantelpiece by vibrations created when Napoli fans cheered their side scoring in the San Paolo stadium in 1990!

Charlton fans formed their own political movement, the Valley Party (named after the disused ground), in 1990. The aim, of course, was to secure enough votes to try and force the side to move back to their old ground. Greenwich Council was already opposed to helping renovate the stadium but the Valley Party, fighting on two fronts, forced a dramatic U-turn by securing nearly 15,000 electoral votes!

Nottingham Forest's Teddy Sheringham scored the first top flight goal shown by Sky TV, the company having recently invested heavily in the new Premier League. At halftime the striker apparently made his way back to the dressing room and downed a bottle of orange juice. He knew immediately that something was wrong, not least because Brian Clough was giving him the look that always spelled trouble. Clough then had to explain to Sheringham that he'd just necked his vodka and orange. Teddy was then a little unsteady for the second half…

On the day that Avi Cohen joined Kenny Dalglish's Liverpool, he reportedly ended his first conversation with the manager by saying:

"You. Me. Same"

Dalglish apparently looked a little confused so just nodded. At training the next day Cohen again came out with the line. This time Dalglish replied:

"What are you talking about, Avi?"
Cohen: *"You. Me. Same. Both learn English"*

Isn't it strange how many people reach for the TV remote to turn the subtitles on every time King Kenny is interviewed?

I didn't believe this when I read it, but I'm ashamed to admit I did find it extremely funny. Sorry. Twenty-five-year-old Indonesian footballer Mistar was killed when a stampede of pigs thundered across their training pitch in 1995. Now you know what happens when they don't get their Domino Stress Ball…

Cameroon's Roger Milla became spokesman for the country's pygmies in 1995. His celebrity status assured at Italia '90 and USA '94, Milla felt he could bring attention to the plight of the little people from his homeland.

Two England fans were hospitalised with broken bones after over-celebrating Alan Shearer's goal against Germany in the semi-final of Euro '96.

Real Betis goalkeeper Joaquin Valerio was sent off 40 minutes before his side's match against Albacete had even kicked off. Valerios reportedly insulted referee Fidel Valle Gil in the tunnel and the official immediately showed him the red card!

Italian pensioner Ivano Bonetti endeared himself to the Grimsby faithful by helping to fund his own transfer to the Mariners in the mid-'90s.

Manager Brian Laws was less than impressed with his performance during a defeat to Luton in 1996 though, and launched a plate of chicken wings at him after the match. Though he knew his contribution hadn't been paltry, Bonetti certainly had good reason to cry foul as the plate smashed into his cheekbone and fractured it.

The Guinness Book of Records lists a match in Paraguay where twenty players were sent off. During the League encounter between Sportivo Ameliano and General Caballero, two Sportivo players were sent off for fighting and then a huge brawl erupted involving everyone but the two goalkeepers. The referee was forced to dismiss the other eighteen outfield players and the match was abandoned.

Watford and England striker Luther Blisset was enjoying his retirement when he received word that four youths in Italy had been arrested for having no tickets while on a train. Why on earth would the former AC Milan player have anything to do with this incident, you might ask? Well, somewhat bizarrely, all four gave their names as Luther Blisset. They were taken to the local police station and questioned, then, eventually appeared in court, still insisting their names were Luther Blisset. It became apparent during proceedings that an anarchist movement gaining popularity among disaffected teenagers and young people in Italy decided to call themselves 'Luther Blisset', though quite why doesn't seem to have been established. The man himself believes it must have something to do with his time at the San Siro.

Arsenal's Gael Clichy supposedly died on the operating table after a freak accident on Friday the 13th 2001 when he was just 15 years old. He was trying to get into the French football academy when he caught a finger while climbing a perimeter fence and tore it off. He managed to scramble to hospital where surgeons reattached the digit. During the operation his heart stopped for 20 seconds after he developed a problem in his lungs.

Milan Rapai missed the start of a Hajduk Split season after sticking his boarding pass in his eye at the airport and damaging the lens. Kevin

Kyle once scolded his testicles with boiling water and missed a couple of games as a result, while Freddie Ljungberg sidelined himself with a slice of cheese. Perhaps he was thinking about a transfer to Sheffield Wensleydale, now under the control of captain Robbrie Fowler - a great cheddar of the ball - and new manager Peter Stilton. Just as long as they do the double over Gloucester, the board will be delighted. Their first European tie is against Parma (San Siro).

Peterborough United goalkeeper Fred Barber ran out at Wembley for a play-off final wearing a Freddie Kruger mask from the film *A Nightmare on Elm Street.*

In 2001 Villareal's Martin Palermo scored a goal in the Copa del Rey and then ran over to the crowd to celebrate. Sadly for him the wall surrounding the pitch collapsed and he broke his leg and was out for six months.

Sevilla's Midfielder Francisco Gallardo helped team-mate Jose Antonio Reyes celebrate a goal against Valladolid in 2001 by biting his penis. Presumably he then became known as a player who went down too easily after a tackle…

The tannoy announcer at Elland Road once asked for a Mr Smith to:

"Go home because your wife is stuck in the toilet"

Tough Sevilla defender Pablo Alfaro apparently tried to stick his fingers up Atlético Madrid's Toché's backside to put him off during the 2003-04 season! Luckily he didn't feel Turdo…

Ray Houghton fell into a verbal trap entirely of his own making in 2005. While discussing why he was late for an interview on talkSPORT radio, he ambushed himself with:

"I've been at a charity golf day to raise money for a boy who was seriously injured in a car crash. I had to drive like a lunatic to get here"

Once it had emerged that Wayne Rooney used to be found trawling for hookers in Liverpool's seedier nightspots, Welsh fans taunted him with:

"Score in a brothel, you only score in a brothel!"

In the Juventus - Lazio match at the Stadio Del Alpi in 2006, one of the Juve players collided with the away dugout. The whole structure then keeled over backwards!

A new signing was welcomed to Italian side Parma in early 2007. The 52-year-old local comedian, Gene Gnocchi, always dreamed of playing in Serie A so wrote to all the clubs in the League. Parma, in deep trouble and facing relegation, agreed and signed him for two months, though it's extremely unlikely Gnocchi will get a game. President Tommaso Ghiradi stated he would be used as a lucky charm instead.

Italian Fabio Capello, then manager of Spanish club Real Madrid, vowed that once David Beckham had signed for LA Galaxy he would never play for Real again. With the axe hovering over him though, and the prospect of being sacked looming ever closer, he recalled Beckham for the game against Real Sociedad in early 2007. The Englishman then ensured the Italian kept his job - presumably alongside Noel Coward and Michael Caine - capping a fine display with a beautiful free-kick in the 2-1 victory.

A lucky, but clearly wealthy, man was celebrating dinner for 16 at Claridge's, hosted by Sir Alex Ferguson and cooked by outspoken chef Gordon Ramsay, after outbidding all-comers at an HMV-sponsored football extravaganza in March 2007. The price (like the salad): a cool £45,000.

During the Manchester United - Blackburn match at Old Trafford in early 2007, defender Rio Ferdinand was pulled up by the referee's whistle after making a strong run towards the Blackburn box. In a fit of petulance he then smashed the ball into the crowd from close range. The ball caught a woman full in the face and almost knocked her out. Ferdinand's reaction was a casual wave and he didn't even check if she was okay. How do they get away with it?

A statue of Southampton's legendary player, manager and president, Ted Bates, costing £112,000, was pulled down only three days after being unveiled in March 2007. Though he'd served the club for nearly seventy years and thoroughly deserved the memorial, Bates, who died in 2003, wouldn't have been too impressed with sculptor Ian Bennett's decision to lengthen his arms and shorten his legs, making him appear, as one observer noted, like the comic character Jimmy Krankie. Lawrie McMenemy was at the ceremony but replied, cautiously and diplomatically, to questions about the statue with:

"I couldn't tell what people thought of it. It was dark that evening"

McMenemy, incidentally, was involved in one of football's most famous bust-ups. After a match, in which he thought defender Mark Wright had played pretty poorly, he delivered a scathing report in the dressing room. Wright was none too pleased at the tirade and roughly shoved the manager into the showers, whereupon they reportedly slapped each other about a bit, to the astonishment of team-mates.

The winners of the 2007 Champions' League Final in Athens in May took home £27 million in prize money. The win bonus per man was rumoured to be around £250,000 for that match alone. If Chelsea had pulled off the miraculous quadruple, they could have been looking at ten times that or more each! Sadly for them, they lost out in the Champions' League to

Liverpool and the League to Manchester United.

Liverpool's full-back John Arne Riise has allegedly been declared bankrupt at the city's county court for not paying a £100,000 debt. Though the defender reportedly earns about £50,000 a week, he is now listed as a bankrupt on the government's Insolvency Agency Service website. The player has been involved in a legal battle with his former agent, Einar Baardsen, over how his salary was invested.

The Dutch FA has asked its referees not to give any reaction during their matches after Eric Braamhaar appeared to punch the air with delight when Ajax scored against PSV Eindhoven recently.

West Ham players were warned about gambling by manager Alan Curbishley in 2007. One member of the squad reportedly lost £38,000 to team-mates in one sitting on the bus going to an away match. Defender Anton Ferdinand tarnished his image twice during the same season. Firstly, he was said to have told club officials he was visiting a sick grandmother while actually on a drinking binge in America, and then he was involved in a nightclub incident after someone supposedly stole one of his rings.

As one commentator put it:

"Footballers: They're a pampered set of preening prats"

Having read this, it's difficult to argue, isn't it? But just in case you needed further proof, here are a final few quotes to get you thinking: honestly, what made them say it?

"I don't believe in luck, but I do believe you need it"
ALAN BALL

"There's no way Ryan Giggs is another George Best. He's another Ryan Giggs"
DENIS LAW

*"The Uruguayans are losing no time in
making a meal around the referee"*
MIKE INGHAM

"Some of the goals were good and some were sceptical"
BOBBY ROBSON

"He's one of those footballers whose brains are in his head"
DEREK JOHNSTONE

*"The one thing that never changes is that John Terry plays, and
he's back today after missing those games"*
CHRIS KAMARA

*"Ivan Kaviedes has played in five countries in the last twelve
months, including Crystal Palace"*
SIMON JORDAN

*"You just can't hypothesize about something that may or may not
happen"*
RODNEY MARSH

"It's lovely to see two strikers playing with each other"
DAVID PLEAT

"As positive as Arsenal were, I thought they were quite negative"
PETER REID

"He's gone down as if he's been felled by a tree"
ANDY GRAY

"He didn't realise it but he had acres of time"
LIAM MCCANN

"Beckenbauer really has gambled all his eggs"
RON ATKINSON

"We scored first and still lost 10-0"
MARK TURNER

German World Cup winner Franz Beckenbauer had just transferred to New York's Cosmos towards the end of his career for a substantial sum. Not realising that positions on a football pitch are quite important, one of the club's executive directors was less than complimentary about Beckenbauer's knowledge of the game, and so he gave us this delightful quote:

"Tell that Kraut to get his arse up front. I'm not paying a million bucks for a guy to hang around in defence"

*

I'll leave the last word to a friend of mine, a quote that, had she been famous, would have graced the middle pages of this book and would have guaranteed her a scholarship to the Keegan School of Excellence (Geography Award). While watching Japan play Korea she asked:

"Is this Euro 2004?"
Sophie Powell

I consulted a number of sources while writing this book. They are listed below:

www.fchd.btinternet.co.uk
www.soccerjones.com
www.footballsite.co.uk
www.dangerhere.com
www.footballchants.org
www.funnyoldgame.net
www.news.bbc.co.uk
www.pubquizhelp.com
www.goalkeepersaredifferent.com
www.football.guardian.co.uk
www.uk.sports.yahoo.com
www.telegraph.co.uk/sport
www.en.wikipedia.org
www.google.co.uk
www.theage.com.au
www.observer.guardian.co.uk
www.fantasysportnet.blogspot.com
www.sport.independent.co.uk
www.rte.ie
www.sportinglife.com
www.ave-it.net
www.channel4.com/football
www.turkishdailynews.com
www.uit.no
www.soccerphile.blogspot.com
www.sportsanswerbank.com
www.football-league.premiumtv.co.uk
www.flaweb.org.uk
www.worldinconflict.wordpress.com

The Cassell Soccer Companion by David Pickering
The Big Book Of Sports Insults by David Milsted
The Big Book Of More Sports Insults by Jonathan L'Estrange
Football's Strangest Matches by Andrew Ward
Classic Football Clangers by David Mortimer
Shit Ground No Fans by Jack Bremner
Talking Balls by Andrew Delahunty
Nuts Magazine
FHM Magazine
Zoo Magazine

Nick Hancock's *Football Nightmares*
Mark and Lard's *Football Nightmares*
David Seaman's *Goalkeeping Nightmares*
Ian Wright's *It Shouldn't Happen To A Footballer*
Bradley Walsh's *Soccer Shockers*
Rory McGrath's *Own Goals and Gaffs*
Rory McGrath's *More Own Goals and Gaffs*
Freemantle Media's *History of Football*
National Geographic's *Most Amazing Moments*
Sky TV's *Sports Disasters*
Sky One's *Sport Uncovered*
BBC TV's *Inside Sport*
BBC TV's *Football Focus*

Acknowledgements

I would also like to thank, in no particular order:

Johnny Collins, Jeremy Pettit, Graham Turrall, Steve Wilkinson, John Devine, Bryn Jones, Rachel Harrison, Gavin Carter, Jo and Niki Haynes, Gordon von Abben, Gavin, Mark and Stuart Turner, Dan Church, Seamus McCann, Dave Archer, Rory McCann, Cam Brown, Fran McCann, Lisa Fairbrother, Yulia Sultanova, Anthony Alaga, Malcolm Couch, Sophie Powell, Barry McCann, Andrea Harrison, Gary Marshall and Russell Staves. My special thanks go to Stefan Nekuda (Niki).

If you have enjoyed this book why not try
Liam McCann's best-selling cricketing title:

The Sledger's Handbook
How to Deliver the Perfect Cricketing Insult

ISBN 9781904332640
£6.99
available from some bookshops, most online retailers
or direct from the publisher
http://www.aappl.us/catalogpage6UK.html#SLEDGE

Also available from Facts, Figures & Fun

Golf Facts, Figures & Fun
Wimbledon Facts, Figures & Fun
Cricket Facts, Figures & Fun
The Olympics Facts, Figures & Fun
The Sledger's Handbook
Dogs Facts, Figures & Fun
Cats Facts, Figures & Fun
Whisky, a Brief History
Beer Facts, Figures & Fun
Sci Fi Movies Facts, Figures & Fun
Noir Movies Facts, Figures & Fun
Animated Movies Facts, Figures & Fun
Vampires
Witches
Werewolves
Love & Romance Facts, Figures & Fun
Rock & Roll Facts, Figures & Fun
Musicals Facts, Figures & Fun
Country Music Facts, Figures & Fun
Christmas Facts, Figures & Fun
Pirates
Unicorns
Our Universe, an Introduction
1000 Jokes You Could Tell Your Mother
1000 Jokes You Could Never Tell Your Mother
Discarded Science
Corrupted Science

For further information contact **info@ffnf.co.uk** or write to us at:
Facts, Figures & Fun, Church Farm House, Wisley, Surrey, GU23 6QL

www.ffnf.co.uk